Praise for Brian Gewirtz and
There's Just One Problem...

"Brian Gewirtz's THERE'S JUST ONE PROBLEM is a fascinating and hilarious inside look into Brian's unlikely yet incredible rise to sports entertainment 'insider' fame and what I would describe as a true WWE Hall of Fame career as a writer and, for years now, a tremendous success as our lead Seven Bucks executive. His long, storied, and unbelievable tenure in WWE is truly what legends are made of. Brian's one of my best friends, one of my most trusted partners, and a real unsung legend in the wild world of pro wrestling. Congratulations on your fantastic new book, Brian! Please don't tell all our crazy stories—save some for the next book."
— **Dwayne "The Rock" Johnson**

"This is the best book I have read in years. If you're a fan of WWE—heck, even if you're not—this inside look into the life of one of the most intense jobs in all of entertainment (a WWE writer), hilariously detailed by one of the most impactful writers and creative contributors in WWE history. is nothing short of fascinating. It's a laugh-out-loud, can't-put-down, sad-that-it's-over kind of book, and I loved every second of it. Apart from, of course, when it was over."
— **Becky Lynch,** WWE Superstar and six-time WWE Women's Champion

"In THERE'S JUST ONE PROBLEM, written by the most talented writer in the history of WWE (my opinion), Brian takes you on a roller-coaster ride in regards to his amazing time writing in WWE. Brian even discusses his 'day' in wrestlers court, where he was the first and only writer in WWE to have to go in front of a judge (actually a wrestler) and pay his debt for 'allegedly' favoring to write for his favorite wrestlers. He survived!!! This book is as entertaining as the scripts Brian wrote during his amazing career in WWE. This book is a must-read."
— **Kurt Angle,** WWE Hall of Famer and Olympic Gold Medalist

"I simply could not put this tremendous book down, finishing it in two sittings within a single day—and lost count of how many times I laughed out loud along the way. Brian Gewirtz has an instant wrestling classic on his hands here; a very enjoyable romp down memory lane, with a unique perspective from a man who was either in the middle of, or very close to, some of the greatest (and not so great) moments in WWE history. With unfettered access to WWE boss Vince McMahon, and as one of Dwayne 'The Rock' Johnson's closest confidants, Brian Gewirtz is the perfect person to chronicle the hectic and sometimes surreal behind-the-scenes chaos of the WWE creative process—and he delivers the goods in insightful and hilarious fashion."

—**Mick Foley,** WWE Hall of Famer and
New York Times bestselling author

"I never met someone in the wrestling business who wasn't a wrestler that had as much knowledge and insight as Brian. There would not be a King Bookah without a Brian Gewirtz."

—**Booker T,** WWE Hall of Famer and
five-time WCW Champion

"Every wrestling fan will love this book. The stories are truly amazing! I couldn't put it down."   —**Ken Jeong,** stand-up comedian,
actor, producer, and writer

"Brian and I are kindred spirits. Amidst allegations of Flash action figure payolas, the infamous wrestlers court, multitudes of laughs, made-up words, 5-second poses, roasting local sports teams, and battling at *WrestleMania* in my hometown over a Japanese shampoo endorsement (you knew I had to mention it), we've both ended up where we needed to be. Keep the world smiling, Brian. As you do in this book. Wrestling's version of *War and Peace*. Or a great, comedic book that involves writing outlandish scenarios for men in tights. Whichever. I'll be over here, still wearing spandex."   —**Adam "Edge" Copeland,**
Canadian professional wrestler and actor

"Not nearly enough Miz."   —**The Miz**

THERE'S JUST ONE PROBLEM . . .

TRUE TALES FROM THE FORMER, ONE-TIME, 7TH MOST POWERFUL PERSON IN WWE

BRIAN GEWIRTZ

TWELVE

NEW YORK   BOSTON

Twelve
Hachette Book Group
1290 Avenue of the Americas, New York, NY 10104
twelvebooks.com
twitter.com/twelvebooks

First Edition: August 2022

Twelve is an imprint of Grand Central Publishing. The Twelve name and logo are trademarks of Hachette Book Group, Inc.

The publisher is not responsible for websites (or their content) that are not owned by the publisher.

The Hachette Speakers Bureau provides a wide range of authors for speaking events. To find out more, go to www.hachettespeakersbureau.com or call (866) 376-6591.

Library of Congress Cataloging-in-Publication Data
Names: Gewirtz, Brian, author.
Title: There's just one problem : true tales from the former, one-time, 7th most powerful person in WWE / Brian Gewirtz.
Description: First edition. | New York : Twelve, 2022. | Includes index. |
Identifiers: LCCN 2022004464 | ISBN 9781538710531 (hardcover) | ISBN 9781538710555 (ebook)
Subjects: LCSH: Gewirtz, Brian. | World Wrestling Entertainment, Inc.—Employees—Biography. | World Wrestling Entertainment, Inc.—History. | Television writers—United States—Biography. | Television producers and directors—United States—Biography. | Wrestling—United States—History.
Classification: LCC GV1196.G48 A3 2022 | DDC 796.81209—dc23/eng/20220321
LC record available at https://lccn.loc.gov/2022004464

ISBNs: 978-1-5387-1053-1 (hardcover), 978-1-5387-1055-5 (ebook)

Printed in the United States of America

LSC-C

Printing 1, 2022

To Roddy, and to my Dad, who, despite his better judgment, always took me to see him

CONTENTS

THERE'S JUST ONE PROBLEM . . .

CHAPTER 1

Wrestlers Court

"You're being taken to Wrestlers Court."

When those words left Stephanie McMahon's mouth, on April 3, 2001, at a *Smackdown* taping in Oklahoma City, I was blindsided. Coming off what I considered my finest moment as a WWE writer, contributing to a hugely successful *WrestleMania 17* and a historic *Raw*, I thought my newly promoted boss would be giving me something else—a bonus, a promotion, maybe even the clippers my hero Roddy Piper once used to shave Little Beaver's head for having the gall to be friends with Mr. T. Instead, her expression was one you'd reserve for breaking the news that a beloved pet had just been fatally electrocuted.

"This is not optional. Make sure you bring beer...maybe some pizza."

Immediately, a number of questions went through my head. *What kind of pizza? What brand of beer?* And perhaps most pressingly: *What the hell is Wrestlers Court?* As word spread throughout the locker room, I quickly learned that "Wrestlers Court" was a time-honored tradition going back several decades. It was a way for the wrestlers (commonly referred to as the "boys," though it included the women wrestlers as well) to let off steam and police themselves when someone violated an unwritten backstage rule, aka the "Wrestler's Code."

Eat fried chicken in the locker room and leave behind crumbs over people's luggage? You're going to Wrestlers Court. Sit in first class and not give up your seat to a veteran who's flying coach? Wrestlers Court. Give up your seat to a veteran who's flying coach but then complain about

1

having to give up said seat to anyone who will listen? Most definitely Wrestlers Court.

It's a way of "ribbing on the square," which means having fun with someone while also making a serious point in the process. But why make that point when there's a golden opportunity to get the entire locker room to fuck with them first? I had never been part of this rite of passage, mainly due to one key word: *Wrestler.* For decades, Court was conducted for the boys, by the boys. In the history of WWE, no writer had ever been taken to Wrestlers Court. Until now.

Stephanie told me I was being accused of accepting gifts from the popular tag team of Edge and Christian in exchange for television airtime. Don't let anyone tell you different: Championship belts are not the most precious commodity in WWE; television airtime is. The more exposure you get on TV, the more promos you get to cut, the more backstage scenes you're in—the more the audience gets a chance to see your character, the greater chance you have of "getting over." To be "over" means the audience is reacting strongly to you (positively or negatively) and you're making money. Lots of it. But you can't "get over" if you're not on TV, and the idea of someone essentially bribing a writer for a promo here or a backstage bit there is actually a serious charge.

Was it true? Not at all! The charges were completely baseless...and by "completely" I mean "mostly."

If there's one tradition in wrestling that dates back even further than Wrestlers Court, it's older veterans being upset that someone newer and younger is taking their spots. I had bonded with Edge and Christian almost immediately when I started with the company back in November 1999. We were all the same age, had similar senses of humor, and of course, tremendous physiques (two out of three of those things are true, but I'm not saying which ones). Other than these guys putting their bodies on the line three or four times a week, every week for the past ten years, and me putting my body on the line...never, we were very similar. I was told early on that much like how *When Harry Met Sally* postulated that men and women can't be friends, wrestlers and writers can't be friends, either. Not because the sex gets in the way (even wrestlers have their standards) but because the relationship is not based on actual friendship but rather "What can you do for my career?"

When I started, Edge and Christian were the classic "great matches, no personality" tag team guys. In reality, they *had* personalities, but they were never given the chance to show them. In fact, when Edge first came up he was told his character was going to be a deaf mute and would express "Silent Rage." Thankfully the real-life Edge, Adam Copeland, expressed clear audible rage over that idea, and he and Jay Reso, aka Christian, were instead cast as brothers and part of "the Brood"—cool, hip vampires who wore flowery pirate blouses and tights, the perfect ensemble for hand-to-hand combat. It wasn't who they were in real life but at least they had characters, a kickass entrance, got to drink fake blood from a goblet, and had acquired the ability to (occasionally) speak.

Adam and Jay weren't actually brothers but they might as well have been, having known each other since grade school. Most of WWE management during this time were in their fifties and sixties, so when a fellow twentysomething came aboard, it didn't take long for the bonding to begin. We brainstormed on ways to make their characters meld more with their actual personalities—hence they became shit-stirring smart-asses. We had a blast coming up with different ways to antagonize the hometown crowds, the centerpiece being the Five-Second Pose. I threw this concept out to them as a way for each of their promos to have a big finish, where "For the benefit of those with flash photography" (flash photography still being a thing in 2000–2001) they would insult the audience in a creative way and then stand in the ring and "allow" the audience to bask in their greatness and take all the pictures they wanted (for five seconds—anything more would be gratuitous).

Yes, it was "cheap heat" as far as insulting local sports franchises or the crowds' lack of hygiene, but it was creative cheap heat and it finally made them stand out. As their characters got more popular, they were getting more comfortable on the mic, getting raucous crowd reactions and, as a result, plenty of TV time. Of course, when someone gets more

TV time that means someone else is getting less, and therein lay the crux of the problem.

Weeks earlier, Edge* had gotten some distressing news—his girlfriend's father had passed away and he needed to leave the TV taping to be with her. Before he left, he handed me a ~~doll~~ badass action figure of my favorite superhero, the Flash, that a fan had given him at a comic book store signing (Edge is more of a Daredevil guy). He was going to hand it to me in private, but in his haste to leave, he gave it to me in the arena hallway. Little did we know Bob "Hardcore" Holly was watching. Hardcore Holly is always watching!

Bob was a veteran, ten years older than us (though he looked like he could be our dad) and was one of the guys seeing his TV time diminish while other, younger talent like Edge and Christian were being booked in multiple segments a night. He was a legit tough guy who was usually pissed off on-screen and even more pissed off backstage. His character was intimidating because *he* was intimidating. He wasn't shy about expressing how he felt about you, and it was clear he wasn't particularly enamored with me. Once I had made some off-the-cuff comment asking someone why he changed his tights from blue and yellow to blue and pink. Nothing against the color pink; I just thought the yellow worked for him. Next thing I know Bob's confronting me backstage in the arena hallway.

"Hey! I heard you're going around telling everyone I'm a [redacted]! How 'bout I [redacted] you in the [redacted]?! Would that make me a [redacted]?!"

There's really no right way to answer that question, and since this was in full view of everyone and his point had been made, Bob stared me down and walked away. And that was one of our more pleasant conversations. So even though the gift in question was not in exchange for airtime

---

*Note: Nobody in wrestling calls wrestlers by their actual names. Once you've got your wrestling name, that's pretty much what you are for the rest of your life. Sorry, Duke "The Dumpster" Droese.

and even though Christian wasn't even involved, Bob believed he had witnessed proof of payola. A clear violation of ethics that he reported, and the wheels of justice were set in motion as Edge, Christian, and I were set to face trial together.

I did not put Edge and Christian on the air because I got a cool Flash action figure, but I was clearly becoming friends with the talent and was writing them onto TV. Granted they deserved to be on TV, and no one gets on the air without Vince McMahon's approval (and Vince shockingly does not accept superhero toys for airtime), but the point was made—you're getting too chummy with talent at the expense of others, and you need to get taken down a notch. Hence while the charges themselves were completely baseless, there was at least some truth to why Bob was angry.

Back at the arena, I made my case to Vince to avoid this thing altogether. Surely with a two-hour show to produce with a major angle to shoot (the biggest star in the industry, Stone Cold Steve Austin, had just turned heel two days earlier and was going to beat up his best friend, "Good Ol' JR" Jim Ross, in JR's hometown) he'd call the whole thing off or at the very least postpone it. Instead, Vince cackled, "Good luck," then went into his office. Nobody on the planet gives off a better dismissive cackle than Vince McMahon.

That failed plea to Vince was midafternoon, and Court time was fast approaching. So, heeding Stephanie's advice, I ran up to the empty arena stands where I bribed a concession worker for a large pizza and a six-pack of beer. My assumption was this was going to be less a full-blown court and more a tribunal—a panel of veterans who'd hear the case and render a quick verdict, then we'd all go back to the more professional things WWE was known for at the time, like yelling "Suck It" to large crowds filled with children. I couldn't imagine anyone would actually give a crap about this whole incident.

I cautiously entered where I was told the trial would be, and my heart dropped to my stomach. This was no tribunal. Every wrestler, producer (former wrestlers who put the matches together), and referee in the company was there. I think I saw the seamstresses and caterers. It was easily over a hundred people now, all staring at me as I walked in holding my single box of pizza and six-pack.

* * *

As I surveyed the crowd (and de facto jury), I noticed one person who should not have been there. His presence immediately set me off. Jamie Morris was a writer who was hired about six months after I started. I didn't have anything against him personally, but seeing an actual fellow writer there, settling in to enjoy the slaughter (and actually eating popcorn years before all the memes!) was something I couldn't accept.

I immediately went to Stephanie and told her point-blank, Jamie can't be there. Literally every other person was fine, but not him. I had no idea what was in store, but I wasn't going to have another writer smirking at me in every writers meeting going forward, telling every new writer this story behind my back. Something about his face in that moment truly incensed me. I was actually prepared to walk out and quit. Had Steph said *Too bad*, I honestly would've grabbed my bags and left WWE for good right then and there. That was how much his presence triggered me. Stephanie must've seen the crazed look in my eyes because moments later she was pulling Jamie aside and escorting him out of the room, a gesture I'll always appreciate. With the first "win" under my belt, I took a deep breath and prepared to face the music.

Edge and Christian were already in the defendant's box (three chairs set up next to the Undertaker's "Judges Table") where I joined them, sitting in the front of the room facing the entire roster. To our far right was the prosecutor, John Bradshaw Layfield, one of the loudest, most bombastic, and toughest guys in the entire locker room (just ask him!). Bradshaw was pure Texas bravado standing six foot five, 275 pounds. Of all the officers in this court, he would be considered the small one.

Behind us was the bailiff, Glenn Jacobs, otherwise known as the Big Red Monster, Kane. He wasn't wearing his iconic Kane mask, but with a stoic look and folded arms he made an intimidating presence nonetheless. I believe his job was to make sure no one physically attacked us . . . okay, me.

Finally, directly to our right, the judge...the Undertaker. It made sense—he was the most tenured and respected man in the locker room. He was also the one "top guy" I had never really interacted with much, as behind the scenes he typically worked with veterans Bruce Prichard or Michael Hayes. I could feel my heart rate rising as I turned to Edge and Christian, who seemed oddly calm. They were even smiling, which I noted could not be a good thing.

To compound matters, sitting in the front row, directly across from me, was Triple H. While I had at least a cordial relationship with Bradshaw, Kane, and Taker, Triple H truly did not think I had any business being in a backstage position of power at the time (and he wasn't alone). This was a guy who looked up to tough, take-no-shit legends like Killer Kowalski (the man who trained him) and Harley Race. I was the guy who owned *The Best of "Match Game"* on DVD, was often seen in catering eating Froot Loops and, despite having no wrestling experience, inexplicably had Vince McMahon's ear. To HHH, my main function seemed to be finding unique and unprintable ways for guys like the Rock (probably my biggest ally, and absent from the trial as he had left to shoot *The Scorpion King* after *Raw* the night before) and Chris Jericho to make fun of him and his on-screen and soon-to-be actual wife, Stephanie McMahon. Months earlier, when Vince came up with the idea of having HHH lose to the Brooklyn Brawler in a three-on-one handicap match, Triple H stormed into the production meeting, looked me in the eye, and said "This *had* to be you." Now he was looking at the single box of pizza and six-pack of beer I had embarrassedly stuffed under my chair and shaking his head in disgust.

Undertaker brought the court in session as Bradshaw laid out the charges—we were being accused of giving and accepting gifts in exchange for television airtime. Edge and Christian pleaded not guilty to the charges, and then it was my turn. Bradshaw asked, "How do you plead Mr. Ger-witz?"

John was no dummy. He knew it was a pet peeve of mine when someone mispronounced my name, which happened 90 percent of the time. It set me off like calling Marty McFly "chicken." Bradshaw had laid the first trap, baiting me. Would I take the high ground and ignore it? Or would I come out of the gates swinging and wow everyone with my courage?

"My last name is pronounced 'Gewirtz,'* so if you're going to proceed with this sham of a trial, the least you can do is get my name right."

The crowd instantly leapt to their feet. Many *ooooh*'d, some *aaaaah*'d, and all were impressed with my sheer chutzpah.

Actually, none of that is true. Instead, there was only dead, soul-crushing silence. As I waited for the slow clap that never came, Undertaker cocked his head and turned with a look that said, *The fuck did you just say?* Even the ever-silent Kane managed to utter a "ho boy" under his breath.

Bradshaw turned his attention back to Edge and Christian, who once again seemed to be having the time of their lives. Christian said, "Not only are we not guilty, but we have an announcement. A lot of the talent have been getting book deals. We probably should just tell you now so you're not surprised when you find out, but because of the stuff we're doing on TV, we've received a book deal, too."

I had no idea what they were talking about, but I could see the natives getting very restless. It was bad enough these guys were taking their spots, but *now* after being in the company for less than three years they were getting a book deal!? Triple H, who decidedly did *not* have a book deal, looked like he legitimately wanted to kill someone. Even more so than usual.

Edge reached into a bag and produced an oversized book: *Edge and Christian: How to Kiss Ass! Our Road Trip to the Top.* They were both Photoshopped on the cover sporting the cheesiest shit-eating grins imaginable.

There was a moment of confused silence and then uproarious laughter. No wonder they had looked so calm—they had been tipped off! No way they could've made that book in less than an hour and now, unlike me, they had the crowd on their side. They went the "we're going to be found guilty

---

*Pronounced "guh-werts," in case you're super curious. I don't get it, either.

no matter what we do, so might as well have some fun and entertain the boys" route (a route they did *not* clue me in on). Maybe I should've been more vocal about stopping a segment where Big Show and Rikishi rubbed their asses in Edge's and Christian's faces months earlier. Live and learn.

With Edge and Christian seemingly in the Court's good graces, prosecutor Bradshaw turned his attention back to me and called upon a number of wrestlers to testify as character witnesses. He essentially wanted to know: Would I be the type of guy to favor Edge and Christian and/or blatantly violate locker room rules?

Taz, the cohost of *Sunday Night Heat*, produced at WWF New York, the company's onetime restaurant in Times Square, was asked whether I had bothered to show up to produce the show.

"Once," Taz replied.

"And who were the hosts of that particular episode?" Bradshaw asked.

"Edge and Christian."

He was right. It didn't stop me from tossing my new orange Taz shirt directly in the trash the next day when I got home, but technically it was true. Jamie Morris was the main producer of *Heat*. He wanted to produce it and considered it his baby but was on vacation the week Edge and Christian hosted. If only he was here, he could explain…oh, right.

Perry Saturn, who in the past was *not* happy when he heard I supplied the Rock with a joke about his crossed eyes, was called on next.

"I've been in the company for 427 days and he said hello 236 of those days but only shook my hand 139 of those days and one time he went into a room and didn't shake my hand or nuthin even."

I'm paraphrasing, but you get the idea. There were a bunch of times I had greeted wrestlers but didn't actually shake their hands. That was actually a big no-no. I didn't realize it when I first started, but shaking hands is a very big deal in the locker room. It was an issue that would rear its head in an even bigger way later in the trial.

As an aside, while Perry, a great guy, had several gimmicks over his career, many WWE fans knew him as the non sequitur–spewing, mop-loving character who'd randomly say "You're welcome" at the end of every sentence. There was a widespread belief that this gimmick was punishment for Perry after he roughed up another wrestler in the ring after a botched move, weeks earlier. Neither of those things are correct. It had nothing to do with that incident and it wasn't done as a punishment. That character came about as a result of me imitating Perry's testimony to my friends (with each account getting more and more ridiculous) and then actually trying a version of it on the air. Perry had been treading water as a singles wrestler at that time, and I thought he could make this new character work. Perry was actually super-entertaining in this new role, and people genuinely enjoyed him. It even took a strange turn in real life. Perry thought we—"the office"—were messing with him, so he decided to mess with us. Outside the ring, he took "Moppy" with him everywhere—restaurants, hotels, flights—as if he and the mop were an actual couple.*

But I'm getting ahead of myself. At the time it didn't take much to decipher Perry's problem, and what was once a case of simple gift acceptance was now turning into a full-on character assassination. Not only was I favoring my friends, but I was big-leaguing everyone else! Even I was starting to think I was an asshole!

In reality my general shyness almost always stopped me from making the first move. Not just in backstage handshaking but pretty much everything. Still, in WWE perception is reality, and it didn't matter if it was a case of an introvert awash in a sea of extroverts with healthy egos—the perception was that "Hollywood boy" didn't have time for anyone but his friends. This was about to turn into a company-wide burial. And with that, I saw Sean Waltman, aka X-Pac, rise from his chair.

Even though Sean was only a year older than me, and even though I was there at the Manhattan Center for *Raw* in 1993, cheering as loud as anyone when he (as the 1-2-3 Kid) beat Razor Ramon in one of the biggest upsets in WWE history, I rubbed him the wrong way almost immediately. Not only did I never work with him on promos, but usually

*I'm not sure how treating a mop like a real-life spouse off-camera is a "lesson" to us, but who am I to stop true love?

I was writing the material when wrestlers were making fun of him. I also didn't recognize Les Thatcher once backstage in catering. Les is a wrestling legend and someone Sean deeply respects and admires, so his anger was justifiable. One time when I wandered into the Male Talent Locker Room, Sean shouted my name and said "What are you doing in here? The sign on the door says *Talent*." That was our relationship in a nutshell.

I don't actually remember specifically what X-Pac said, but he was so livid he actually left his seat and headed toward me before Kane stepped in to stop a full-fledged riot from breaking out.* All I remember was him spewing a bevy of profanity and the tension in the room growing to such uncomfortable levels I was hoping for Bradshaw to call upon literally anyone else. The good news is, he did. The bad news? It was Bob "Hardcore" Holly.

Bob provided the eyewitness testimony of the incident in question—the Flash action figure went from Edge's hands to mine, where it was received warmly! I blurted out that while I did take the figure it had nothing to do with who goes on television. Bob nodded reflexively, apologized, and quietly sat down. I'm kidding. I think the words he chose were "You calling me a fucking liar!?"

My instinct was to deflect with humor, so I made the regretful decision to speak tongue-in-cheek about how great the Flash was. Despite everyone in the room needing to get ready for a two-hour television show seen in person by over twelve thousand people and by millions more at home, I told one hundred pissed-off and visibly confused wrestlers the tale of police scientist Barry Allen getting hit by a bolt of lightning and doused with chemicals, thus becoming the fastest man alive.

To the shock of no one (but me) my dissertation on the origin of the Flash did *not* go over with the group. Nor did my other attempt at humor—offering to call my mother to deny the other charge against me: that I had invited Edge and Christian to my parents' house on Long Island

---

* Something I later found out had *never* happened in the history of Wrestlers Court— just another social norm shattered by yours truly.

for a home-cooked meal. Not only was that charge completely false, the likelihood of it ever happening was quickly dwindling as I could sense Edge and Christian giving the assembled a look as if to say *We're not with him.* I was drowning badly, and each attempt to rectify the situation only made things worse. I believe the wrestling term is "burying yourself." At that moment I was a human shovel.

* * *

Amidst the groans and blank looks of confusion during my (admittedly fantastic) Flash story, I could see one of my closest allies, Kurt Angle, shaking his head in anger. But not at me. Kurt could sense this was going too far. WWE producer Gerry Brisco took notice and quickly piped in. "It looks like Kurt Angle has something he wants to say."

Kurt *did* look like he had something to say, and I was more than ready for him to say it. Kurt and I started with the company at roughly the same time. After winning a gold medal in the 1996 Olympics in Atlanta (with a broken freaking neck) he made his WWE debut at *Survivor Series 1999,* my first pay-per-view in the company. Together we collaborated on all his promos and backstage vignettes. I wrote a story line where he, Edge, and Christian become friends, something we called Team ECK (Edge, Christian, Kurt). He was probably my closest friend among the sea of wrestlers I was facing. If anyone would stand up for me and give me a much-needed shot of support it would be our Olympic Hero.

Bradshaw asked "Kurt, do you have something to say on behalf of the defendant?"

Kurt rose up, opened his mouth for a brief second, then shook his head no and sat down.

In the grand scheme of things, risking permanent paralysis while wrestling with a broken neck was actually a less daunting act than saying something in my defense at this trial. Kurt later explained to me that if he said something on my behalf it only would've made things worse. For both me *and* him. The praise wouldn't have helped me, and he would have come off as a suck-up or a stooge. He was probably right, but in that moment I felt a tremendous sense of betrayal.

This was a slaughter, to be sure, but despite the wave of testimony against me (no one had brought up a single thing against Edge and Christian since the reveal of their fake book) I was still hanging in there. I truly believed I had a puncher's chance of coming out of this, if not found innocent, at least somewhat still intact. Most of the charges levied against me made me look ignorant or even entitled but not necessarily a *bad* person. Then Paul Heyman was asked to testify.

* * *

Paul had joined the company just a few months earlier, and even though he was on the writing team, he was also the *Raw* color commentator and a veteran, so it wasn't the same as Jamie. Paul was a very affable guy and easy to like, but at the time he had, let's say, a "reputation." He was kind of like the Lando Calrissian of wrestling*—charming, a bit of a scoundrel, and depending on who you talked to, not exactly 100 percent trustworthy. We would butt heads many times over the course of our tenure (foreshadowing!), but at this point we had been pretty friendly. I even went with him to a mall in Houston a week earlier to help him pick out his *WrestleMania* suit. Things went south when Paul came out with his outfit and the salesman asked me, "How do you think your dad looks?" Paul is eight years older than me.

"I tried to mentor this young man, take him under my wing, but when I told him it's important to shake hands with Funaki, he flat-out stated, 'Why do I need to do that? What does shaking Funaki's hand have to do with me succeeding in this business?'"

Oof. Any semblance of sympathy from the crowd-jury completely vanished, and justifiably so. What an obnoxious thing for me to say. Funaki, a wrestler *everyone* loved, was not a main eventer, and by not shaking his hand I came off as an elitist at best and a prick at worst, and it confirmed what Sean, Perry, and everyone else was intimating earlier.

The only issue was, it wasn't the truth (though it wasn't a lie, either). Paul did try to show me the ropes when he first came on. One day as we

---

*Had Lando lived in Scarsdale, New York, and traversed the galaxy donning a skullet instead of a cape.

passed Funaki in the hallway, Paul stressed how important it was to shake everyone's hand and how it would be detrimental to my job and reputation not to. I explained to him that I saw Funaki earlier in the day, said hello, did a RNOR (Respectful Nod of Recognition), and basically did everything *but* shake hands. So my point was if you're saying hello and being respectful, why is a physical handshake so important? I was genuinely curious. Not that I had an issue shaking hands, but if you missed someone and still greeted them, wasn't that essentially the same? In the wrestling world it wasn't. The shake is *everything*, and as much as I tried to dance around it, the fact is I didn't do the act.

The problem was—questioning the method of your greeting versus thumbing your nose at someone because of their stature on the card is a pretty big discrepancy. Paul knew exactly what he was putting out there, and it was probably the most damning testimony anyone could give. It was doubly hurtful because Paul really was acting as a mentor then, and I felt he took something I'd asked him about in private and used it as a way to eviscerate me in front of the entire company. In vintage Paul-ese he later explained to me what I said was in earshot of Bubba Ray and D-Von Dudley, who were in the vicinity, and therefore it was fair game to repeat it to everyone.

Bradshaw saw my agitation and pounced, immediately asking, "Are you calling Mr. Heyman a liar?"

This time I didn't hold back. "Uh . . . *yeah*!?!"

At this point two things happened. Stone Cold Steve Austin, arguably the biggest star in the history of the business, seated in the last row, had enough and walked out of the room. I was honestly surprised it took him this long. Just as Steve walked out, legendary backstage producer Pat Patterson walked in. Pat was completely oblivious to what was going on. In his forty-plus years at WWE he had been to his share of Wrestlers Courts and knew it was pretty much a tongue-in-cheek, "we rib you because we like you" kind of affair. Not this one. Pat could read a crowd and read an opponent, but he could not read a room.

Bradshaw caught Pat coming in and asked him what he thought of the accused. Skipping Edge and Christian, Pat looked at me and in his thick

French-Canadian accent (which always sounded like Dracula mixed with Super Mario when I did it) shouted, "Dat little shit, he fucks with my matches. Changes da finishes!"

John asked pointedly, "Pat, how long have you been in this business?"

"Over forty years," Pat proudly replied.

Bradshaw turned to me. "And the defendant?"

I pathetically muttered, "A year and a half."

And then, Judge Undertaker, like he did to many an opponent, decided to mercifully end the suffering. He found all three of us guilty and asked if we had anything to say before he passed sentence. Edge and Christian kept their self-deprecating humor alive with their final statement, though the room had now gotten decidedly more intense and uncomfortable, so it didn't quite land as well as the book routine earlier. Tonally the "fun" vibe of the room had gone from *Anchorman* to *Apocalypse Now*. Now it was time for my closing statement.

For once I didn't try to deflect by being sarcastic or excruciatingly unfunny. I stood up and spoke from the heart as I addressed the entire company.

"I know what the perception is, but the truth is I'm not stuck up, I'm shy and I know I need to get over that and do better. What I can honestly say is I am writing for every single talent in this room. I know this is your livelihood, I know how important airtime is, and I know this show is better when everyone's involved. I care about and respect this business. I wouldn't be here if I didn't. I know I need to get out of my comfort zone and work with everyone when I'm on the road, and if you'll give me a chance, I know we can make something great."

The reaction wasn't a standing ovation but it wasn't eye-rolling scorn, either. Hopefully they could tell that I did mean what I said. The truth is I *was* trying to get as many people over as possible,* even if I chose favorites

---

* "Get over" means attaining popularity with the fans and getting a reaction. To "go over" means to win a match, and to "put someone over" means losing to them or having them "go over" in order to "get over." Nothing confusing about that.

to work with on TV. It took me a while, but I realized it was actually an *honor* to be the first writer brought into Wrestlers Court. Despite what I thought at the time, just being taken to Court *did* mean that they liked me or at the very least thought I was worth teaching a lesson to. Not every writer—hell, not every wrestler—gets that same respect. If they didn't see any value in me, guys like Triple H or Taker could've easily walked up to Vince and said, "This one's got to go." I saw it happen to others on the writing team over the years, but thankfully they saw enough in me to administer some needed tough love. It really wasn't about the Flash action figure (okay, for Bob it probably was); it was about a change in attitude. About opening up and making more of an effort to get to know and work with everyone instead of retreating to my safe space.

Court was adjourned, and I have to admit I was pretty shaken up. I could hear Pat Patterson from the back saying, "What?! No, I don't hate da kid, I taut we was ribbing!" Pat actually came up to me right after to apologize, which he didn't have to do. That's just the type of guy Pat was. I responded by doing something I had never done before nor since, and smoked one of Pat's cigarettes right there on the spot.

I got back to Vince's office a little shell-shocked and saw that Vince had a big smile on his face.

"I heard Court went well." Vince gave me one of his big booming laughs. Before I could regale him with stories, his expression immediately changed as he asked, "So where are we with the show?"

* * *

The following week it was time to learn what our sentences were. Edge and Christian got their sentences lifted after buying Taker a giant Harley Davidson coffee table book, a DVD set of boxing legends, and an expensive bottle of liquor. It was common knowledge (to all but me) that sentences could be lightened or lifted based upon the bribes one gives the judge.

Even if I'd known, it wouldn't have mattered. Whatever the punishment was, I was ready to accept it. I was about to understand why the Undertaker was so awesome. In my final testimony I had said how much

I respected the business, so Taker wanted me to write a two-thousand-word essay on *why* I respected the business and also take Funaki and other talents I had supposedly dissed out for a drink.

I can honestly say I had never written an essay with so much passion. I wrote about going with my dad to Nassau Coliseum to see Roddy Piper when I was a kid. I wrote about watching in awe over the amount of work it took the ring crew to actually set up the ring, the producers to put together a match, and the wrestlers to absorb so much mental and physical punishment, day after day, year after year, in the name of earning a living and giving the audiences something special to remember. I also pointed out how, despite looking like a trampoline on TV, in reality the mat is hard. Like *really* hard (something I had learned firsthand—more foreshadowing!).

Taker read it, smiled, and ended up giving me an A.* I should've left it at that, but of course I had to push my luck. Feeling emboldened, I sought out Hardcore Holly, who was still wearing his blue-and-pink ring gear. Now that a week had passed, I was hoping a mutual respect had developed. (The good news is that it totally had! The bad news is that it didn't really kick in until fifteen years later, after we had both left the company.)

"Hey Bob!" I said as I made sure to shake his hand. "I know it was kind of crazy last week, but I just wanted to ask: Are we cool?"

Bob thought about it, then shouted "Fuck no!" and stormed off.

It wasn't ideal, but I considered the fact that there was no loud, verbal threat of [redacted] to be a definite sign of progress!

---

*I really wish I'd had the foresight to keep a copy of that essay. Hopefully the Undertaker has it framed and proudly displayed on his refrigerator.

CHAPTER 2

I AM the Mountie

Like most twentysomething wrestling fans in 1998, I was captivated by WWE and WCW battling it out head-to-head on live television every Monday night for over five years. The Monday Night Wars featured elite performers in their prime, shocking real-life twists as wrestlers jumped from one show to the other, Vince McMahon being acknowledged as the real-life owner of WWE, Hulk Hogan being revealed as the evil third man in the nWo (and growing an evil beard to match!). It was unprecedented. Every show became a must-see event. As someone who was antisocial, a huge wrestling fan, and with no significant other,* this was a glorious time with even more incentive to stay home!

Despite my rabid fandom, back in '98, you could've given me a thousand guesses of what I'd be doing in five years and "alone in a room with the Rock and Bill Goldberg backstage at *Monday Night Raw*, writing their first-ever face-to-face confrontation" would not have been one of them. And yet, here I was, for better or worse, ready to contribute to wrestling history.

We were in Seattle, Washington, on March 31, 2003, the day after *WrestleMania 19*. The Rock (cocky, bad-guy, Hollywood Rock) had finally beaten his adversary Stone Cold Steve Austin on the biggest stage possible and now was letting the crowd know he had done it all at age thirty and there was no one left for him to beat.

---

*A friend once sat me down and explained, "You have neither the capacity to love nor feel love," which I thought was fair.

Backstage, earlier that day, Rock and I met with Goldberg, whom Rock had actually helped bring into WWE. Goldberg, based on his experiences in WCW, had an understandable, healthy distaste for writers, but this wasn't going to be a long, drawn-out "promo."* Rock had most of the promo solo; all Bill had to do was make his pyro-fueled entrance, tell Rock he's "next," then hit him with a spear. The only question was staging. Where would Rock and Goldberg physically be when the verbal exchange took place?

Harkening back to the epic Rock–Hulk Hogan promo in Chicago a year earlier, I suggested they stand face-to-face in the ring and let the tension build. Rock seemed down for that, but Bill was hesitant.

"There's just one problem...I ain't Hulk Hogan."

Rock and I exchanged a quick side glance, but no worries. Perhaps feeling a false sense of kinship with Goldberg based on the fact that we both had had a bris, I confidently cited a Rock–Chris Jericho promo from a few years back where Rock was in the ring and Jericho was up on the stage. Maybe Goldberg can say his line then slowly walk to the ring, letting the tension build, for the physicality. Again, Rock was good to go but once again, Bill paused.

"There's just one problem...I ain't Chris Jericho."

O-o-okay then. After much discussion we landed on Rock and Goldberg circling each other in the ring. Thankfully no one could cite another example of anyone in the history of wrestling doing that. In that surreal moment (along with the time I found myself at a Waffle House at 2 a.m. with the Million Dollar Man, Ted DiBiase, dissecting the plot and worldly ramifications of *Brokeback Mountain*), I had to take a step back and quote my inner David Byrne by asking myself, *Well...How did I get here?*

More specifically, how did someone who just years earlier was writing for a teenage werewolf Fox Family show become the head writer for WWE?** How did a guy go from attending a *Monday Night Raw* show

---

* Shorthand for whenever a wrestler has a microphone and talks—be it in the ring or backstage.

** Even coming in at #7 one year on a wrestling newsletter's highly prestigious / completely meaningless "20 Most Influential People in Wrestling" list.

holding a homemade poster of Madonna saying "Even *I* respect D'Lo Brown" to sitting in a *Monday Night Raw* creative meeting with Vince McMahon and actually writing for D'Lo Brown? And way more important, how does one go from Hardcore Holly wanting to kill you to ultimately exchanging genuine, non-ironic holiday well-wishes with the man a decade and a half later?

Well, to quote Vince McMahon, sometimes in order to take two steps forward, we need to take one giant step back.

* * *

Of the many misconceptions about "Hollywood writers" in WWE, the most common one is that they're plucked from soaps or sitcoms with zero knowledge about wrestling and given the keys to the creative kingdom. Even worse is the rumor the McMahons actually prefer it that way. Neither is true. Yes, there have been plenty of writers over the years who fit that description, but in reality, if you're joining WWE completely cold, it's extremely hard to make it work.

WWE is unlike any other form of entertainment with its mix of the verbal and physical, the fact that it's on fifty-two weeks a year from a different city every week, has a cast of over sixty characters, and a history/backstory that spans decades, which makes it almost essential you have a general working knowledge of the show. Even if you don't know the history of the business, you should at least know the current product. There have been many writers with extremely impressive IMDb pages who came in only to get completely overwhelmed. That's why so many writers are there either for a minute or a lifetime. In order to succeed, it helps to have that moment from your past when you became hooked.

For me it was while watching Hulk Hogan vs. Rowdy Roddy Piper for the WWF Championship in the *War to Settle the Score* on MTV. It was 1985 and I was eleven years old. Like most kids, I cheered when Hogan beat the Iron Sheik to become WWF Champion, but the more I started watching Rowdy Roddy Piper, the more I gravitated toward him, even though he was a bad guy. Actually, his character was more than just bad; he was a horrible guy. But he was also so brash, fearless, and funny, it didn't matter if he'd often do unspeakable things like kick Cyndi Lauper in the head. I didn't mind. In fact, I bought my first "Hot Rod" shirt at Madison Square Garden right before Roddy confronted and attacked the Living Legend, Bruno Sammartino, as my friend's mother looked at me like I was a future serial killer.

The War to Settle the Score featured celebrities of all kinds, including *the* top names in pop music,* all weighing in on Piper vs. Hogan. Unbeknownst to us fans, the match itself had been designed to set up the main event of the first-ever *WrestleMania*. As Piper battled Hogan, something happened that I had never seen before—a "ref bump." In the course of the action the referee got knocked unconscious. This blew my eleven-year-old mind. An official was knocked out in the middle of a match! The action then continued, as literally no one (not the wrestlers, fans, nor announcers) cared!

With the ref out of commission, Piper and his ally, "Mr. Wonderful" Paul Orndorff, ganged up on Hogan, laying him out. Then Cyndi Lauper got on the apron to try to stop them as Mr. T watched on from the crowd. One of the biggest pop stars and *the* biggest TV star at the time were all part of the story. (To put it in 2022 terms, imagine Taylor Swift jumping up on the apron as Baby Yoda watched from the crowd.) Piper and Orndorff slowly stalked Lauper as Mr. T jumped from his seat and actually got in the ring! Piper and Orndorff attacked Mr. T as Hogan came to, and a huge melee unfolded.

Once again, mind blown. I burst into my parents' room and gave them a detailed rundown about what happened, including the part about the referee getting knocked out, which, again, I found indescribably fascinating. From that moment on, I was hooked.

I would either watch the WWF pay-per-views at a friend's house or listen to them on a scrambled cable channel, savoring the intermittent seconds of clear audio and video that came on the screen every four minutes. I begged my dad to take me to Nassau Coliseum to see Piper vs.

---

*Tina Turner! Dee Snider! Ted Nugent! Geraldine Ferraro, for some reason!

Adrian Adonis with Andre the Giant as the special guest referee. I had all the classic WWF dolls and ring. I'd watch the Saturday Morning cartoon, the weekend syndicated shows, stay glued to MTV to see when they'd play "Land of 1,000 Dances" off the WWF *Wrestling Album* (which of course I owned on vinyl). I'd buy both the *WWF Magazine* and *Pro Wrestling Illustrated*, where I'd learn of other non-WWF wrestlers. I remember seeing this one guy who I found extremely strange and disturbing, drinking Jack Daniel's and sticking out his tongue. It was Michael "PS" Hayes, who I'd eventually spend a decade and a half working with and to this day find extremely strange and disturbing.

As I entered my senior year of high school I'll admit my interest in wrestling started to wane. Even with the knowledge it was all a show, I thought Sgt. Slaughter siding with Iraq during the actual Gulf War was in poor taste, and with Piper no longer wrestling regularly (plus WWF hitting a creative low in the early '90s) I spent less time watching WWF and more time trying to figure out how to date Meg Ryan.*

When I got to Syracuse University and attended the S. I. Newhouse School of Public Communications (the "Harvard of communications schools," as I've told hundreds of eye-rolling people), my wrestling interest was at an all-time low. If I had been placed in a different dormitory on a different floor it might've stayed that way, but as fate would have it I befriended a fellow student named Mike Konner, who was about the biggest wrestling fan on the planet. He single-handedly pulled me back in.**

While other college freshmen were engaged in deep philosophical arguments or experimenting with recreational drugs, Mike and I debated then WWF president Jack Tunney's decision to bar all reptiles from ringside after Jake Roberts's snake bit Randy Savage on the arm. On a side note while at WWE, I always wanted Chris Jericho to lose the

*This was peak *Joe Versus the Volcano* period. Don't even think of judging me.
**For those wanting to send hate mail for any crappy angle you saw on *Raw* in the 2000s, you can send it to him.

Intercontinental Championship only to appeal the decision and win back the title because his opponent was wearing snakeskin boots and was thus in violation of Tunney's reptile ruling.

While others in our dorm actually went down to Florida and appeared on *MTV Spring Break* engaging in all kinds of salacious behavior, we were offering a girl $5 to stand on the table in our dining hall and yell one of the most iconic wrestling catchphrases of the era, "I *am* the Mountie"! (College hijinks on par with someone hell-bent on dating Meg Ryan.)

Freshman year happened to be the greatest *Royal Rumble* of all time, when Ric Flair entered at number three and won the WWF Championship. I found myself once again hooked, strutting down the hallways of my dorm, "wooo-ing" to no one in particular. Even Roddy came back into the fold during this time, beating the aforementioned Mountie and becoming Intercontinental Champion!

As I found myself getting sucked back in, two new favorites caught my attention. I found the heel iteration of Bob Backlund to be hypnotically entertaining. Like all good heels he was technically in the right (children *should* be valuing their education and reading their dictionaries), but his crazed delivery and impressive (if slightly off) use of SAT vocabulary words made him an instant hero in my eyes. Years later, I was thrilled when I convinced Vince to bring "Mr. Backlund" back for the 2000 *Royal Rumble*. Even more thrilling was when I discovered he did in fact appear to be slightly legitimately insane.

I also gravitated to Owen Hart. As a kid, I always liked the secondary characters more than the main ones. The ones who were infinitely more interesting but never got any of the attention or glory. While I thought Bret Hart was great, I found Owen to be far more my style. I got a lot of grief from family members when I made Owen's entire three-minute promo about "kicking Bret's leg out of his leg" my outgoing message on my answering machine, oblivious to how it felt to those calling long-distance.

One night, junior year, WWF was making a house show stop at the Syracuse War Memorial (name since changed). My friends and I decided not only were we going to go, somehow, some way, we were going to meet Owen face-to-face.

As your typical oh-so-clever college-aged wrestling fans, we cheered the heels obsessively, thinking they'd love it (they don't). When Owen came out we did everything in our power to get him to acknowledge us. In fact, long before Roman Reigns made it a catchphrase, we screamed:

"Acknowledge us! Put meaning into our otherwise empty lives!"

We were close enough for Owen to hear as he actually turned and raised a fist at us in support (something heels almost never do). In that moment he actually *did* put meaning into our otherwise empty lives.

After the show we waited by where we thought the wrestlers parked, determined to meet our hero. Unfortunately, we were a little off in our calculations as we saw Owen and Jeff Jarrett approaching their rental car a block away. At this point our friend Max made a beeline to their car in an effort to stop them before they left. This was perfect because either Max was going to be successful in stopping them or Owen was going to kick his ass! We would've been happy either way!

We watched Max approach Owen, but instead of beating him up, Owen...engaged in friendly conversation with him! No way!

We all raced to their car and took turns shaking Owen's hand, expressing what big fans we were and proudly telling him *we* were the ones chanting our support (somehow, I had a feeling he knew). Then someone in our group said Bret cheated and Owen should've won, which instantly mortified us, but Owen let it slide. We gushingly called him awesome and started to exit until my friend John politely said, "Ummm...you too, Double J" to Jeff Jarrett, who was waiting in the car, having been ignored by all of us the entire time.

* * *

Our obsession with Owen led us to hunting down *WrestleMania 10* tickets and taking the four-hour road trip from Syracuse to New York City in the first of what would eventually become hundreds of four-plus-hour road trips to attend a wrestling show in my lifetime.

We sat in the upper section of Madison Square Garden as Owen took on Bret and cheered so loudly when he won, a ten-year-old girl took a swing at Max. Unfortunately, she missed. On a side note, years later I actually got Max hired as a writer at WWE. He was eventually fired after he was deemed to not be a "cultural fit," which is either an extreme insult or a compliment, depending on who you talk to.*

The next year, as luck would have it, *WrestleMania XI* was in Hartford, Connecticut, which meant another *WrestleMania* road trip! A friend of ours who had graduated and now worked at ESPN got us tickets—literally the last row at the Hartford Civic Center, but we didn't care. He brought along some work friends, including up-and-coming *SportsCenter* anchor Craig Kilborn. About halfway through I heard Craig say, "Where are the midgets? I came to see midgets," and he eventually left before the show ended. In his defense, it was a pretty poor *WrestleMania* devoid of midgets. We watched as Big Daddy Cool Diesel stood victorious in the ring with a bevy of celebrities, including Jenny McCarthy. Little did I know I'd be writing poorly received material for both within the following decade!

My friends and I graduated Syracuse in 1995 and took our "Harvard of Communications School" degrees to Los Angeles, where we all got jobs as production assistants on sitcoms with the hopes of becoming writers. I was the writer's production assistant on a CBS sitcom called *Almost Perfect* starring Nancy Travis. It was an incredible learning experience being able to eavesdrop on two seasons' worth of writing sessions and hearing such prolific writers like Ken Levine and David Isaacs (who wrote forty episodes of *Cheers*) and Robin Schiff (who wrote *Romy and Michele's High School Reunion*). They even put me on the show and gave me a joke in the season one finale, stretching my acting ability as I played a production assistant named Brian. The premise of the series had Nancy Travis as a TV writer trying to balance her romantic and personal life (which was Almost Perfect!), and on the season one finale the show within the show, *Blue Justice*, gets cancelled. At the wrap party everybody started turning

*To be fair, Max would not be considered a "cultural fit" in nearly any occupation.

on each other. My character walked up to the pampered star of the fictional show and said:

"You know that bottled water you had me getting you all season? I got it out of the toilet."

To this day I've never actually watched the episode (I'm told it's on YouTube), but at the end of the show when everybody in the cast came out for a curtain call in front of the studio audience, I took a bow like one of the popular wrestlers of that year in 1996, Greenwich blue blood Hunter Hearst Helmsley future Triple H (that, thankfully, is *not* on YouTube).

My friend John Beck—he of the kind words to Jeff Jarrett—got a job as a production assistant on *Boy Meets World*. Once again, luck was on our side as WWF superstar (the man they call) Vader was guest-starring. John somehow managed to finagle *WrestleMania XII* tickets from him as the show was taking place in nearby Anaheim. That would be three *WrestleMania* trips in a row! We didn't sit in the last row but pretty close to it as we cheered on Roddy in his Hollywood Backlot Brawl against Goldust. The show itself was a big step up from the prior year, and now we were attending not as weird-ass college students but as weird-ass professional Hollywood production assistants! What twenty-two-year-old doesn't dream of living in LA and eschewing all the clubs and fancy parties in favor of driving to Anaheim to see the return of the Ultimate Warrior and holding a homemade sign reading "I would like a Mantaur sandwich"?*

Between 1996 and 1999 my friends and I would congregate for pay-per-view parties as we pursued our dreams of becoming actual television writers. My writing partner Dave Feeney and I were fortunate, landing a spot in the Paramount Studios writers program (now defunct) and getting placed on a show called *Claude's Crib* (also defunct) on the USA Network. No one has heard of this show, not now and not even when it actually

---

*Technically it was my friend Jason Oremland who wrote and held up the "I would like a Mantaur sandwich" sign. He would go on to co-write Disney's "The Princess and the Frog" but I find this way more impressive.

aired, but so what? We were no longer PAs and were actually getting paid to write television.

The next gig we had was as staff writers on NBC's *Jenny*, which at the time was a much-hyped show with one of the hottest talents of the late '90s, Jenny McCarthy. This was a very special moment for me, not because I could now finally talk to Jenny about *WrestleMania XI* (which of course I never did) but because my uncle, Howard Gewirtz, was co-creator and executive producer of the show (Edge and Christian: "Nepotism rules!"), and it had been my dream to write on a TV show with him ever since I was a kid. He was what I aspired to be since third grade, having written for the legendary show *Taxi* and also for *Three's Company*, and Tom Hanks's first show, *Bosom Buddies*, in addition to *The Larry Sanders Show*, *Wings*, *Everybody Hates Chris*, and *The Simpsons*. The show itself was not a success, and my pitch of Jenny volunteering at a seniors home and losing an old man at a Spice Girls concert—while capturing the essence of the '90s perfectly in one sentence—never made it out of the writers room.

I did learn a ton, however, including how to pitch a joke without being terrified. As previously noted, I was/am an introvert by nature, and my tendency was never to pitch a joke out loud in front of the entire room—which is a problem, as that's exactly what the job entails. If I had a joke I thought was funny I'd quietly pitch it to the writer next to me, hoping to get approval, and then *maybe* bring it forward.

My uncle had to sit me down once and make a point of telling me it didn't matter if we were related—I needed to step up. There are a ton of aspiring writers who'd kill to be in my position. It wasn't enough to be on staff and think of jokes and stories while at the office. I needed to be making an extra effort, poring over the script after work when I got home, looking for places to punch it up and come in prepared the next day. And I needed to be more vocal if I was going to make it. He made it clear that if I didn't, Dave and I wouldn't last the season (awkwardness at future family functions be damned).

That talk really woke me up. From then on, I was a lot more vocal in the writers room, actually getting jokes into the show without having to "test" them first. The lessons of that talk proved to be invaluable at WWE and pitching to Vince McMahon. Vince can sniff weakness better than anyone, and you need to not only bring your work home with you, but you need to exude confidence even if you're just faking it.

With a newfound outlook, I tried to make my mark at *Jenny*, but the show was cancelled midway through its first season. It was just not connecting with the audience. Ultimately young adult males who tuned in to see an unpredictable, sexy, outrageous Jenny on *Singled Out* did not have any interest in seeing her as an earnest girl from Utica, New York, moving to Hollywood with her best friend and becoming the next *Laverne and Shirley*.

It was a damaging blow, but that was the nature of life in Hollywood. Once a show gets cancelled, you start looking for your next gig. Even though I was young with two writing credits under my belt, getting hired on a third show did not come easy. Dave and I were writing our spec scripts, taking our meetings, and going on our job interviews. We were told we were finalists for a gig on the show *Malcolm and Eddie*, starring *The Cosby Show*'s Malcolm-Jamal Warner and comedian Eddie Griffin. Had we gotten staffed, I can say with certainty I never would've worked at WWE and Kurt Angle never would've driven to the ring and sprayed the Alliance with milk. Thanks, Malcolm and/or Eddie!

We didn't get the job, and I found myself out of work for over a year. I went from a professional high to an extreme low very quickly, collecting unemployment, not knowing when the next job would be or if there would even be one. But everything would change in June 1999. I got a call from my sister, who was interning at MTV. They were producing a series of WWF specials leading up to 1999 *SummerSlam* . . . and as luck would have it, they needed a writer.

CHAPTER 3

MTV and Fast-Food Espionage

As someone who hadn't watched MTV since being psychologically damaged by the human cake scene in Tom Petty's "Don't Come Around Here No More" video, it's amazing how instrumental it was to my career.

First with the *War to Settle the Score* and then with what I'll refer to as "WWE Week 1999." For the sake of simplicity I'm just going to assume that everyone knows WWF became WWE in 2002 and just refer to it as WWE from here on in. Your brain will thank me.

In July of '99, WWE was at the height of the Attitude Era. It was dominating the Monday Night Wars and was about a month away from launching *Smackdown* on UPN. Looking to cash in on the nationwide phenomenon, MTV made a deal to air a series of five specials over the course of a week that would lead into the *SummerSlam* pay-per-view.

Apparently, there were not many wrestling fans working at MTV at the time, since they needed to find a writer from the outside to work on them. A mixture of luck, coincidence, and multiple instances of nepotism brought me into the fold. See if this tracks:

At Syracuse, my favorite professor was Dr. Robert Thompson, authority on all things television. *He* happened to teach a young student at SUNY Cortland years earlier, named Mick Foley. Professor Thompson would invite me and my friends into his office and cold-call the father of Cactus Jack Manson (as he was then called) in attempt to look cool, which totally worked. (We had another professor who came over and jumped on the giant trampoline we had bought who looked cooler, but it was still quite impressive.) After I graduated, Professor Thompson decided to teach summer classes at Cornell where my sister Randi attended. She liked his class so much she decided she wanted to go into television. She called my uncle—who, as mentioned, was co-creator and executive producer of NBC's *Jenny*—and he helped her get an internship at MTV. That internship led to her finding out about the need for a writer who needed to be a WWE fan.

At this time I hadn't watched WWE in months. As I mentioned, Owen Hart was one of my favorites, and when he tragically died at the *Over the Edge* pay-per-view in May, I just decided to stop watching cold turkey. Every second of WWE television reminded me of Owen, and I couldn't bring myself forward to watch it.

Careerwise I had hit a low point. Needing a job, I decided to embark on a profession I never knew existed: "fast-food spy" for Jack in the Box. My writing partner, Dave, and I had answered an ad in the *LA Times* (never a good sign if you pride yourself on being a working television writer) that promised "free food and fun." We and a bunch of, shall we say, "colorful LA characters" met at a Burbank airport hotel to work in the exciting field of fast-food espionage! The job would entail hiding outside a Jack in the Box with a stopwatch to report on how fast the drive-thru was, going inside under the guise of regular customers and seeing how clean the restrooms were, how competent the staff was, and how long it took to get an order. They were especially interested in me because I could visit the truck stop Jack in the Box, several hours away, then order beer and see if they'd card me. It was not the job I envisioned when graduating college, but on the bright side, the food we ordered we were allowed to eat! On the downside, the food we ordered we were allowed to eat.

Right before my first weekend of assignments, my sister called with news of the WWE-MTV job. I took a leap of faith and quit the Jack in the Box gig before I could go on my first mission—which admittedly is slightly disappointing, as the stopwatch I purchased was nonrefundable.

I quickly cram-watched *WWE Raw* and sent some writing samples to

MTV. Thankfully, I was hired, my first paying writing job since *Jenny* was cancelled. I don't remember all the specials. One of them (shot last) was Mick Foley (as Mankind) on the set of *Total Request Live* with Carson Daly hosting "I Wanna Be a WWE Superstar." A ring was set up in the studio as hopefuls trotted out and cut promos looking to impress. At one point the producers asked me to stand in for Carson for blocking purposes. I looked out the window of the *TRL* studios and saw hundreds of young fans (mostly women) shrieking in excitement only to fall silent and look very confused when they realized it wasn't Carson but some guy who might or might not have been Bud Bundy from *Married with Children*. I became very used to that feeling riding in limos with the McMahons. The limo would pull up, a crowd would gather, screaming as the door opened and then...who the fuck is *that* guy?

The other show involved a live match taped exclusively for MTV. The match they were given was Edge and Christian vs. the Hardy Boyz. I remember MTV being very disappointed and trying to get another match (without success). They were hoping for Stone Cold Steve Austin or the Undertaker and felt a bit cheated, which is funny considering the E and C–Hardys rivalry is now considered one of the greatest, if not *the* greatest, in WWE tag team history.

The biggest show was something we'd record at a WWE live event at the Meadowlands in New Jersey. The premise was having fans' favorite Superstars doing commentary over their favorite music videos.* Here WWE went all out and provided three of the biggest names they had: Triple H, Mankind, and the Rock.

The only issue was that MTV was selecting their "favorite" videos, and there was a good chance that (a) these videos were *not* the wrestlers' favorites, and (b) the wrestlers probably had never seen or heard of the chosen songs before. It was my job to write some fun commentary in the voices of these characters as they talked over videos from Limp Bizkit,

---

*This was before MTV dropped music videos in favor of twenty-hour blocks of *Ridiculousness.*

Kid Rock, and Korn, among others. I myself wasn't even familiar with the videos in question, but despite not having watched in months, I knew these characters and knew how to write in their voices. I pored over every line, every joke, just knowing I would blow everyone away. Nothing could stop me the day of the shoot—and then Triple H walked in with Chyna.

I should've assumed this would be the case, since they were an on-air duo at the time, but no one told us Chyna would be there, so I hadn't written anything for her—which Triple H immediately pointed out upon receiving the script. He was completely professional and we got through it all right, but with no material for Chyna plus Triple H not exactly wild about endorsing "Nookie" as his favorite music video, it made for a tense affair. It had me wondering if I was better off checking the toilet paper supply at the Jack in the Box in Calabasas.

The mood lightened considerably when Mick Foley, aka Mankind, went next. I couldn't blurt out Professor Thompson's name fast enough, and that worked as an icebreaker. I don't remember much about the material itself, but I do remember writing Mankind to be obsessed with finding actual corn in the Korn video. Lo and behold, it did seem to feature something resembling corn, which we freeze-framed as Mankind celebrated.

Finally, it was time to meet the Rock. Having considered myself one for two at that point, I was eager to make a good first impression. This scene with the Rock would determine whether the day was a failure or success. He looked over what I had written and thankfully thought it was pretty good. Then, in a moment that would repeat itself every time we worked together for the following twenty-plus years, he wondered, "How can we make this even better?"

That led to him suggesting we shoot a vignette on the spot where he'd tease that the Rock was coming up next. He'd walk up to some jabroni on the backstage pay phone, ask him what he thought of the Rock's $500 shirt, and when said jabroni tried to answer, Rock would hit him with a classic "It doesn't matter what you think!" before teasing that the Rock was moments away from electrifying MTV.

That jabroni would be me. It would be the first and only time the Rock and I would appear on camera together. (After not being able to find this clip for two decades the Rock actually found it on Instagram earlier this year.)

After the shoot was over, the Rock pulled me aside and asked if I had ever considered writing for WWE before. I hadn't. WWE was so far off the grid as far as Hollywood was concerned. I knew nothing about their creative process or if they even employed writers. It was just not something I considered to be a viable career option. I had always treated WWE like I did a delicious hamburger from Jack in the Box (yes, I still feel guilty about quitting on them last second and insulting their food earlier)—I just wanted to consume and enjoy it without ever thinking about how it was actually made.

Still, the Rock was impressed enough to have a WWE official take down my information. Despite the hiccup with Triple H and Chyna, I felt pretty good about the day. I certainly didn't think it was going to lead to anything, but once all the specials were shot I got a call from Human Resources at WWE asking if I could come to Stamford for a series of interviews for a job on their creative writing team.

It really wasn't a tough decision—of course I'd go interview. What did I have to lose? Even if they offered me a job, it wasn't like I had to take it. The experience alone would be worth it. I said sure and was given a date and time to come to Titan Towers, WWE HQ in Stamford, Connecticut. It wasn't just one interview I'd be having, I was told it would be a series:

- Interview one: WWE Human Resources
- Interview two: WWE writers Vince Russo and Ed Ferrera
- Interview three: Shane McMahon
- Interview four: Linda and Vince McMahon

As someone who a year earlier had dressed as Corporate Mankind (regular Mankind but with a white shirt and tie) for Halloween, this was a pretty big deal.

* * *

Even though an itinerary like the one I had would be any wrestling fan's dream come true, I wasn't even sure if this was a job I even wanted. Ever since I saw my uncle's name in the credits of *Taxi* in third grade, the plan was to make it as a Hollywood television writer, and going to WWE would be a major detour.

At that time as far as Hollywood was concerned, working for WWE even as a top writer carried little to no weight. You might as well be working at Costco. Truthfully, even after all the strides WWE has made as a legitimate form of entertainment, I don't think a WWE writing credit to this day gets you any buzz. A staff writer on the lowest-rated show on Tubi probably gets you an easier path to another writing job than being lead writer of *Raw* or *Smackdown*. Which was why I went into the day of interviews with an ulterior motive:

"Are you guys developing any shows starring wrestlers for sitcoms or dramas in the near future?"

That was my first question to WWE writers Vince Russo and Ed Ferrera after my initial "get to know us" interview with HR. Russo and Ferrera had taken WWE out of their creative doldrums with a fresh, innovative style of storytelling. Their reward? A brand-new show called *Smackdown* to write on top of *Raw*, *Sunday Night Heat*, and a pay-per-view every month. On the surface it seemed like they needed some help, but the impression I got from Russo in that interview was that he wasn't interested in that help coming from me.

Granted, I was told the two had just come off the road, which can make anyone a little cranky, especially when they have to sit down and interview some kid who wasn't even asking about the actual task at hand but was looking ahead to try to make sitcoms (which I was told pretty quickly that they weren't). I felt Russo wanted to get the interview over with and move on. Ed was definitely friendlier (he was a former Hollywood writer himself) but my hesitation of wanting to even join them in the first place was probably showing.

The meeting wasn't especially memorable, at least from their end. In fact, years later after I talked about the meeting on a podcast, Ed Ferrera reached out to me on Twitter to say he had no recollection of the meeting at all. I get it. In fact, I've read firsthand accounts from writers who *I've* actually interviewed with no recollection of said meetings. The world of WWE moves at a breakneck pace with multiple meetings every day (including meetings to plan for future meetings), so something would truly need to stand out to make it memorable. That was why we eventually hired a guy who had a glass eye and took it out during the interview.* Okay, back to *my* interview...

The meeting with Shane McMahon didn't go much better. Shane was in charge of WWE.com at the time and was a major on-screen character as well. It's funny, once I came onboard I'd find Shane to be one of the warmest, most considerate, egoless people I've ever known in my life, but that day I found him to be a little cold. It probably was my own fault. I sabotaged myself pretty early. When he asked me why I wanted to move back to the east coast and work for WWE, I replied with the first thought that popped into my head:

"It's crazy how no one knows how to operate a satellite dish in Los Angeles. I go to sports bars asking them to put on the Mets game, and they look at me like I'm asking them to split an atom."

Not only was that one of the worst possible answers you can give when someone named McMahon asked you why you'd want to join their company, it also didn't help when Shane replied:

"Yeah...I'm a Yankees fan."

The second he said that I realized I am seriously bombing these interviews. All that was left was one more meeting with Vince and Linda McMahon. Honestly, I'm surprised they didn't just cancel the last interview, give me a complimentary Steve Austin foam middle finger, and send me home. Here was an opportunity to join a company I grew up loving, and I was talking about sitcoms and baseball games on satellite. As I made my way to the fourth floor of Titan Towers I was told Linda had a last-second conflict, and it would be just me and Vince.

---

*And of course, eventually had him take out in the ring on live television.

Just the most powerful and influential man in the history of wrestling and me—the guy who without a lucky phone call from his sister would be hiding in the bushes of a Jack in the Box parking lot.

As daunting as it would seem on paper for a lifelong twenty-six-year-old WWE fan to be meeting Vince McMahon in his office for a job, I had this unusual sense of calm. In my mind I had already botched these interviews, so I truly had nothing to lose. I made up my mind that I wasn't going to fish around about potential WWE sitcoms and I certainly wasn't going to talk about the Mets. I was simply going to walk in with the mindset of a professional writer, open up about being a lifelong fan, and see where it went.

Vince's office was spacious, with a red-and-black interior, and it had this weird, splotchy black-and-white design along its side wall, as if a group of Dalmatians were mowed down with a machine gun. This was years before an actual dinosaur skeleton head (a birthday gift from Stephanie and Triple H) would adorn the room, but it was pretty impressive nonetheless.

Vince had a presence. Fortunately, I returned his handshake with a firm one of my own, maintaining eye contact the entire time (I believe HR gave me the heads-up to do that). I talked about how I loved watching WWE as a kid, my infatuation with Piper, my attending various *WrestleManias* (essentially an abridged version of the previous chapter) and how WWE is like nothing else on television as it combines all the great elements of entertainment—action, drama, suspense, humor, compelling characters, but in a live setting with no safety net. I could see Vince nodding along as I listed them off (ironic, since Vince himself hates when people do that). The conversation got so loose and comfortable I even segued into the *Royal Rumble* pools we'd do in college. We each put in ten bucks, put all the wrestlers' names into a hat, and then picked two at random. One year a friend of ours randomly picked Timothy Well and Steven Dunn of the little-used tag team Well Dunn. Vince let out a genuine laugh.

"Ha ha haaaaaa, *that* guy's not going to win."

It didn't even seem like a job interview, more like two people discussing their love of WWE. And yet I was still surprised by the words that came out of Vince's mouth as I got up to leave.

"So…we'll make you an offer you can't refuse and you'll come work for us."

Damn, this day turned around in a hurry.

Not only was I about to get an offer from WWE, straight from Vince McMahon himself, but when I got back to my parents' house* I saw that my agent had called—I had an offer to write on another sitcom: *Big Wolf on Campus* on the Fox Family channel (please hold your applause).

It was a more comedic, more kid-friendly *Buffy the Vampire Slayer*–type show about a teenage werewolf fighting goofy supernatural bad guys while going to high school. Yeah, it wasn't exactly *Frasier*, but it was a tremendous opportunity to work on a "real" show again.

So now I had a decision to make. Actually, I didn't, since Vince's offer was in fact quite easy to refuse.

WWE HR called back and let me know I was being offered a job writing for WWE.com but not the actual television show. I don't know if that was always Vince's intention or if he had gotten underwhelming feedback from Russo and Ferrera, but it didn't matter. There was no way I was packing up and leaving Los Angeles and a television writing career to work on WWE's website.

I joined the room of *BWOC*, where my writing partner and I wrote two episodes, one about an evil wrestling promoter and his evil wrestling protégé (Dr. Apocalypse) who upon winning his 666th match would bring about the end of the world. Someone pitched calling the promoter "Manny McVincent" but I nixed that idea. In the 1/100,000,000 chance Vince McMahon watched *Big Wolf on Campus*, I didn't want to risk offending him. Either way, the MTV experience was a fun little detour into the world of WWE, but as far as I was concerned nothing would actually come of it.

---

*After I had gotten lost driving back to Long Island and somehow wound up in the Bronx.

And nothing did for the next several months. Then came the phone call.

One morning in October of '99, my college roommate and now real-world roommate Mike Konner (again, the biggest wrestling fan I knew) asked me if I heard the news. He read online that Russo and Ferrera were leaving WWE to go to rival WCW. I hadn't heard but I condescendingly told him if that was true, I probably would've been the first to hear about it. I went to shower, and when I came out there was a message on my answering machine. It was WWE HR:

"Brian, it's Palma from WWE, can you give us a call? Something's come up that we'd like to discuss with you as soon as possible."

Turns out Mike was right—Russo and Ferrera had left, and WWE had anywhere between five and eight hours of programming a week to fill with nobody left to write them. I called WWE back. Forget WWE .com—they were offering to move me out to Connecticut, ship my car, put me up in an apartment, and offer me a full-time job writing for WWE TV.

Now I had a *real* decision to make.

The *Wolf* show had just wrapped up, and once again I'd be looking for my next gig. Here I was being offered a job writing for the hottest show on cable, in one of the top positions (I honestly didn't even know if there were any other writers working for them) on a show I truly loved and knew I could do.

Plus, that stuff about the Mets I disastrously told Shane was part of a bigger issue. I missed the east coast. I had spent four and a half years out in Los Angeles and it never felt right. I missed New York's energy and vibe.* I found the stereotypes of New Yorkers being brash and obnoxious with Los Angelinos being phony and status driven quite well founded, and given a choice I'll take brash and obnoxious every time.

I was tired of the on-again, off-again nature of TV gigs, tired of the

---

*Shout-out to the woman in my Upper East Side neighborhood who roams the streets screaming at the top of her lungs and spits at children.

LA scene, and, yes, I'll admit I was one of those people who even missed the weather changing with the seasons. Now, despite all the caveats I listed about writing for WWE, I would be joining them. It actually seemed like a safe, smart move. Sure, this wouldn't lead to getting hired by *Everybody Loves Raymond*, but I was going on a show that was in no danger of being cancelled. Stability is a big deal if you're coming off of working only four of the previous twenty months. If anything, with *Smackdown* starting that fall, WWE was only going to grow. Besides, as I told myself, it'll only be for a year. Two years, tops. There was no way this was going to be anything but a short-term gig.

I called back WWE HR, and in my best DX voice, said I had two words for them:

"I'm in."

CHAPTER 4

First Day on the Job

I'm often asked, of all of Vince McMahon's famous words to live by, which resonate with you the most? The answer is easy:

"Hippos *eat* people?!"

That's what I heard the Chairman exclaim while sitting in a crowded limo in 2004. I was listening to my iPod as one song faded into another, and I really should've hit pause. I have no idea of the context of the conversation, but Vince genuinely seemed shocked and, for reasons unexplained, angry. It was almost as if he wished he had this information earlier. But that "Vince-ism" is kind of an outlier. The more common one that permeates the entire WWE is this:

"Treat every day like it's your first day on the job."

Meaning, don't get too comfortable and think you already know it all no matter how long you've been working. Be eager, enthusiastic, and always willing to learn. Vince would talk about how he never stops trying to learn even after decades of success. Good words to live by, but does it hold up? To answer that, I thought long and hard about my actual first day on the job.

WWE arranged for me to fly into Washington, DC, for *Monday Night Raw* on what would be my first official day as a WWE employee—November 1, 1999. Nowadays they usually sign new writers to a trial period (typically three months) to see if they're working out, but that wasn't the case back then. Vince Russo and Ed Ferrera had gone to WCW, and now there was only one writer on staff, Tommy Blacha, who had just been hired weeks earlier from *Late Night with Conan O'Brien*. With anywhere between five and eight hours of television to produce per week, fifty-two weeks a year, WWE needed the bodies. That being said, I had neither officially moved from Los Angeles to Stamford, Connecticut, nor signed my WWE contract. If this trip turned into a disaster this first week could be my last.

I flew in on Halloween night. The flight attendants were in costumes and the pilot was making Halloween puns like "Sit back, relax, and have a pleasant fright." I don't like it when the airlines try to have "fun." I like my flights to be like the impression I leave on most of my dates—a cold, hollow experience, devoid of human emotion.

Where the hell was I going with this? Oh yeah, my first day.

The next morning, I arrived early at the MCI Center, eager to make a great first impression. I walked to the backstage loading dock area where I had been instructed, ready to change the business forever. Unfortunately, I was immediately stopped by security, who refused to let me into the building. Who would've thought looking like an eager sixteen-year-old fanboy with no credentials (WWE hadn't supplied me with any) would've been a problem? A WWE official came out after I refused to leave, and he also didn't believe me. Thankfully, before the police were called, always a good sign when starting a new job, I produced a printed-out email (I did not have a cell phone then) from Vince's assistant with my travel itinerary. It having been determined the letter wasn't a fake, I was given a temporary ID and finally let in. My career was off to a flying start. I'm almost certain Andre the Giant never had to go through this.

The first thing on my schedule was the *Raw* production meeting. I headed to the room and found only one other person there—Dr. Tom Prichard, one of the greatest trainers WWE ever had, sitting alone at one of the tables. We had a nice little back-and-forth until he asked me what it was I did. That was when Dr. Tom's expression changed.

"Wait, you're the new writer? If that's the case, I think you're supposed to be sitting up there," he said, motioning to the head table facing all the others.

Not one to argue, I got up and sat at the head table. Just me and Dr. Tom alone in the production meeting room, staring at each other in silence. That would end up actually being the *least* awkward part of that morning.

Vince and his inner circle were running late, which meant the room started filling up as some strange guy nobody knew stared at them from the head table. Producers, production staff, announcers, all taking a seat looking up in confusion as I smiled nervously. For the second time in as many hours, the idea of alerting the authorities had been debated. If only I could've wowed them with an interesting fact about the dietary habits of hippos.

Of course, what I *should've* done was get up and start introducing myself to as many people as possible, but my natural introverted instincts weren't allowing for that. Instead I sat there like a moron for several agonizing minutes. Finally, Vince, Shane, and Stephanie McMahon, along with executive producer Kevin Dunn and Tommy (who I had never met nor spoken to), entered the room. Shane and Stephanie sat among the others while Vince, Kevin, and Tommy joined me at the head table. I greeted Vince, who might or might not have remembered our interview from two months earlier, then turned to the near fifty people in the room, trying to decide what I'd say once Vince introduced me, the strange guy sitting next to him. It turned out to be a moot point because…he didn't.

With the meeting already running late and a Monday Night War to win, we didn't have time for such trifling matters. Instead, Vince went straight into the segments of the show, reading them off of what looked like a piece of scrap paper or a large napkin. The planned main event was huge and couldn't have epitomized the Attitude Era any better—future real-life brothers-in-law, Shane McMahon vs. Triple H for the WWE Championship (with DX at ringside, along with Mr. McMahon, Kane, and the Rock with Stone Cold Steve Austin on commentary!).

By the time Vince ran through the show, I looked up and surveyed the room to see if everyone was as impressed as I was. If they were, I couldn't tell. What I could detect was the same general expression aimed my way: *Seriously, who in the fuck* is *that guy?!*

After the meeting ended, I was introduced to Stephanie McMahon, who couldn't have been friendlier. I made some stupid comment about being glad she wasn't sacrificed to the Undertaker months earlier, and she was relieved to hear I was a fan. She gave me the grand tour of the entire backstage area, including the production trucks, catering, and the locker room area. I met legends like Sgt. Slaughter ("no one's really sure what Sgt. Slaughter actually does," Tommy whispered to me) and the Fabulous Freebird Michael "PS" Hayes, who wished me luck. I got reacquainted with the Rock and Mick Foley, having last seen them at the MTV shoot months earlier. They were involved in several segments that day, so I ambled over to Edge and Christian, who were talking hockey. After I introduced myself, they asked me if I was a hockey fan, which I lied about immediately. "Oh sure…um…I really like…Dale Hawerchuk." I hadn't watched an Islanders game in about a decade, so I threw out the first random hockey name that popped in my head. I think they bought it.

Everything was going fine. Tommy, despite having just been hired by WWE himself, took me under his wing and handed me a yellow notepad and a pen. We weren't assigned anything to write, so we just went up to wrestlers and asked if they wanted any help with their promos. I mainly observed, taking in the atmosphere, which was pretty incredible. Despite a production meeting that had everyone in the company basically hearing the show for the first time, backstage was a frenzied but well-oiled machine, with people shooting backstage vignettes, preparing for their matches, and figuring out what they were going to say on the mic. As I was marveling at the scope of everything, Tommy asked me if I was set for the drive to Philly for *Smackdown* once the show was over.

Oh crap. I didn't realize we were leaving for *Smackdown* that night. In hindsight, *of course* that was what we'd be doing, but like an idiot I'd left my luggage at the hotel.

For reasons still inexplicable to me to this day, when the question of *Should I leave the arena right now to go grab my luggage?* came up, I didn't ask Stephanie, who had been doing nothing *but* answering my questions all day. I didn't ask Tommy. I didn't ask Gerald Brisco, whom I had accidentally called Jack—his brother's name—earlier in the day. I didn't even ask Michael Hayes, who someone had introduced me to for what had been the third time that day and was now getting annoyed.

"Jesus Christ, I've met him three times! I hope you get fired so I don't have to meet you again!"

Nope, instead I walked up to the chairman of the company, who in a few minutes would be appearing in multiple segments on a live show, hitting his son in the head with the WWE Championship and asked, "Um...hi! Is it okay if I run back to the hotel to grab my luggage?"

This is a stark reminder that sometimes it's best *not* to treat every day like it's your first on the job. Sometimes on your first day you do stupid things that makes the boss look at you like you're the dumbest person on the planet.* I took his confused yet perturbed look of annoyance as a yes and made a mad dash back to the hotel.

After a successful show, and luggage now in hand, I asked Tommy what would happen next. I didn't know if there was a bus or if he had a rental car or just what. Instead, he told me to hop in the SUV with him and the McMahons. As previously mentioned, literally one year earlier I was dressed as Corporate Mankind for Halloween. Now I was sitting in the back of an SUV next to Stephanie McMahon, on my way to Philadelphia for *Smackdown* with Shane McMahon at the wheel and Vince McMahon riding shotgun.

It was a 150-mile drive in the dead of night, but with Shane driving it would easily take less than two hours. Maybe even an hour and a half. Shane and the speed limit really weren't on speaking terms. As Shane attempted to break the sound barrier, Vince turned and asked me what I thought of my first night.

"Well considering my apartment is filled with inflatable WWF

---

*Though, in fairness, the average WWE writer receives that look from Vince multiple times per week.

furniture, I'd say pretty surreal." This thankfully elicited a hearty chuckle from the boss, and it was true. My roommate and I not only had one of those inflatable WWF chairs but an inflatable Stone Cold Steve Austin "Battlin Bop Bag." You know, like most cool kids in their midtwenties living in LA.

It was a fun, breezy conversation. Tommy, myself and the McMahons recapped the show. As we got near Philly we entered an eerie tunnel.

"This is where we kill you and stuff the body if you do a bad job," Vince said jokingly.*

I don't know what possessed me to say it, but the words "Is that what ended up happening to Koko B. Ware?" came out of my mouth this time to dead silence. It got so quiet I thought I might've accidentally stumbled upon something I shouldn't know about.

We rode in relative quiet until we passed through a residential neighborhood at around 1:15 a.m. Suddenly Vince leaned over Shane and started frantically honking the horn, over and over again. I had no idea what was going on until Vince stopped honking and turned to the back with a devilish grin.

"*That'll* wake 'em up!" Vince followed that up with a classic "Ha-ha-haaaaaaaaaa!"

As I thought about the multiple Phillies fans waking up in the dead of night, frightened and confused, all I could think was—you had to love this guy.

We got to the Philly Holiday Inn at around 1:30 a.m. I still had no idea what was on tap for *Smackdown* tomorrow. Despite reading the segments of *Raw* off a napkin earlier, I had just assumed they had already written the show. I assumed wrong.

"We'll meet at 8:00 a.m. in my room. Brian, make sure you tell Steph what you want for breakfast," Vince said as he grabbed the keys already waiting for him at the front desk.

It sounds incomprehensible to say today, with WWE having two

---

*I think it was jokingly.

writing teams of over thirty people and scripts written in advance, but back then we'd meet in Vince's hotel room suite on a Tuesday morning and write the show from scratch, with hours until that day's production meeting and Stephanie McMahon taking orders for breakfast. Though technically she wasn't officially a writer, a year from this time she'd be the head of the entire creative team.

And now the scandalous part. This is not meant to be any kind of McMahon tell-all, but I can't ignore the truth. I realize this will send shock waves throughout the wrestling community, but it needs to be stated in print—the entire McMahon family are *incredibly* patient when it comes to eating pancakes. Once pancakes are set in front of me, I'll pour the syrup and attack immediately. This family, no matter how hungry they are, will very methodically cut their pancakes into tiny squares before applying the syrup, resisting the urge to eat right away.

"The syrup penetrates the entire pancake this way," Shane explained, and he was right. You can accuse Vince of making many decisions on the spur of the moment. Plenty of times I'd hear we were changing a title or turning someone heel/babyface day of the show, and all I'd think was *The Pancakes! Remember your patience with the pancakes! For the love of all things holy, apply that here!*

Okay, I'm glad I got that out in the open. Back to *Smackdown*.

That morning we came up with a stacked main event that flowed perfectly from the night before. An eight-man tag team match of the newly formed D-Generation X (Triple H, Road Dogg, Billy Gunn, and X-Pac) vs. Shane McMahon, Kane, the Rock, and Stone Cold Steve Austin!

The carryover story from *Raw* was Mr. McMahon accidentally hitting Shane with the WWF title belt, causing Triple H to gain the victory. Or *was* it an accident? That was what Jim Ross postulated on commentary, and it set us up for a show-long story of whether Mr. McMahon's actions were on the level or he was secretly in cahoots with DX.

In fact, Triple H and DX were set to come to the ring and make a startling announcement—Mr. McMahon was the newest member of DX! They brought out a DX jersey with "McMahon" written on the back, and the plan was for Vince to come to the stage and rebuke them. Keep in mind this was during a rare time when the Mr. McMahon character was a good guy (babyface) and not too long after real life WCW head Eric Bischoff had joined the evil nWo, so story line wise it wasn't far-fetched.

Backstage, moments before the segment, Vince was looking for something he could say back to Triple H. He headed to Gorilla Position (named for Gorilla Monsoon, it's the area backstage just before wrestlers step through the curtain into the arena) and asked, "Dammit, what's something ridiculous I could join? The Girl Scouts? The circus?"

This was my chance. I had still been in observation mode for most of the day, but now I had the opportunity to make an actual contribution. And not just any contribution but a line for Vince McMahon himself in the main-event angle. Taking the lessons I had learned on *Jenny*, I didn't pitch anything to Tommy first, I decided to just walk up to the Chairman and go for it...

"What if you said you'd rather join WCW?"

There was a brief pause as Vince took that in. Over the years I'd get used to that pause as he tried on the idea and either accepted it or rejected it. This time he nodded and said, "That's it."

Moments later Mr. McMahon's music hit and he rebuked Triple H's offer to join DX, saying he'd rather join "Dub-ya Cee Dub-ya." It got a tremendous pop from the Philly crowd and from the announcers, who were obviously hearing the line for the first time.

I snuck out into the crowd to watch this all go down and felt a tremendous rush. You can get a big laugh on a sitcom with a studio audience who are supposed to laugh on cue, but hearing a sold-out arena react so viscerally to a line that had come out of your head minutes earlier was a feeling that was unique to wrestling.

I had actually done it—I had made my first real contribution to WWE programming. I carried that high all the way back to Los Angeles, got back to my apartment, and sat proudly in my WWE inflatable chair like it was the Iron Throne. Then Tommy Blacha called.

"So I was talking to the McMahons after the show. They asked me what I thought of you and I said, 'I like him.' They said they did, too! Guess we'll see you next week!"

The truth was, I liked them as well, and I had enjoyed the two days on the road. Awkward first day aside, I thought, *Maybe this can work. After being out of a job for over a year it would be nice to have some stability back in my life.*

Then Tommy continued: "Hey I almost forgot. Keep this to yourself, but Steve Austin needs to have neck surgery. He may never wrestle again. We need to figure out a way to write him off the show. Bye!"

Okay so maybe *stability* wasn't the right word, but it was definitely a challenge worth taking. After four and a half years out in Los Angeles, I was moving back to the east coast, and I'd never look at wrestling, television, hippos, or pancakes the same way again.

I would experience the thrill of wrestling without having to endure the physical pain of it...

Or so I thought.

CHAPTER 5

The Bump

G o backstage at any wrestling show in the world, from WWE to an independent show on a used car lot, and you can divide everyone you see into two categories—those who take bumps and those who don't. To take a "bump" technically means you've fallen to the mat in some form on your back, but really it's to be on the receiving end of any wrestling move. Bump takers aren't just limited to wrestlers. Managers, authority figures, ring announcers, commentators, referees, celebrities, sometimes accidentally cameramen and medics, have all found themselves having to take a bump at some point.

But not writers. At WWE, writers and pretty much anyone who's an employee and never seen on camera are off-limits when it comes to physicality.*

For the most part, Hollywood actors have had stuntpeople to take the bumps for them. Plus, even if you are, say, Jackie Chan or Tom Cruise on the *Mission: Impossible* set, you're not having to perform your stunt live on television in an arena filled with ten thousand–plus screaming people. Wrestlers truly have no safety net, and it was something a writer like myself, just starting out in 1999, needed to be cognizant of. No matter how painful it may be when a promo you've written gets cut, it's not the same hit as what the wrestlers actually go through. When it comes to

---

*Even the Undertaker didn't throttle the pyro guy who accidentally set him on fire live on pay-per-view.

49

bonding with wrestlers, you can laugh with them, be friends with them, drink *way* too much alcohol with them, but unless you're out there taking bumps you'll never truly be *one* of them. And that can occasionally cause some unspoken but undeniable tension.

When it becomes painfully obvious that some writer who's never been in a real fight and never taken a bump in their life is putting a wrestler in no-holds-barred Tables, Ladders and Chairs matches, some feelings of resentment can emerge. The issue of *How can you truly write this stuff when you don't even know what it feels like?* always exists.

Experiencing what the people you write for are actually going through in some capacity helps lessen that tension. It's why you sometimes hear about Hollywood writers taking acting classes. But it's not that simple in wrestling. Sure, you can write yourself onto the show and take bumps that way, but that almost always ends in disaster and causes way more problems than solutions (as I will allude to multiple times throughout this book). You can hop into the ring during the day and just start asking wrestlers to hit their finishing moves on you, which sure will make *them* happy but would surely get you fired and/or hospitalized.

Writers taking bumps just isn't the natural order of things. It would take a person who was crazy enough not to care about protocol or potential lawsuits to find a solution.

Enter Shane McMahon.

Shane is probably the most famous huge bump taker in WWE history who's technically not a wrestler. Shane has no fear, and he gained a lot of respect from the boys and fans alike for doing things in the ring that no sane person would ever attempt. He is the walking epitome of YOLO and FOMO. I'm the exact opposite. I'm LOMO—I actually have a *love* of missing out on things. I've turned down invitations to do things on New Year's Eve because as long as I had an invitation and technically *could've* done something, then I can turn it down, relax, stay at home, and not feel like a total loser. It was why I always took my WWE vacation weeks during International tours and didn't even get a passport until years into my tenure. Why experience all life has to offer when you can do nothing?!

Anyway…it was therefore not a shock when, in January 2000, Shane burst through the writers room door in Stamford, Connecticut, like the Kool-Aid Man and told the four-person writing team, "We're going to take some bumps."

The creative team was working out of the WWE studio at the time. This was the building where all the television production took place (as opposed to the corporate offices a few minutes away). There was a spare ring set up at the studio, and Shane wanted us to gain some appreciation for what the men and women of WWE went through. Sure, us writers had our own set of unique difficulties, churning out hours of television fifty-two weeks a year on the whim of a man known to change his mind on things he had previously loved twenty-four hours earlier. But no matter how hard you try to rationalize it (and trust me, I've tried) physical wrestler bumps are just not the same as psychological writer bumps. This was Shane acting as our own personal Morpheus, getting us to take the red pill.

I didn't really know what Shane had in mind, but secretly, despite my general preference to avoid pretty much everything, I was kind of excited. It's every wrestling fan's dream to step into an actual ring. On TV it looks so much fun! Plus, our toy WWF rings from childhood gave the impression that it was one step below a bouncy castle.

I stepped through the ropes as my idols had done and immediately realized something was wrong—as I would later point out in my man-dated Wrestlers Court essay, the mat was hard. Like *really* hard. It almost felt like walking on a set of wooden planks with a thin sheet of canvas layered over it. Which makes sense, because that was exactly what it was.

Years before it became an *Arrested Development* catchphrase, I realized I had just made a terrible mistake.

Shane showed us how to run the ropes (which were also surprisingly hard) and take "flatbacks," the act of dropping oneself backward onto the (again, deceptively hard) mat. He showed us some simple individual moves, then had us string them all together. I was the youngest of the quartet going through writer's boot camp, and I'm not exactly proud to say I was the first one to tap out.

About ten minutes in, I started getting winded and nauseous. I ran the ropes, did a few flatbacks and one lousy Hurricarana,* and I wanted to throw up. If Shane's goal was to make me sit on the ring steps asking, *How in the living hell do these people do this every night?* then mission accomplished!

Now I had a greater appreciation for the men and women taking bumps for our enjoyment, plus I had a fun story to tell all my friends (in that version, I did not bail in ten minutes and bitterly watch the others while eating Goldenberg's Peanut Chews). Regardless, lesson learned on the physical toll wrestlers take, and the best part was I'd never have to deal with anything like that ever again...

Until two weeks later.

It took a massive blizzard and local Baltimore officials literally banning people from driving on the streets to postpone *Smackdown* in January 2000. As word was getting out that the show had been postponed, I saw Shane, the Dudley Boyz, and others talking to writer Tommy Blacha in the ring. After some gesturing and nodding, I saw Tommy being lifted up, about to take a suplex! Being the supportive friend that I was, I immediately turned around and attempted to get the hell out of Dodge before someone saw me. That was when I heard Shane's voice.

"Hey, Brian! Why don't you come into the ring?"

I froze like Ed Rooney hearing Ferris Bueller was on line two.

There was no choice but to turn and get in. I saw Tommy in the corner recovering from the suplex, and he didn't look well. I needed to think fast and proceeded to tell the now-growing crowd of wrestlers about the impromptu session with Shane and how much I appreciated the physicality they put into their craft. Then Bubba Dudley stepped forward and said four words that would change my life forever:

"Let's do a Powerbomb!"

This was now a pivotal moment. A simple *thanks but no thanks* would do irreparable harm to my reputation. I'd be labeled a gutless phony and

---

*Okay, it was a very slowly executed somersault.

would have no leg to stand on when trying to convince a performer to do something they weren't feeling. On the other hand, a simple *Sounds good!* would result in a Powerbomb. It was the lesser of two evils, and it really wasn't a choice at all—I needed to take the Powerbomb.

For context a Powerbomb, as defined by Wikipedia, is: "a professional wrestling throw in which an opponent is lifted [usually so that they are sitting on the wrestler's shoulders] and then slammed back-first down to the mat." Fun!

Again, the thought of something like this happening today would be ludicrous, but at the time, no one seemed to be worried about things like "liability" or "violation of company policy" or "potential multimillion-dollar lawsuit." There were no cell phones recording video and no social media to post it to even if there were. I sucked it up as I saw Shane pumping his fist and Bubba making his way to the corner of the ring. This was going to be not your standard Powerbomb, but a Powerbomb from the second rope! Seemed like a perfectly safe thing to perform on a guy who got queasy getting lifted in a chair at his bar mitzvah.

Now the crowd at ringside was growing larger. D-Von Dudley lifted me up to Bubba's shoulders so that Bubba was facing forward and my back was to the mat. It was well known in most wrestling circles backstage that D-Von was "the nice one" while Bubba was…well…kind of a prick. The truth was, Bubba could be a prick if he wanted to be, but mainly he was an outspoken, passionate guy who said what he felt and didn't have a problem letting you know it. In a position like this you're putting your body in the other guy's hands, and I didn't really know what to expect next, though I started to regret writing Bubba to lose to Jeff Hardy the previous week on *Raw*.

As I looked up at the ceiling and braced for impact, wondering how the hell I ended up in this position (nothing like this was happening to the writers on the teenage werewolf show), I heard Shane McMahon screaming from the outside.

"Tuck your head in!"

"What?" I shouted back.

"Your head! Make sure you—"

Before he could finish the sentence, we were airborne. I managed to tuck my head in at the last second as we landed with a thud. Even though by all accounts Bubba took care of me, his ass taking the majority of the impact, I still felt like the wind was knocked out of me.

I honestly don't remember much of what happened next. Did the boys start slow-clapping in a sign of mutual respect? Did they get upset at Bubba for taking it too easy? I have no recollection.

The next active memory I have was being in my hotel room afterward, still feeling it. It was a very strange feeling. On the one hand I wasn't feeling pain, but I also was not *not* feeling pain. I started to figure out what was going on. Whatever pain I might've had was replaced by something new to me—pure, unbridled adrenaline.

I had never experienced anything quite like this before. I paced in my hotel room and realized upon further reflection that taking that bump was...incredible!

I felt a surge of pride, toughness, and a strange desire to get into a street fight. Back then I tended to keep to myself and shy away from the hotel bar after a show, but this time I marched down feeling like the second coming of Mick Foley after Hell in a Cell. A mix of the boys and the staff greeted me with a hero's welcome, and it truly felt like the dynamic had shifted. There was a modicum of newfound respect over the fact that I didn't chicken out. I wasn't one of the boys, not by a long shot, but, for one night, in their eyes I was a man! A man who celebrated by drinking not one but *two* light beers at the Baltimore Sheraton before heading back to his room—but a man nonetheless!

I now had the slightest bit of credibility when it came to describing bumps to normal civilians. In fact, when Seth Green guest-hosted *Raw* years later and we met in his hotel room to go over the show, I could tell he was a little nervous about being in a match, so I decided to set his mind at ease. I told him not to worry about having to take a bump, for I had taken a bump myself. He asked what it was like.

"Remember when Joe Pesci and Daniel Stern got hit with the pipe and then fell through a hole and landed on their backs on the basement floor in *Home Alone*? It's kind of like that."

Seth gave me a quizzical look as I realized standing in the room, hanging out and listening to this story was none other than Macaulay Culkin, one of Seth's friends and a huge wrestling fan. Seth turned to Mac (his friends and other people who randomly tell anecdotes about him in books call him Mac) and said, "Heeeey, *you* were in that movie!"

Mac nodded. "Yeah, I believe I was."

But even the awkwardness of that moment couldn't take away the pride I felt being able to recount the tale of my single bump. And sure, the adrenaline from that night had worn off the following day, and once it had, I had no desire to ever take another bump again. But thanks to Shane O'Mac's blatant disregard of the WWE employee handbook, one of the worst snowstorms in Baltimore history, and Bubba Ray Dudley's ass, I finally earned my *b* card.

And that was how I found a way, for one night at least, to win the wrestlers' respect. But it was kind of an isolated incident. I'd ultimately find far more unique ways to piss them off.

CHAPTER 6

If You Smelllllll . . .

W hen Dwayne Johnson, aka the Rock, came back to WWE in 2011, Vince McMahon looked me in the eye and said something...curious.

"You get to work on the Rock's promos. That's the easiest job in the world."

That statement is 100 percent accurate and 100 percent ridiculous. What Vince meant was that the Rock was so "over" it didn't matter what he said since the crowd was going to go crazy. And in a way, he was right. Writing a thirty-second backstage "insert" promo (when you see a character pop up in a little box during their entrance) for someone with no distinct personality is way harder than writing a twenty-minute promo with the Rock. But what Vince was wrong about was that it very much *does* matter what the Rock says.

(Note: In our current day-to-day lives I usually call him "DJ." I'm not nerdy enough to go with "Dwayne" but not cool enough to go with "D." Whenever we're back at WWE, I revert back to "Rock," as that's what he's still called by everyone there.)

The Rock holds himself to an extremely high standard. He goes into each backstage interview, each in-ring promo, and each movie and non-wrestling-related project today with the same mindset he had when I met him at that MTV shoot in '99: "How can we do something no one's ever done before? How do we raise the bar higher than it's ever been?"

Trying to live up to those standards from the man himself, much less to the expectations of a global audience spanning multiple generations, does not qualify for "easiest job in the world." But it is exciting. Working with the Rock has always been one of the most exhilarating parts of the job. There were times we'd have something ready to go days in advance. Other times the promo would be finalized seconds before his music hit. It can be intense, unpredictable, at times heat-getting, but in the end it was *always* fun.

Most of that is due to the Rock himself. It's funny how over the years I gained a reputation as "the Rock's writer" because if there was anyone who never needed a writer it was him.

Whenever I meet someone new and the topic of what I did in wrestling comes up, I'm always hit with one of two things. Either that person will mock-shout, "You mean it's all scripted?" (I've heard that roughly 872 times) or I'd get asked which of the Rock's catchphrases did I come up with.

The fact is the Rock came up with *all* his famous catchphrases.* When I first started, the Rock was already considered one of the best on the mic. He very easily could've seen a new writer coming in and said, *Yeah, I'm good*.

A lot of the "over" wrestlers had that attitude, and it was understandable. Wrestling had existed and thrived for decades without writers. Just using one, especially one who inexplicably went through a phase of carrying a yo-yo backstage despite knowing *zero* tricks, would be a slap in the face to tradition and all that made wrestling pure. Ric Flair, Dusty Rhodes, Roddy Piper—none of the great talkers needed "writers." Just the thought of it was laughable. Rock, while being a third-generation star and old-school in his own right, had a different point of view. His attitude was "I'm going to give this guy a chance, and if he sucks I'll still be fine, and if he can help me, even better."

There's a misconception among some that the Rock has all his promos

---

*Actually, that's not true. I did come up with "the People's Strudel," without which, let's face it, he'd be nothing.

fully scripted for him. Not true. Our formula was simple: If there's a Rock promo on the show, we'll start the process early. I'll ask him what he's thinking and what points he wants to get across. I'll also share my thoughts, as well as some potential lines and themes. He'll review and provide feedback, telling me what he likes, what he doesn't, plus what he'd like to add and achieve. He'll then go over his match while I go put something down on paper. Then we'll meet and go over everything, beat by beat, until we have something we're happy with. If it's a promo with multiple people, we'll involve them as well.

This can take some time, but it's really the ideal way. Having the talent heavily involved in the creation of the promo will almost always result in a better promo than just handing them a piece of paper. I realize back in the day when there were no writers, most wrestlers would speak off-the-cuff, with often brilliant results. There are plenty of wrestlers out there right now who can certainly do that, but it's often (and I can speak only for WWE) not that simple.

Sometimes a wrestler doesn't have the entire scope of that night's show and where certain angles are going. As a wrestler you can have a great idea in your head, but you might not know if Vince already has that same idea planned for someone else or how he sees your character. Sometimes what you want to say would take ten minutes but your promo is only allotted for five. Or sometimes you've got a great line in your head but you don't know if someone else is using that same line (or something similar) later, which means you saying it first would kill its impact.

There are other factors as to why a writer can be useful as well. Maybe you've got a huge match you need to concentrate on,* and your life would be made easier if you can have someone you trust take a stab at the promo until you have time to look at it later and make it your own. Maybe you actually *prefer* to not have to worry about what you're going to say and

---

*Writers have nothing to do with the putting together of actual matches. How wrestlers memorize entire bumps, spots, sequences, false finishes, and more has always been beyond my comprehension.

want someone to write it out for you. These are all decent reasons for writers to exist in wrestling, and it's ultimately up to that writer to bring something to the table. That was my situation with the Rock, and it mirrors his situation when he first started in WWE—here's your opportunity, now it's up to you to either sink or swim. That mindset led to some incredible moments both in front of and behind the camera. Here are a few:

In early 2000 the Rock was looking for something new he could say to his longtime rival Triple H. As we met backstage early that afternoon, I pointed out a particular speech pattern that I, as a fan, always noticed. He had a habit of attaching a big "uhhh" to his words.

"So tonight-uh . . . in this very ring-uh . . ." That kind of thing.

We all have our personal verbal tics. Announcer Michael Cole used to say "now" at the end of every sentence. "Jeff Hardy, into the ropes now . . ."

Vince took it upon himself to fine Cole every time he ended a sentence with the word "now," and sure enough Cole stopped doing it.

I admit, my goal in pointing out Triple H's *uh*s wasn't altruistic. I just wanted the Rock to have something he could sink his teeth into and make fun of. I explained this all to Rock, and even imitated Triple H's voice. Rock found it hilarious and wanted to use it in his promo with Triple H that night. All we had to do was get it approved by Vince.

We strode into Vince's office to find Hunter and Stephanie . . . and all of DX—Road Dogg, Billy Gunn, and X-Pac. I hadn't exactly endeared myself to DX at that point. It was just weeks earlier when I was supposed to produce a DX vignette backstage. I walked in feigning confidence, outlining the scene, the camera positioning, and the blocking, as I asked if anyone had any questions.

"I got one," Billy Gunn replied. "Who the fuck are you?"

So it wasn't exactly a warm room when Rock and I strode in. Vince asked what we had in mind. With Triple H looking on intently, Rock took over.

"Hunter, you're going to love it. You guys are out there doing your thing when my music hits. I go to the top of the ramp and tell you how every single week you come out here, stand in the middle of the ring, and every time you open your mouth, it sounds like *this*..."

Rock gave a dramatic pause then turned to me and said "Brian, do the voice."

My heart momentarily stopped as Hunter, Steph, and all of DX turned their heads in my direction. I tried to turn it back around on Rock:

"Well, you know you're going to be out there, maybe you should do it..."

"Yeah, but you did it so well before, everyone in the hallway was laughing."

"It's just that in order to—"

"Dammit, Brian, do the voice!" Vince shouted, ending the argument quickly.

With little choice, I did the imitation.

"Tonight-uh...I am the Game-uh...and in this very ring-uh...for the next twenty minutes-uh...I'm going to be talking-uh...and saying absolutely nothing-uh."

Vince guffawed pretty loudly, as only he can, and gave his approval as DX sat quietly. Triple H just nodded and said, "Sounds good," but I detected actual steam coming out of his ears. It was a look I got from him early and often in my tenure at WWE that eventually dissipated (and it took only sixteen years!).

In the end, the imitation got over huge with the crowd—and lo and behold, shortly after that segment the *uh*s started disappearing from Hunter's promos entirely. I didn't exactly get a thank-you from Hunter that night. In fact, when I got back to my hotel I found my backpack was filled with vegetables from a tray I could've sworn I saw in Vince's office (the writers and Vince inexplicably shared an office at TV during this time). I've always suspected this to be the work of DX, and based on what I heard about the history of wrestlers filling people's bags with things, I'd say I got off extremely easy. As I was emptying broccoli and cauliflower from my bag, I made a mental note—the Rock imitating his opponent *works*! Something Rock and I would put to the test ten months later.

*   *   *

Even though it was always in character and even though the Rock's gimmick was to talk shit about people, it was actually pretty surprising how sensitive some wrestlers were to being made fun of. Not all of them, mind you. Not even most of them. But sometimes "laying the smacketh down" would result in a number of "hurteth feelings."

Two promos stand out as far as pissing talent off, and oddly enough they rank as two of the most popular Rock promos of all time.

The first was in December 2000 before the six-man Hell in a Cell match at the pay-per-view *Armageddon.* Remembering the success of the Triple H imitation in February, I threw out an idea to Rock—if imitating one opponent could be so memorable, how about imitating all five of your opponents? These were some pretty heavy hitters, all of them future WWE Hall of Famers—Triple H, Kurt Angle, Rikishi, the Undertaker, and Stone Cold Steve Austin.* Rock said he was going to buzz all of them to make sure they were cool with it.** Once he did that, we collaborated on the promo which, like all of Rock's backstage promos, he insisted on performing live.

On a side note, I've always been amazed how Rock does this, working live with all the pressure that comes with it. When I was a kid, I'd get so nervous if anyone was watching me do anything. If I was playing tennis and anyone I knew was in breathing distance, I'd make them turn and look away like it was the final scene of *The Blair Witch Project.* It was just too much pressure for me. If I had to do a WWE promo I would demand it be pretaped hours in advance and that the backstage area be clear (with security allowed to use Tasers on anyone not authorized to be there). Rock cared not for such things. There'd be large crowds of wrestlers, WWE employees, people who worked in the arenas, and guests of guests

---

*Yes, technically Triple H isn't officially in the Hall of Fame yet, but fingers crossed.
**The Rock would always let his opponents know what he was going to say beforehand. Maybe not word for word, but he'd give the general idea and when his opponent should respond, should the Rock start ad-libbing.

gathered around on set whenever the Rock had an interview. He never asked them to leave. In fact, it didn't faze him one bit.

Doing promos live is a savvy move for a couple reasons. First, if the crowd is responding, you can go off script and react to them—it just makes the promo feel alive and more electric. Plus, you don't have to worry about doing it take after take nor worry about time. If you're doing a pretaped interview, you'll often have an annoying writer standing by with a stopwatch (like the job at Jack in the Box, here we were also required to carry stopwatches), ready to tell you that perfect take went two minutes heavy and that Vince is going to be upset. It might result in you having to do it over. When you're live you can certainly *try* to hit your allotted time, but if you don't... well, it's no longer your problem (it would become my problem).

So, back to the *Armageddon* promo where Rock proceeds to roast all the other competitors. The Triple H imitation was back as was a spot-on imitation of Rikishi, who had recently turned heel ("I did it for da Rock"). We added a Kurt Angle Viagra joke (*the* in thing in 2000). In addition, there was a cross-eyed version of the Undertaker and a Stone Cold Steve Austin imitation in which the Rattlesnake professes his love of the Backstreet Boys. To paraphrase the late, great Pat Patterson, the crowd went "banana" for it. However, the next day at *Smackdown*, I heard most of the imitated talent were not as pleased. In fact, I believe the words of the Rock were:

"Great promo last night. By the way, the boys are fucking pissed."

Officially I heard that their issue was Rock didn't put over the severity of the Hell in the Cell structure enough. The reality was that despite their "approval" the boys didn't like the way they were made fun of.

Trying to see their side, I get it... kind of. These are top money-drawing talents, busting their asses trying to sell a main event, and Rock's turning it all into comedy. Technically speaking, if you watch the entire promo, Rock does begin and end on a serious note selling the severity of the Cell; it's just not the part people were talking about afterward.

If that had happened today, I'd take the time to approach each talent and see what their issue was (or better yet, take it upon myself to buzz them before the promo). Back then I only approached Kurt Angle, as he was the only guy I considered myself friends with. Kurt, as I suspected, didn't really care about the comedy, but he did confirm the other main eventers weren't exactly among the millions (and millions) enjoying the promo. In one fell swoop, I had managed to piss off a good portion of the top guys in the company, so I chose to deal with the issue as any real man would—I approached no one and hoped it would all be forgotten.

The problem is, people may eventually forgive, but in wrestling, no one ever forgets.

The other promo that caused some waves involved the return of the nWo in 2002. There were some mixed feelings backstage on whether to bring back Hulk Hogan, Scott Hall, and Kevin Nash, but Rock was all for it. He had idolized Hogan as a kid and was a big fan of Hall and Nash and what they accomplished in the wrestling business and in WCW. Hall and Nash basically launched the Monday Night Wars. When they took their seats at ringside on *Monday Nitro* back in May 1996, fresh off exiting WWE, wrestling as we knew it was never the same. Rock had debuted in WWE in November 1996, so they never had the chance to work with each other. Until now.

On their debut night, on the *No Way Out* pay-per-view, we had set up a backstage confrontation between Rock and the nWo. After taking a picture with Hulk Hogan for Hogan's son, Hogan insulted the Rock. That in turn resulted in Rock cutting a promo on all three members. It was quite memorable with Rock calling Hall and Nash by their old WWF personas, Razor Ramon and Big Daddy Cool Diesel (complete with truck honking sound effect, which is never not funny).

The problem came as a result of a difference in philosophy. Kevin felt that since the nWo was supposed to be brought into WWE by Vince McMahon as "poison," why would the Rock be dressing them down on their very first night? You bring in these three monster heels and you immediately blow off all their heat. And I can totally see his point...if the story ended right then and there.

However, the next night on *Raw*, Nash, Hall, and Hogan proceeded to attack the Rock in the back of the head with a hammer, hit all their finishing moves on him, and spray-painted *nWo* on his back. Then Hogan literally rammed the ambulance Rock was in with a semi-truck.* This was all designed to be retaliation for Rock's promo the night before. *You insult us? We put you in the hospital.* It was designed to put a ton of heat on the nWo and set up the Rock-Hogan *WrestleMania* match. Why not do it all on *No Way Out*? Vince's feeling was *Raw* was seen by way more people, so the idea was to introduce the nWo on the pay-per-view, have them come across as heelish but somewhat enigmatic, seemingly not there to cause any trouble only to have them show their true colors the next night on *Raw*.

I always thought of Kevin Nash as pretty cool and the type of guy you want to be friends with. In fact, back in college, after a house show (a non-televised live event), Shawn Michaels, with Nash and Sean Waltman in tow, pulled up to me and my friends as we were walking back to our car and asked for directions to the local hospital. We had no idea why—the only wrestler who seemingly might have been injured (though he could've been just "selling") was Mo from the tag team "Men on a Mission"—but why wasn't important. We followed him to the hospital where we infiltrated the waiting area and "hung out" with Shawn, Kevin Nash, and Sean Waltman (without them knowing) before hospital staff caught on and asked us to leave. Our protest of "But we're here to see Mo" decidedly did not work. Point being, even though he didn't know it, Nash and I went way back.

But any thought to being friends with Kevin pretty much evaporated after that promo and completely blew up the night after *WrestleMania 18*, when Rock called him "Big Daddy Bitch" during a promo segment.

For all the hype and promotion WWE gives its product, I think the one thing they actually undersell is the fact that both their shows are live. Amazing things can and do happen on live television. The Rock loves

---

*We weren't really into subtlety back then.

working live and being in the moment. He'll listen to the crowd, have an idea pop in his head that's not in the script, will say it live on the air, and then watch as the crowd loses its collective mind. That's just how the Rock thinks. In this particular case, seeing Nash in the ring, hearing that crowd, feeding off their energy, the Rock, as he had done hundreds of times before, thought of an insult on the spot... "Big Daddy Bitch."

In Kevin's mind this was completely unprofessional. Now, I could make the argument that, similar to their 2002 debut, Kevin was going to get the last word by Powerbombing Rock through a table that night. Then again, I'm not the one being called a bitch on live television, so I can't really say it wasn't that big a deal.

During their match as Nash worked Rock into a corner you can actually hear him scream, "Who's the bitch now?" Nash was legit pissed. We never talked about it, so I'm theorizing here, but I'd imagine to Kevin this was the last straw. The nWo, one of the biggest angles in wrestling history, one that he was the face of, was being bastardized in WWE. Rock was facing Hogan and Steve Austin was facing Scott Hall, so Nash found himself not working a match at *WrestleMania 18* (if something were to befall Scott, Vince wanted a big name like Nash ready to step in). And now, he was being hit with an off-the-cuff remark on live television. I don't think being called a name by the Rock in the heat of the moment would normally faze him, but I do think it was the cherry on top of a shit sundae that he'd been force-fed since coming back to WWE.

Having said that, the insult and reaction to it was something special. When you watch the physicality between Rock and Nash it feels *intense*. It feels *real*. Mainly because it was. Nowadays when you're sitting through a three-hour *Raw*, as a viewer you're begging to see something as visceral as this. And maybe, as the years passed by, that's something a part of Kevin deep down appreciated. Not the "bitch" part, but being front and center in a battle of real-life, high-level gamesmanship that had everybody talking.

Why do I feel this way? Well, there was a lot of resentment that went on for years between myself and Kevin Nash. Nothing overt, but a simmering tension anytime we had to work together. There was an aura of *Oh no, not this fucking guy* that came between us. Then, a decade later, at *WrestleMania 30*, something changed. I saw Kevin at the *WrestleMania* hotel. Our eyes locked, and it would've been way too awkward for one of us to just turn around and walk in the opposite direction. I looked at Kevin's face and could tell there was a moment of *fuck it* as he approached and asked if I wanted to get a drink with him, to which I said, "Sure."

This was it. The moment I had been waiting for since ~~stalking~~ hanging out with "the Clique" in that Syracuse ER. Maybe I'd ask him if he ever got to check in on Mo. Either way, I was finally going to put "Bitch-Gate" behind me!

I thought it was a very cool gesture by Kevin. Naturally, just as we approached the hotel bar, the manager announced they were closed. I turned to Kevin and said, "Now *that* guy is a bitch!" and we laughed for hours.

Okay, that didn't happen. In reality we went our separate ways and haven't seen each other since. So close, yet so far. I really do hope that drink happens one day.

Did those Rock promos ruffle some feathers backstage? Absolutely.

Did it result in *years* going by before certain individuals saw me as more than just "the Rock's personal writer"? You betcha!

Did it lead to instances of mistrust, paranoia, and resentment? Pretty sure!

Would I do it all over again? Well, based on the most important thing—the audience's reaction, a reaction that echoes in my head twenty years later—to steal another guy's catchphrase that I had nothing to do with, "Oh hell yeah!"

Rock's attitude then, when cutting a promo, taking part in an angle, or even pissing some people off, was based on two principles: Will the audience enjoy it? Will it draw money? If we had to step on some toes backstage to create something the fans would be talking about and ultimately pay to see, then it was always worth it. When you have an angle or a character that's drawing money, then the entire company benefits. It's very easy to get people to *not* talk about wrestling or wrestling characters. Just ask the Miz (I kid).

It's a much bigger challenge to get them talking and energized and when that happens, everyone wins.

The Rock would do or say anything in the name of entertaining the people, even if the person being embarrassed was himself. It's time to revisit what was perhaps my favorite stretch of working at WWE. I'm referring to that glorious period when the Rock the "People's Champion" became the arrogant bad guy known as "Hollywood Rock."

* * *

It started at the *Raw* tenth anniversary show in 2003. Rock's movie career was taking off, and he couldn't physically be in the WWE Times Square restaurant where the show was taking place. As a nominee for "Superstar of the Decade," he sent in a pretaped promo. As much as Rock doesn't like to do pretaped promos, the audience really doesn't like it. You can put up all the "live via satellite" graphics you want, they know the difference. The promo was met with a lukewarm response, which was obviously very rare for him. On top of that, the fans voted for Steve Austin. That was all Rock needed to initiate something he'd been thinking about for a while— turning heel.

There were times when we'd be working on a promo in the past where I'd throw out a line that insulted the fans just to pop the Rock backstage. "Oh man, if I was a heel, we'd be able to have so much fun." The problem was back then with Steve Austin and the Undertaker out with injuries, Shawn Michaels retired, and Bret Hart in WCW, it was hardly the ideal time for the Rock to be a heel. But now the timing was perfect, even with Rock's big movie, *The Rundown*, set to be released later that year.

The old-school mentality was you can't turn heel if you're promoting a movie. Why would anyone want to support an asshole who's insulting them and beating up on their favorites? Rock had the foresight to know that if you're entertaining they're going to want to see you regardless of whether you're a babyface or heel. The idea of a pompous star "gone Hollywood" was too tempting to pass up. All the pieces fit. The audience *did* resent him going into movies and leaving WWE behind, they *did* boo him in his match against Hogan at *WrestleMania 18*,* and a character like the Rock always responds to the people. When Stone Cold turned heel two years earlier it was shocking, but despite Steve putting everything he had into it, the audience just wasn't willing to accept it. Rock's turn was more organic. Much like Hulk Hogan's historic heel turn in 1996, the audience *wanted* this to happen.

Like everything else, Rock wanted to do a heel turn in a highly elevated way. Rather than just coming out as a heel or doing a specific dastardly heel act, he wanted to put this on the fans. The People's Champion always had a special bond with the "people," which the people had broken. With that in mind, the Rock stood in the ring in Indianapolis in 2003 as he asked the fans the questions that would dictate the direction of his character.

"Ask yourselves. Do you really want to boo the Rock? Do you understand the line we're going to cross? The ramifications of booing the Great One? You're going to make the decision right here tonight. One last time, do you want to boo the Rock?"

As the chorus of boos rained down, instead of acting in mock heel outrage, Rock looked out to the crowd, contemplative. Almost hurt. And while I never actually talked to him about it, similar to the fans turning on him early in his WWE career, maybe deep down he was. Not so much for the fans booing him but for the pockets of those stubborn fans who could never understand why he'd "leave" WWE.

"Understand this. You have no idea, and the Rock means no idea, what's about to happen."

This opened the floodgates. Now we can take classic wrestling tropes and upend them, starting with the hometown crowd popping for a wrestler mentioning their city. In Toronto, where one year earlier fans cheered

---

*And a sizable section of people in his *SummerSlam* match against Brock Lesnar months later. Though, to be fair, that match was on Long Island and those/my people would boo anyone showing the faintest sign of a soul.

Hogan in their *WrestleMania* match, Rock stood in the ring and declared "Finally, the Rock has come back to Toronto."

As the people predictably cheered, Jim Ross, not knowing what Rock was going to say, commented, "Rock sucking up to this crowd, if you ask me." Rock then started mock-clapping and affecting a baby voice:

"Hooray! He said Toronto! Dat's where we live. We live in Toronto! Aaaaah, shut up!"

It's common knowledge that all bad guys deep down believe they're in the right. Rock blamed the fans for cheering Hogan (true), he blamed them for voting for Austin as Superstar of the Decade (true), he singled out one fan and commented on how he can get more "pie" in a week than that fan can get in a lifetime (don't know the guy, but I'm willing to bet heavy money on...true). He even hit the fans with the ultimate insult, telling them, "It doesn't matter what you people think."

It was hard to argue with the Rock's logic. Heels being completely correct always fascinated me. As a teenager, I'd watch the wrestler I.R.S. condemn fans who didn't pay their taxes, and I'd yell at the TV in agreement: "He's absolutely right! People *should* pay their taxes!"

In college, I'd soundly agree as Mr. Bob Backlund condemned children for not taking their education seriously. "Children absolutely *should* read their dictionaries! Procure the Cross-Faced Chicken Wing, Mr. Backlund!"*

To counter that truth, all Rock needed to do was turn the arrogance up to 11 and call the fans out on their own hypocrisy. "Heel" Rock can do what the babyface version of Rock could never do but with the same intensity and charisma. Plus, now he could interact with a brand-new set of talent, the unlikeliest being Shane "Hurricane" Helms.

When Shane came over from WCW, I was probably the only one who recognized the tattoo on his arm was the insignia of Green Lantern, and we quickly formed a friendship. It didn't take long for him to transform into "the Hurricane," a highly entertaining superhero character. Like

---

*I didn't date much.

Edge and Christian, Shane was my age. Unlike Edge and Christian, we were not taken to Wrestlers Court when I invited him to my apartment for Thanksgiving with my family. He was stuck in NYC with nowhere to go after participating on the WWE Thanksgiving parade float.* This marked Shane's first experience with matzo ball soup. After it was served, he stared at it for a while before turning to me in this thick North Carolina accent:

"What exactly is in the matzo ball soup?"

"Matzo balls."

Long pause...

"Okay then."

I knew pairing Rock and the Hurricane together would pay dividends, even if it were only for one night. Unlike all the drama we had experienced with others in the past, all egos would be set aside and it would just be about entertaining the audience. But even I was surprised at the crowd reaction when Hurricane mentioned the one superhero he could beat: "The Scorpion King!"

A lot of this had to do with the Rock selling it. He reacted like that was the most shocking thing anyone could say to him. The other thing Rock did (which no one told him to do) was subtle but genius. Whenever Hurricane would exit a scene, he'd leap out of frame with the production truck adding a "woosh" sound effect as if to imply he was flying away. As he leapt out of frame, Rock would look up as if Hurricane actually possessed the power of flight. It allowed fans to completely suspend disbelief and get wrapped up in the story.

What was intended as one vignette turned into several live bits spanning over a month. You know it's a good sign when heel and babyface are actually giving each other material to insult them with, as Hurricane did when he suggested Rock call him "nothing" then answer his cell and say, "It's nothing, he says he knows you."

This type of thing almost never happens. Rock was coming off a

---

*Yes WWE had a float in the Thanksgiving Day parade, the same month Triple H simulated sex on TV with a mannequin in a casket.

number one movie in his first starring role in *The Scorpion King* and had a *WrestleMania* match with Stone Cold Steve Austin on the horizon. But knowing where we were going, with Rock finally beating his nemesis at *WrestleMania*, was freeing in a way. Without the drama of "who's going over at *Mania*," Rock could sink his teeth into drawing money with Austin *and* doing some of the most entertaining things in his career with Hurricane, to the point where Rock actively wanted to do vignettes with the Hurricane and (with Austin's help) actually have Hurricane beat him in a match on *Raw* (which Hurricane has occasionally since talked about).

Most top guys would have an issue with losing to a guy lower on the card on the road to *WrestleMania* or any other road, for that matter. But when you have confidence in both yourself and your ability to stay "over," a loss, done correctly, isn't going to hurt you.

Not everyone would be enthralled by Hollywood Rock's antics. Vince would infamously sum up his problem with "Heel Rock" as such:

"When he shits on the people, he's shitting ice cream."

What that means (aside from ruining ice cream forever) is that fans can't truly hate you if they're smiling and having a good time. Look, it's hard to argue with that logic, it truly is. But in an era where heels would give lengthy serious heat-seeking promos, sometimes to boos, sometimes to silence—or worse, "WHAT" chants—occasionally you just want to rummage through your mom's purse for change, run outside, and find the damn ice cream truck.

The apex of the heel Rock run culminated in Sacramento in the first "Rock Concert." Anyone who's followed the Rock's career knows how much he likes to sing. Be it dressed as Bigfoot and singing duets with Will Ferrell's Neil Diamond on *SNL*, to performing "You're Welcome" in *Moana*, to belting out Taylor Swift's "Shake It Off" on the first episode of *Lip Sync Battle*. What not many people knew (myself included) was that he could actually play a little guitar. Rock asked me what I thought of the idea of him playing a series of songs that ragged on the fans and Steve Austin. As the proud owner of every Weird Al Yankovic CD in existence, I found this idea extremely appealing.

If you go back and watch this first Rock Concert, it's clear how much fun the Rock is having, and it was here where we produced arguably one of the greatest moments in cheap heat history.

"Cheap heat" is the act of getting the crowd to react negatively by going the easy route, like making fun of their sports team or home city. It's like cocaine to a new writer. You hear a loud reaction to something that came out of your head and find yourself wanting to do it over and over again. It can be intoxicating, but it can also be an extremely lazy crutch.

Vince and I would get into many arguments over the years when it came to cheap heat, but my stance was if it's done in an entertaining, creative way that makes the crowd react so negatively that it becomes fun for the people watching at home, then it's worth it. I always cite Pete Rose at *WrestleMania 14* in Boston as one of the most brilliant displays of cheap heat ever. Of course, it made sense for the all-time hit king and conqueror of the Red Sox in the 1975 World Series to rag on Boston. Conversely, having a midcard heel talk about the Blue Jackets' losing record for no reason other than the fact that WWE just happens to be in Columbus, Ohio, is predictable and boring.

So when Rock was singing a parody of the classic song "Kansas City" and coming to an ultimate moment of cheapness, even he had to pause because he knew this was going to be good.

"Sacramento, Sacramento I won't stay . . . (check this out, check this out) but I'll be sure to come back when the Lakers beat the Kings in May."

This was coming a year after the Lakers beat the Sacramento Kings in a grueling seven-game series. The wound was obviously still fresh as the crowd lost their freaking minds. In no other form of entertainment can you get a crowd of fifteen thousand people to react like this. It was just as much fun for me watching backstage as it was for Rock to perform. By the time Stone Cold came out and destroyed the Rock's hand-signed Willie Nelson guitar (inspired by his real-life Willie Nelson hand-signed guitar, which remained safe), the fans were like Forrest Gump after he got shot in the ass—enjoying all the ice cream they could eat.

We had so much fun with the Rock Concert, we made sure there were encore performances with Goldberg, Vickie Guerrero, and John Cena (more on that later). Vince—and really all of us—knew from the start that the heel run of "Hollywood Rock" wouldn't be a long-term thing. When the Rock returned a year later to team up with Mick Foley to take on Evolution at *WrestleMania 20*, the fans were more than happy to have the People's Champion back on the side of the People. And even though Rock appearing on WWE TV would never again be a fifty-two-weeks-a-year thing, I knew the adventures were far from over.

CHAPTER 7

I Am Not Ready for Some Football

In early 2000, when Vince McMahon told Tommy Blacha and me that he was starting his own football league, we really didn't give it much thought. For one thing, that was at least a year away, and we had *Raw* to do that night! Plus, truth be told, we both thought there would be a pretty good chance neither of us would be in the company by then, both thinking we'd be back writing for more traditional television shows. It's like when you read about the sun burning out in a few billion years—sure it'll suck for the people who have to deal with it, but that's their problem.

For Tommy, his indifference was justified, as he left WWE that same year. For me, the reality hit hard in early 2001 as the XFL was debuting right in the middle of *WrestleMania* season. That's the unofficial name given to that glorious time between late January and the end of March, when there's no *Monday Night Football* to compete with, no NBA or NHL playoffs, and baseball is out of sight out of mind. Sure, we compete against all other television shows, but there's a reason why the ratings always spike during this period as we head into our biggest show of the year.

In February 2001, Michael "PS" Hayes and Bruce Prichard officially joined the creative team. Of course, they'd both been in the business forever in many different roles but never as writers. For a creative team that was (and still is) constantly being complained about both backstage and online for having no wrestling experience, these were valuable additions.

Michael had been working strictly as a "producer," the people who

74

put the actual matches together, something writers—and this can't be stressed enough—are *not* qualified to do.* Now Michael (who is probably one of the most accomplished, innovative producers in WWE history) would be pulling double duty working as both a producer and a writer. Bruce, who had done it all in his career, was working in Talent Relations. I had gotten along with both of them and now we were united in our one major fear—the XFL was going to take Vince's focus off of the wrestling product.

Vince was still very much intent on approving everything that went on his show, perhaps even more than before, since WWE would now be in the spotlight and scrutinized. But less time with Vince meant less things approved, which meant a lot of uncertainty the day of *Raw*. If Vince hadn't seen the script, there was no telling what he'd keep in and what would get cut. There's nothing more awkward than when you're reading the show in the production meeting to an entire room of people and Vince pauses, leans toward you, and asks, "Where are we going with this?" Now you have to have this side conversation where you have to spew out a monthlong angle in about thirty seconds as Sgt. Slaughter watches, silently judging you.

Getting a story line approved is *much* easier if you're meeting during the week in the seclusion of Titan Towers in Stamford, but sometimes even that isn't enough. Seeing Vince take out his pencil and mark a giant *X* over a promo or backstage segment you had worked on all week, as you're reading it in a production meeting, does wonders for your psyche. Often I would read a segment and then see the pencil come out. I'd pause and say, "Aaaand this segment is apparently brought to you by the letter *X*." Vince would chastise me for reading over his shoulder, but it was hard to miss. I would come to hate that pencil, but it turned out having Vince's attention stretched was not the biggest of my problems.

---

*Though I never "produced" a match, I did suggest the finish of William Regal hitting Big Show with brass knuckles and then getting pinned when Big Show's unconscious body lands on him.

"What do you know about football, Brian?" Vince asked me on the corporate jet.

This was a trick question. If I lied and said I knew nothing of football, he'd see right through it. Tell the truth and talk about how I'm an avid Buffalo Bills fan* and how I won my 2000 fantasy football league, and I'd get sucked into an XFL vortex I might never come out of.

"That's the one with the running backs, right? I'm kidding. You know the Mets and Knicks come first for me. Then Syracuse basketball. I used to play tennis as a kid. I actually have a two-handed backhand in Ping-Pong. But yeah, I guess football is okay."

It was the best I could muster as I hoped not to get caught in the tractor beam. It didn't work. My football knowledge wasn't important—what was important was that there would be lots and lots of prerecorded bits which needed to be clever, and that was where I would come in. I'd join Bruce, Michael, Stephanie, and Shane on a weeklong odyssey. We'd get back home from producing *Smackdown* early Wednesday morning, fly to Las Vegas Wednesday afternoon, have meetings, produce the inaugural XFL vignettes Thursday and Friday, produce the XFL games Saturday and Sunday, then fly back to Atlanta for *Raw* and *Smackdown* Monday and Tuesday. Oh, and *Raw* and *Smackdown* actually needed to be written at some point, too.

The corporate plane ride from New York to Vegas, where the New York / New Jersey Hitmen** would face the Las Vegas Outlaws, had some pretty heavy hitters. It included the entire McMahon family (including Linda), commentator Matt Vasgersian, legendary television producer and Vince's good friend Dick Ebersol, and of course me, Bruce, and Michael. We were the "others" as in, if the plane went down, the headline would read "McMahons, Ebersol, and Others Perish in Crash."

---

* Ever since the Jets left Shea Stadium for New Jersey and, like the charlatan Giants, had the nerve to still call themselves "New York."

** Say what you want about the XFL, but at least they had the courage to admit the Hitmen played in Jersey and were named after criminals.

The flight time was listed at around five hours. Approximately four of those hours would be dedicated to trying to come up with the name of the opening play. The XFL had a lot of funky new rules, one of which was instead of a traditional coin toss, a ball would be placed in the middle of the field where two opposing players would race to grab it first. Whoever grabbed it would decide possession. With the first game days away, this thing needed a name, and all suggestions were welcome.

Shane McMahon was heavily endorsing "Suicide Scramble." Michael Hayes was behind "Ball or Nothing" because, as Michael pointed out multiple times, "you either get the ball or you get nothing."

Just as Dick Ebersol seemed to be leaning toward "Suicide Scramble," Vince's face turned sour.

"It just doesn't make any sense. There's no actual suicide involved."

Shane leapt from his seat. "Dad! When a hockey game goes into 'Sudden Death' nobody actually dies—it's just a cool name!"

As the debate raged on, Vince turned to me. I hadn't said a word at this point, instead trying to figure out what eleven segments we'd be doing on *Raw*. Vince said "You have any new ideas?"

Nowadays I'd probably just state my honest opinion (truth be told, I was a "Suicide Scramble" guy). Instead, despite not drinking anything on this flight, for some reason, I decided to say this:

"I see two options. One—'That thing when the two guys go running to grab the football then whoever gets the football chooses what they want to do with the football, pending approval of their coach.' It's a little lengthy but it definitely explains what it is. The other idea is to create an air of mystery and just call it 'Fuck a goat.'"

For reasons I still can't figure out, Dick Ebersol, iconic producer of NBC Sports and *Saturday Night Live*, found this hilarious. For the rest of the week, whenever I passed him in a hall or in a meeting, he'd look at me, smile and say, "Hey! Fuck a goat!" I took an odd sense of pride in that. For the record we ended up simply calling it "the Scramble," which sounds more like something you'd order at Denny's than a cutting-edge football innovation, but whatever.

Once we landed in Vegas, Matt Vasgersian assumed we'd go straight to the hotel, working later in the evening or even the next morning. How little he knew Vince. We got out of the plane to waiting limos and headed straight to Sam Boyd Stadium, home of the Vegas Outlaws.

The field itself looked...incomplete. It hadn't been fully painted, the mechanics of the moving jib camera, which was a real innovation the NFL would steal, was still being figured out, and an assortment of players were standing around wondering what the hell was going on.

I turned to Bruce and Michael and asked, "Anyone else getting a *Jurassic Park* vibe here?" I had a foreboding sense of dread even though I couldn't quite explain why. Vasgersian, already miffed he had to go to the field where there was literally nothing for him to do, had enough. As Vince and Dick were sidebarring, Matt voiced his frustration, telling Bruce and me there was no reason why *he* had to be there. He was exhausted and hungry! He was going to march up to Vince and tell him he was going to take one of the limos back to the hotel and then send it back to the stadium. Bruce, having worked with Vince for decades, just smiled and told him that was an excellent idea.

Bruce and I watched as Matt marched up to Vince and Dick, and gestured he was going to head back. It was far enough away that we couldn't hear the conversation but could see Vince was not exactly keen on this plan, first looking puzzled, then annoyed, then angered. Moments later Matt walked back, the bravado he had moments earlier completely eradicated.

"I'm just going to wait in the limo until they're ready to go," he said, a defeated man. Bruce and I feigned empathy for Matt, who was essentially the cow being lowered into the velociraptor pit.

Every minute of the day for the rest of the week was devoted to nonstop wrestling and football. Michael, Bruce, and I would attend the morning XFL production meeting, then go to a conference room to write *Raw* and *Smackdown*, then head to the stadium to shoot XFL vignettes. We were in Las Vegas, but with the amount of work we had to do it might as well have been Boise, Idaho. Don't get me wrong, we weren't being paid to go to Vegas to have fun and gamble,* but it was still pretty maddening for me. I had never been to Vegas before and was perfectly willing to obtain a life-altering gambling problem.

But none of that was important. We had a job to do. We had to produce the vignettes that would introduce America to the XFL players and cheerleaders! Vince made it clear in the production meeting:

"Think about how much more invested people will be if they knew their personalities! Plus, they were encouraged to date! What's Tiffany going to think when she sees her man Todd get hit with a brutal sack! Think of the drama! This is no different than WWE—we need to be storytellers!"

Armed with that mindset, Bruce and I met with the XFL cheerleaders to shoot their vignettes. The idea was that these women would have interesting, dynamic jobs during the day but at night they just wanted to let their hair down and have fun. At night...they were XFL cheerleaders! So if one of them was a doctor (as we were told some were) you'd see them in their doctor's scrubs as they said the first part of their line, then a camera transition as they transformed into their official XFL cheerleader outfit.

Sounded simple enough. The complication came when Bruce asked them what they did for a living.

"I'm a dancer."

"I'm also a dancer!"

"I'm a college student...who dances part-time!"

Bruce then asked: "Just out of curiosity, do any of you happen to be doctors or lawyers?"

Years earlier, I had met a girl named Erica and instinctively (because it was true) told her, "That's what I would've been named had I been born a girl!" The mix of confusion, fear, and an intense desire to flee that was displayed on Erica's face was the same as the expression on the cheerleaders' faces when Bruce asked his question. None of them had any idea what he was talking about. I started humming the *Jurassic Park* theme.

---

*Though when it came to the XFL, we technically weren't being paid anything.

With no other choice, we decided to get creative, asking the group to tell us something about themselves. Literally anything.

One of the women said she recently got a puppy. "Great, you're going to be a veterinarian," Bruce said.

Another told us a story of how she recently contested a parking ticket. "Excellent! You're now a lawyer!"

And thus, we ended up getting our doctors and lawyers during the day, XFL cheerleaders at night. These were pretty tame compared to the much more salacious NBC-produced promos that aired prior to the first game. They were also completely independent of the bizarre halftime cheerleader dream sequence that aired the following week featuring Vince, cheerleaders giving each other sponge baths, and, for some unknown reason, a half-naked Rodney Dangerfield. But we did them, giving these women brand-new identities and skillsets, waiting (hoping?) that they'd now start dating the players so the drama could unfold.

Speaking of the players...

Bruce and I also had to produce the player vignettes. These were a bigger challenge because of the nature of their awfulness. We were told they should be in the spirit of *Love, American Style*.* For instance...

VO: Meet [name], XFL Quarterback.

QUARTERBACK: (*standing next to a cheerleader*) I like to go long and deep!

VO: Meet [name], XFL Tight End.

TIGHT END: (*standing next to and ogling a cheerleader*) I always say there's nothing better than a good *tight* end.

That sort of thing. Unspeakably terrible, and whatever I had written (which thankfully I've erased from my memory) wasn't much better. Some of the players, just happy to be there, recorded these. Others had different ideas. There was one player in particular who was studying the

---

*Always the first thing on the mind of young adult football fans in 2001.

one-sentence script with an intense seriousness, as if he were about to audition for a Paul Thomas Anderson film. He got up, stood in front of the green screen, and shouted, "I ain't saying this shit!"

Instead he delivered a profanity-laced diatribe that was equally crass, indignant, and magnificent (and completely unairable). We recorded a bunch of these when Stephanie came in to check them out. Followed by Shane. Then Vince. Then Dick Ebersol. Each person giving a different set of notes and comments to poor Bruce as I slowly walked away like George Costanza during one of George Steinbrenner's rants. For the record, I don't recall if any of these vignettes actually aired, which in itself is an accomplishment as you have to produce something truly awful for this version of the XFL not to air it. I think only a couple of the cheerleader vignettes saw the light of day as well.

Those vignettes still haunt me even twenty years later. If I meet someone who says, for example, she needs to buy some plants, my first thought will be *Great! You're a botanist by day, but at night you're an XFL cheerleader!*

It was a long Friday after a long Wednesday and Thursday, but at least we had the promise of finally experiencing Vegas that night! That is, until we got back to the hotel and learned Stephanie had arranged a "special surprise" for us. We were told to enter a room at our hotel the (off the Strip) Sunset Station, where we were met with a giant screen, chairs, and appetizers. Our worst fears were realized: Despite the hotel not carrying UPN, Stephanie had arranged for us to watch that week's episode of *Smackdown*.

I couldn't believe it as Bruce and Michael angrily turned their gaze toward…me! *Oh crap, that's right!* Before we realized we would be doing nonstop meetings of football, wrestling, and more football, I had actually asked Steph if we could get a DVD of *Smackdown* to watch! This was actually *my* fault!

It was at this point I quickly started to crack. The nonstop wrestling and football had pushed me to my breaking point. Sensing this, Bruce and Michael decided to have some fun. They told me they were going to call the Rock and Kurt Angle, to tell them I was making fun of them. Instead of rolling my eyes, I lunged for their phones. When that didn't work, I grabbed a chair and actually flung it against the wall. It was shortly after this incident that Stephanie found me and pulled me aside.

"Brian, I don't think you should come to the stadium tomorrow. Don't even work on *Raw* and *Smackdown*. I think it's best if you just took a day off and cleared your mind." I nodded like George "the Animal" Steele. In that moment, Stephanie might've saved my life.

I took full advantage of getting the day off. I gambled (and won)! I went shopping! I saw a movie! I ordered room service! It was like the episode of *The Simpsons* when Homer skipped church. Then I sat back and watched my newly adopted NY/NJ Hitmen, of whom Vince had said, "I don't see how they could lose!" get drubbed 19–0. But so what? Bruce and Michael had said they'd show me the Vegas Strip after the game, so I got dressed up to make this perfect day complete. I waited downstairs as they arrived from the game and encountered two of the most miserable, wretched human souls I'd ever seen in my life. Bruce Prichard and Michael Hayes had also reached their breaking point, and it didn't take much prompting to find out why.

Bruce's and Michael's jobs were to produce the two XFL sideline reporters. Apparently both reporters were having a competition to see who could be the bigger pain in the ass. Each of them complaining incessantly and counting how many lines the other had. It was so bad they were both summarily fired after that very first game. Despite that little hiccup, I asked Bruce and Michael when we were going to the Strip.

"We're not" was their flat reply. All the life had been sucked out of them.

They told me to follow as they parked themselves at the hotel bar and ordered several *bottles* of wine. I foolishly asked if they wanted to be left alone and they told me I'm not going anywhere. I sat and drank with them...in silence.

After about their third bottle of wine, things began to loosen up, and the former Fabulous Freebird and I headed to the Sunset Station blackjack table. I had coined a phrase about Michael that still holds true to this day:

Hair in a tail, no need to bail.
Hair undone, your ass better run!

When the Freebird's hair is in a ponytail he's usually in business mode, and there are fewer minds sharper in the wrestling business. When it's not and the golden locks are flowing, it's usually trouble for whoever is in his path—which at this point was me. Michael decided right then and there that for the rest of the night I was to assume the role of his son. (When the hair is down and bottles of wine have been consumed, it's best not to question anything.)

We found a blackjack table, where a very inebriated Freebird continued to lose hand after hand. Having drunk about a tenth as much, I tried to get him to call it a night, with as much success as the NY/NJ Hitmen had on the field.

"My son doesn't show me enough respect," Michael said to the old woman seated next to him. She nodded politely. He then ran out of chips, and in an act I have never seen before or since, scooped up some chips from this poor old lady.

"Um, Michael, I don't think you should be doing that," I said, trying to defuse a potential incident.

The old woman, now legitimately terrified, countered, "Oh, it's okay, I don't mind."

"See?! She don't care! Now let's deal!"

Thankfully Michael's wife had come down, and she led him away before the cops were called. "Our boy don't listen," I heard him say as he stumbled out of view. "Dad's got a drinking problem!" I told the old woman before giving her some of my chips (though not as many as Michael took) and exiting.

My relative good fortune continued the next day at AT&T Stadium in San Francisco. I was assigned a workspace in one of the production trucks to write the script for *Raw* while Michael and Bruce now had to take care of the new sideline reporter—Stephanie McMahon. Steph wasn't a sideline reporter by trade, but then again the players weren't actors, the cheerleaders weren't doctors and lawyers, and Michael Hayes wasn't my father, so why not give it a shot?

Before she did her first on camera in the stands, Shane pulled Michael and Bruce aside.

"I just want you two to know, I love you both like family, but if anyone lays a hand on my sister, I will legitimately kill you." Just the type of thing you want to hear before leading a famous person into a drunken mob.

As far as I knew, no one laid a hand on Stephanie. The problem was the audience, many of whom were sufficiently drunk before they stepped into the stadium, knew Stephanie for one thing—one half of the evil McMahon-Helmsley regime, terrorizing their favorite babyfaces on *Raw* and *Smackdown*.

An earnest Stephanie, thrust into an announcer role much like her dad was on WWF television decades earlier, gave it her all reporting from the actual stands as a cascade of "slut" chants echoed down. This was something that was actually encouraged in this decidedly un-PC era of WWE but just added to the disaster that was the XFL in 2001. It was just surreal watching a smiling Stephanie McMahon telling the inspirational story on how a player overcame cancer as thousands in unison (men, women, and children) chanted "slut" while they high-fived behind her.

On the plane ride from San Fran to Atlanta, Bruce and Michael seemed even more shell-shocked than the previous night. I couldn't blame them. But of course, being the petty wiseass that I am, I couldn't help but have some fun myself. The plane ride itself was actually pretty celebratory. The ratings from Saturday had come in and the XFL, at least for one week, was a huge hit.

As we started to land, I could see Michael getting serious (hair back in a ponytail). Atlanta was his hometown, and he wanted nothing more than to simply get a good night's sleep in his own bed after a uniquely hellish week. He piped up from the back of the plane as we touched down at around 3 a.m. local time.

"Hey Boss? You think it would be possible to push the production meeting from noon to one tomorrow?"

I sensed weakness and immediately jumped in.

"Are you kidding me? All this week you're telling me to suck it up and be a man and now *you're* asking for a break? 'Aw, please, Mr. McMahon, please let me get another hour so I can rest my Freebird eyes. My Freebird body is ever so sleepy and I want to snuggle in my Badstreet Bed!'"

The whole plane was in stitches except for Michael, who was legitimately pissed and stared a hole through me.

"See this look, boy? You know what this look means?"

I knew what that look meant, but I wanted to see where he was going.

"This look means... [searching for the right words] 'I hate you.'"

That just made the plane erupt in laughter even more as Vince mercifully pushed the production meeting to one.

That ended up being the first and last week I was on the XFL beat. Since I really had nothing to do (those vignettes went away pretty quickly) and I needed to write the WWE shows, Stephanie told me I no longer needed to go. Bruce and Michael did not get off that easy; they had to hit the road for the XFL and be Stephanie's personal protection for several more weeks.

Eventually the ratings would nosedive as the league slowly imploded. The fact that they stopped relying on cheesy vignettes and turned more toward actual football meant it was heading in the right direction, and the 2020 version was actually pretty fresh and innovative. Vince had clearly learned a great deal from 2001, and this felt like an entirely different venture. I was rooting for it to succeed in 2020, but it became a casualty of the coronavirus and had its season stopped short and then cancelled.

I didn't think much of it until several months later. I was now working full-time at Dwayne Johnson and Dany Garcia's* Seven Bucks Productions, and we needed to have a company-wide meeting. My jaw dropped when I found out why—Dwayne and Dany were planning on purchasing the XFL. Try as I may, I just cannot escape this football league!

---

*Dany is Dwayne's ex-wife, current business partner, cofounder of Seven Bucks, and the smartest person I know.

I don't know what the future holds for the new XFL, set to debut in 2023. I do know Dwayne and Dany both have a passion for and love of football, and a distinct marketing and business plan that will make it a completely different animal from what we saw in 2001. I'm genuinely excited and optimistic. But fair warning—if you hear announcers say, "We now go to midfield for the opening 'Fuck a Goat,'" then something has gone horribly wrong.

CHAPTER 8

Old School vs. New School

In 2002, life as we knew it in the WWF would never be the same again. Mainly because the "WWF," as it related to wrestling, would no longer exist. A legal battle with the World Wildlife Fund resulted in the World Wrestling Federation becoming "WWE," or World Wrestling Entertainment. WWE is actually the more apt name considering all the inroads in entertainment the company has made, but I still prefer "WWF." Partially because it's what I grew up with, partially because "Federation" just sounds way cooler than "Entertainment." Anyone can work in "Entertainment"—from doing puppet shows to making balloon animals to starring on *Miz and Mrs.* If you're part of a "Federation," you're mysterious, a bit of a badass, and infinitely more interesting.

But that wasn't the only change. Shortly after *WrestleMania 18*, Stephanie McMahon (now the head of the creative department) came into the writers room with Vince and announced that the company would be undergoing a "brand split" with different talents going exclusively to *Raw* and *Smackdown*. Not only that, but we were going to be operating with two distinct writing teams headed by myself and Paul Heyman (more on that in the next chapter).

I had a somewhat unique relationship with Mr. Heyman. On one level Paul and I were a lot alike—two Jewish guys from the tri-state area who had strength in their convictions and knew how to push an idea through. On way more levels, we were nothing alike. Paul was a wrestling lifer, having entered the business as a teen by pure force of will and taking on all sorts of roles—photographer, manager, booker, head of and spiritual leader of Extreme Championship Wrestling, among other things I probably don't even know (or want to know) about. He had forged decades of relationships for better or worse and was a household name to wrestling fans. For all the modern innovations he brought to wrestling his DNA was decidedly old-school.

I on the other hand, had once brought a dry-erase board to an episode of *Raw* and frantically scribbled "*not* a real doctor" when Dr. Death, Steve Williams, was announced, thinking I was the funniest person alive. If that doesn't qualify as "new-school" as it relates to the wrestling business, nothing does.

Paul and I had gotten to know each other since he started at WWE a year earlier in 2001. While I wasn't really an ECW fan, having never attended a show or regularly watched, I wasn't against it. I did catch it on occasion on cable and enjoyed listening to my friend's audiotapes of Cactus Jack talking about what he was going to do to Terry Funk. I admired what they accomplished but I wasn't a disciple, and it was clear I wasn't going to be Paul's disciple (he usually had one in tow) anytime soon. If anything, I'd go out of my way to make it clear I was no one's disciple, especially Paul's. The way I saw it, even though Paul had decades more experience in the wrestling business, when it came to the WWE creative team, *I* was the veteran, having been there fifteen months before Paul came aboard. After a few cordial "get to know you" months, it didn't take long before Paul and I started arguing over pretty much everything. It just became an accepted part of the job.* I likened it to the old Looney Tunes cartoon of the Wolf and Sheepdog, checking into work, engaging in bloody warfare, and then casually checking out. "Mornin', Ralph. Mornin', Sam."

Why bloody warfare? Because I believe, for Paul, being on the WWE creative team wasn't just a writing job. It was much bigger than that. I'll

---

*For me, at least. I'm pretty sure Stephanie would've *much* preferred her two top writers not behave like complete lunatics.

shift off the Looney Tunes analogy to something more apt—it was like *Game of Thrones*, where you play the "Great Game" and you either win or you die. It's not exactly speaking out of school to say Paul loves a good argument. In the course of our relationship, I found out something I didn't know about myself—I did too. Paul and I would get into it constantly, and it occasionally escalated to the point where we'd find ourselves in the hallways at TV literally in each other's faces screaming at each other.

I should point out that, normally, I am *not* a screamer. I'm more of a passive-aggressive, "wait for the right moment to say something cutting and then hold a grudge forever" type. Yelling was not a behavioral trait I had engaged in before nor after—it was only with Paul.*

One time on the corporate jet Paul got so amped up (over what, I don't remember) that he got up and challenged me to a fistfight, midflight. To be fair, I'm sure I'd said something that made him want to punch me in the face.** Whatever it was caused Paul to stand up, look me in the eye and declare:

"I'll give you three free shots to the face if I could have just one."

Before I could respond to that offer, Shane McMahon jumped up from his seat. It was not to point out having a fistfight on a small plane was a bad idea. Instead he took me into the plane's bathroom to show me how to properly throw a punch ("Stand sideways—you expose less of your body and use your full body weight") as I empathically reminded him I had not actually agreed to this deal. I ultimately turned down the opportunity to have a good old-fashioned plane fight, disappointing most on board—including Vince, who seemed way more interested in this potential match than the Tajiri vs. Albert match from hours earlier. (If, like Tajiri, I'd had green mist to spit in Paul's face, I might've reconsidered.)

I told myself, it's fine. The red wine had been flowing, tempers had risen, and I figured it would most definitely be the last time I'd find myself in a potential physical confrontation with Paul.

---

*He had that way with people.
**I had that way with people.

I figured wrong.

Paul would often tell me, "It's okay! We're meant to fight! I was hired to fight with you!" I have no doubt that Paul was coming on board to provide a different perspective. But Paul's issue (and often mine as well) was fighting over *everything.* We were so often told by the McMahon family to "pick a hill to die on," but there were way too many hills and not enough dying.

Again, everything was part of the Great Game. In a story well documented, *Raw* and *Smackdown* would have separate conference calls with Vince on Saturday, first *Raw* and then *Smackdown.* The two calls were supposed to be with the two separate teams to go over that week's show, but one day on the *Raw* call we learned we had an extra participant. In the middle of the call an automated voice was heard saying, ". . . has left the conference." The pause being reserved for the recording of your name when you dialed in which the person having dropped off the call did not bother doing.

"Dammit, who'd we lose?" Vince said, then he asked for a roll call. Everyone on the *Raw* team said their name. We apparently didn't lose anyone and yet someone had dropped off. The number was eventually traced back to Paul, who, despite indisputable evidence, denied it was him.

He denied this for *years*, the story always shifting. At one point it was "Yes, the number was my cell, but I wasn't using it." Then it was "I simply had it on so when I got the text saying the *Smackdown* call was starting I could hop right on" (to save twenty-two seconds of dialing in?). Then more recently, he said, "I had been listening in on many *Raw* calls, just not that one." That's a relief.

I can only imagine how many times he heard me doing my Paul imitation (which was basically just Martin Short's Jiminy Glick voice, only way more cartoonish).

We'd each have our unique tactics of engaging in writing team warfare. I'd often take a cheap shot at Paul via a babyface's promo, taking (unfair) advantage of the fact that Paul was an on-screen character. "Of course, *I'm* not making fun of you, Paul Heyman, the real-life person! I just happened to have written a promo making fun of the fictional character of Paul Heyman"—totally different!

Equally dubious, it would often be brought to my attention that disparaging things about me were being written in the online wrestling newsletters, aka the "dirtsheets," with information provided by an anonymous someone within the writing team.

"Mornin', Sam. Mornin', Ralph."

For all the yelling, posturing and theoretical plane fighting, Paul and I never engaged in any actual blows until one fateful day in the office. Again, Paul always liked having a young disciple who was honored to be taken under his wing. One particular day, a young writer's assistant Paul was grooming was talking to him about a big idea. Paul stopped what was going on in the room to make an announcement.

"Attention. This young man has an idea he'd like to share. He has been crafting and cultivating this idea for some time, and I'd like each of you to stop what you're doing and hear him out. I want it to be taken seriously and for you all to show him respect. If anyone laughs, I will be deeply offended."

This build-up led me to think this idea was going to be along the lines of the Mega Powers exploding. Instead, the idea was for Torrie Wilson to appear completely naked in the ring.

Don't overreact, I told myself. *This is exactly what he wants.* The assistant explained that she could wear a flesh-colored bottom so it should be easy. Someone then asked even if there was a legit story line reason for doing it—there wasn't—you still can't have someone expose their bare breasts on TV.

"That's no problem," the writers assistant replied. "She'd have—" Paul urged him forward like a proud parent teaching a toddler how to ride a tricycle as the assistant confidently said, "—nip covers."

That was it for me. I violated the "no one laugh" rule as I openly chortled at the ridiculousness of the idea—something Paul did not take kindly to. I saw him stomping across the room headed in my direction.

Some who were there would say I fearlessly stood my ground and didn't move an inch. The truth is, in the rare times I find myself in a situation like this, my tendency is to completely freeze up. That was what I did as Paul made his way closer. There was some yelling, some name calling, perhaps a few poorly attempted slaps, but before anything could escalate the other writers stepped in and broke it all up. (I don't know why. If I were them, I'd have wanted to see what would've happened.) At the time, all I knew for sure was this shit was definitely not happening in the writer's room of *Frasier*.

The next day Stephanie, like the beleaguered captain in a *Lethal Weapon* movie, called us into her office and told us we were each being suspended for one week...with pay! Seeing as this was a pay-per-view week, one of the most work-heavy and hectic weeks in the WWE calendar, it did not seem like such a terrible arraignment.

This was something she did not have to do. Suspension without pay (or worse) would've been totally understandable. Stephanie was in a tough position: twenty-six years old and heading the WWE creative team with a ton of pressure on her as it is. The very *last* thing she needed were her two head writers acting like out-of-control, profanity-spewing Muppets.

She led us into the writers room to announce the suspension to the team, but waiting for us in the room was Ellis, a former stuntman and special effects expert from WCW who had a meeting scheduled with the team to present his ideas. Paul and I, along with Steph and the team, sat in silent tension for nearly two *hours* as Ellis gave us his presentation. We were shown slides for things like "Truck-a-Saurus," a monster truck shaped like a dinosaur. We sat and nodded as we both wished Stephanie had enforced the suspension immediately instead of making us sit through this. I would've docked myself a day's pay if it meant not having a grown man explain, "See it's not *really* a dinosaur, it's a Truck-a-Saurus." (That's the short explanation. The actual one took about forty minutes.)

After the presentation was mercifully over, Ellis left (and was promptly hired!) as Stephanie announced Paul and my suspension to the rest of the team. Michael Hayes then stood up Atticus Finch–style and gave his eye-witness testimony.

"Okay, Steph, but he [pointing at me] didn't do nothing...he [pointing at Paul] did it."

Stephanie duly noted Michael's point, but the suspension remained intact. Kind of. I still called the *Raw* writers and reviewed the week's show with them; I just didn't have to spend the weekend writing it. In fact, on the day of the pay-per-view, I went to the World (formerly WWF-New York) restaurant in Times Square and watched it with Trish Stratus and the Hurricane, who were that week's special guests. The manager who would eventually be caught allegedly embezzling over $400,000 (now there's someone who should've been suspended without pay) served us cookies! Point being, it was a grand old time and something I now look back at completely mortified. It was the "irresistible force meets the immovable object" of stupidity.

But that was the nature of my relationship with Paul back then. He was immersed in playing the game, and while I didn't want to get sucked in, I sure as hell didn't want to lose. I think the McMahons actually liked our passion and our competitive nature (to a point). I'm sure on multiple occasions we probably flew too close to the sun as far as testing their patience, but I think a combination of *Their pluses outweigh their minuses* and *We don't have anyone better to replace them with* probably worked in our favor.

The key was not to cross the line. A line Vince established pretty early on with me:

"I want you to have your own opinion and stick up for your ideas but just remember, if you take the fight to me, you're going to lose...every time."

I think that was where Paul got himself in trouble. He took the fight to Vince one (or several thousand) times too many. No issue too big or small to be championed. But that's a story for Paul's book, which absolutely needs to happen.

I can honestly say there was probably no one in the company who got me so legitimately upset but who I also legitimately liked. Despite our many battles it was hard to actually stay mad at the guy. Ninety-nine percent of the time when someone says "Don't take this personal" it *is* personal, but I really didn't feel that way with Paul. We were the Flair and Steamboat of "Jewish wrestling writers arguing over imaginary nipple covers" of our day. And like Flair and Steamboat, despite all the bloodshed, I'd like to think we garnered a healthy respect for each other. I know I did for Paul. Wrestling backstage needs a good mix of old school and new school. Lean too far in one direction, you risk alienating a large segment of the audience, and that's a hill I'll die on.

Nowadays when I come back to a WWE show and run into Paul, I'm genuinely happy to see him. I think we've both grown as human beings and professionals (it would be almost impossible not to), and Paul is particularly killing it as an on-screen character right now. He's one of the most talented actors and compelling characters in the entire company. We went through the craziness (much of it of our own making) together and came out whole on the other side.

In fact, there was one moment where we even found ourselves on the same side. It started in the summer of 2002, when both of us arrived at work and were immediately summoned to Stephanie McMahon's office. Nothing good ever comes from an office summoning, and this was no exception. You could've spotted us each one thousand guesses as to why we were called in, and neither of us would've come even close.

CHAPTER 9

The Prodigal Son Returns . . . Bro

Before I get to that fateful meeting in Stephanie's office, I want to take a step back and give this time period some context. In retrospect, it's amazing how crazy 2002 was in WWE. From the company changing its name, the returns of Hulk Hogan and Shawn Michaels, the debuts of John Cena, Dave Batista, Randy Orton, and Brock Lesnar, "HLA,"* and of course the first-ever "brand extension."

That was a fancy way of saying "we're splitting *Monday Night Raw* and *Thursday Night Smackdown* into two separate shows, changing the landscape of WWE as we know it."

Technically they were always two separate shows airing on two separate nights, but from a storytelling standpoint they featured the same characters in the same angles, going from *Raw* to *Smackdown*, back to *Raw*, back to *Smackdown*, and then ultimately culminating at that month's pay-per-view, where it would all start again the following night. At a certain point (for me it was as soon as *Smackdown* debuted in 1999), it was decided that people didn't necessarily have four hours** of time to devote to WWE every single week for the rest of their lives. Keep in mind this is also before DVRs, social media, and YouTube were things.

---

*If you don't know what that stands for, look it up on YouTube, preferably at work or at a child's birthday party. You'll thank me later.

**Seven if you included pay-per-views, eight if you included MTV's *Sunday Night Heat*.

You couldn't pick and choose what you wanted to watch unless you were one of seven people in the country who knew how to program a VCR. You either watched or you didn't, and it became a little overwhelming. Even with twice the amount of content the ratings were still good (and would be considered astronomical by today's standards), but creatively it was starting to get unsustainable and repetitive.

We were burning out our top stars by featuring them so often, and burning out the audience as well. So the idea was to split things up. Same amount of content, but each show would be different, fresh, and unique. The decision was made to have *Raw* and *Smackdown* with its own set of characters, story lines, live events, pay-per-views...and writers.

As mentioned, Vince and Stephanie announced that Paul Heyman and I would be heading up *Raw* and *Smackdown* as lead writers, we just didn't know who would be leading which show. The writers, along with Talent Relations, had worked with Vince on splitting up the rosters in a way that was supposed to be an even split, but in terms of wrestlers I personally liked working with, it was pretty one-sided, a development that, selfishly, I was more than fine with.

On the *Raw* side you had what some might call the "tough guys": Stone Cold Steve Austin, the Undertaker, the New World Order (Nash, Hall, and X-Pac), Bubba Dudley, RVD, Brock Lesnar, Bradshaw, among others. These guys were mostly veterans who all had a strong connection to Paul Heyman.

On the *Smackdown* side you had more of the "entertainers": the Rock, Kurt Angle, Hulk Hogan, Edge, Christian, Chris Jericho, the Hurricane, Al Snow, also among others. I had worked almost exclusively with all of them and was excited to have them all in one place. For me, this couldn't have worked out more perfectly. Three years removed from not getting the job of staff writer on UPN's *Malcolm and Eddie*, it was clear to me I was now going to be a lead writer on the number one show on UPN.* I think Paul was also satisfied because the assumption was he would be

---

*Or the equivalent of the forty-seventh highest-rated show on CBS.

reunited with all "his" guys and would now be lead writer on WWE's flagship show. A split like that played to our strengths and our relationships and everyone was happy...

...for about five minutes.

We gathered in the writers room, where we were hit with a bombshell. It was announced that it would be Paul heading *Smackdown*, and me, *Raw*. I was shocked. In addition to the majority of talents on *Raw* being "Paul guys," they were equally and emphatically not "Brian guys." I don't think this decision was a coincidence. Vince likes to challenge you and keep you on your toes. This would get Paul and I out of our comfort zones and force us to become better, more well-rounded writers...in theory.

Vince could have his cake and eat it, too.* Contrary to some revisionist history, this wasn't going to be a true split. While the teams worked all week on their respective shows, both teams were still attending the writers meetings with Vince in Stamford and writing for both *Raw* and *Smackdown* on the road. I found myself still working with guys like Rock, Kurt Angle, and Edge, just on Tuesdays only, the happiest day of my week. The idea of brand warfare might've existed for the talent, but it really wasn't the case for me. I saw it as if the Lakers were playing the Celtics, and then LeBron got to switch sides and play for Boston for the entire fourth quarter.

Once the announcement was formally made, I had mixed feelings. Of course, it was an honor to be the lead writer of *Monday Night Raw* while still in my twenties and having been in the business for just two and a half years. Plus, it showed the tremendous amount of faith Vince and Stephanie had in me. Whether it was their plan all along or just a coincidence, it definitely *did* force me to get out of my comfort zone to work more closely with talents I usually avoided.

But my personal relationships weren't important; what truly mattered was how the brand extension was going to affect the shows. The effect was immediate and not pretty. Ratings dropped as soon as people started

---

*Metaphorically, of course—outside of one "respect bite" for birthdays the man never eats cake.

realizing half their favorites were no longer on Monday or Thursday nights. Vince had foreseen this, saying the company was going to need to take "two steps back initially, in order to take three steps forward in the long run." Still, the natives, in this case our network, TNN, didn't really care so much about the long-term growth of WWE as they were about their current ratings taking a hit.

The *Raw* ratings (a ratings point being equal to approximately a million viewers) had gone from the low 5s and high 4s of January–April 2002 to the low 4s and high 3s of that summer.

Smackdown's ratings had taken a fall as well, so even though we all saw the ratings dip coming, tensions were running high when Paul Heyman and I were summoned into Stephanie McMahon's office that fateful day in June 2002.

We honestly had no idea what this was all about. Were we falling on the sword for the lower ratings three months into the extension? Were we getting fired? Were we both going to be traded to Raymour & Flanigan for a nice two-piece sectional? Any one of those options would've been more likely than what Stephanie told us:

"The company has made the decision to bring back Vince Russo to run creative. You'll still be lead writers of your respective shows, but you'll both be reporting to him. Vince [McMahon] is bringing him in now to meet with you and the team."

Heyman and I looked at each other like Bruce Willis and Ving Rhames in *Pulp Fiction* right before they brought out the Gimp.

For those unaware of who Vince Russo is, here's a quick refresher course: Russo was the first actual writer in WWE. The previous people in the creative department were wrestling lifers and old-school bookers who set up the matches and angles but didn't actually write promos or scripts. The weekly nature of *Raw* almost necessitated a writer to come on board, and Russo and later Ed Ferrara were the two guys steering the creative ship. *Raw* and WWE in general achieved great success with the Attitude Era.

Back then *Raw* would be live on a Monday and a second *Raw* would be taped on Tuesday, and then you'd have *ten days* to write two more shows, often poolside at Vince McMahon's house. In 2002 the schedule was slightly different; we had half the time (five days instead of ten), and double the shows and office meetings that would be endlessly delayed and sometimes not happen at all until a weekend phone call. Ultimately Russo and Ferrara left WWE in October 1999 to join rival WCW. That gig didn't go nearly as well, and WCW programming on the Turner network ceased to exist by March 2001.

Before I get into the story of Vince Russo coming back to WWE, I want to establish a few things. First off, I'll always respect him and Ed because they *did* it. Having lived through the experience of working for WWE, I will always respect those who logged the hours on the road, in the office, backstage, etc. Not only did they do it, I thought they did it quite well. WWE during the height of the Attitude Era had me hooked every week. I know that's a combination of a lot of elements—the talent, Vince McMahon, the production team both on the road and back in Stamford, but a big part of that was undeniably the writing. The Rock's turn at *Survivor Series 1998* remains a masterpiece in storytelling.

Russo's problem, in my opinion, is he let the success of his WWE run get to his head and had no one to rein him in at WCW. The first telltale sign was the fact that he made himself an on-screen presence immediately. Ten minutes into the *Nitro* broadcast, announcers hyped "Vince Russo and Ed Ferrara, part of the creative team at WWF, became part of WCW, and this is their first show." When you're watching a show and suspending your disbelief, pointing out that there are writers immediately causes confusion. To add to the problem, Vince and Ed soon became on-air characters, seen from behind a desk as "the Powers that Be." Their faces were never exposed, but Russo's unmistakable voice was heard. Over his tenure, Russo's on-screen presence would increase; he eventually become a major character,* and at one point he actually wrote himself to win the WCW Championship, which he'd often refer to as being merely a "prop."

---

*I think toiling in anonymity, something I personally found delightful, actually tore at his soul, like Henry Hill at the end of *Goodfellas*.

When defending that decision, and the decision to put himself on television, I'd hear him say to critics, "Unless you've been in that position, pencil in hand, trying to write the show, you have no idea."

Well as someone who *was* in that position, pencil in hand, trying to write the show, I can honestly say making yourself an on-air character of a wrestling show, much less becoming Champion, even if it's only for a few days is...what's the right way to put it...fucking insane.

He also let his love of combining fiction with reality get out of control as he introduced insider lingo and out-of-character "shoot interviews" in the middle of shows, taking audiences completely out of what they were watching. At one point there was a story line of Goldberg refusing to take a move, as announcers shouted, "He's not following the script!" That wasn't meant to be metaphorical. That was literal. I mean, if Goldberg's not following the script, then what the hell is everyone else on the show doing?

Again, in my opinion, it was incredibly convoluted. In fact, when WWE had a west coast *Raw*, instead of meeting the next morning to write *Smackdown*, we'd congregate in Vince McMahon's hotel suite that night to get a head start. We'd put TNT's replay of *Nitro* on and laugh at it. There was one moment in particular that had us in stitches. It was an outdoor *Nitro* and Hulk Hogan was in the ring.

Suddenly Hogan reacts in fear as announcers point out the wrestler "the Wall" is watching him! Standing on the roof of another building at least three blocks away.

The camera did a zoom to a tiny shot of the Wall pointing menacingly as announcers screamed: "The distance! Look at the distance!"

After that whenever an idea was pitched in one of our writers meetings where it was so bad you had to laugh, Vince would start pointing and yell, "The distance!"

* * *

I debated putting the story of Russo's return in this book, but after hearing Russo's version multiple times—the one where he reached out to Vince McMahon because the *Raw* numbers had fallen to under a 3 (false), and met the team of over twenty writers (not even close), most of them "nameless and faceless" (what does that even mean?), and everyone's jaw dropped to the floor when he laid out his incredible creative vision (true, but not for the reasons he thinks), I figured: Why not?

This would be the literary equivalent of putting the WCW Title on myself—no one asked for it, no one particularly wants to see it, and it'll probably do more harm than good, but I'm doing it anyway! Back to 2002...

Before Stephanie dismissed Paul and me from her office, she gave us a direct order from Vince McMahon—"When Russo comes in, you need to set the tone for the rest of the team and work with him. Don't get into petty arguments or tell him why something *can't* work. Show him how it *can* work. Vince is counting on both of you to provide leadership by example."

With that we went back into the writers room. The building was already buzzing as WWE.com had announced Russo's return—which was weird because neither WWE.com nor WWE, for that matter, *ever* mentioned the writers. Ironically, Russo never being acknowledged for WWE's success was one of the many reasons he left WWE in the first place, and now it looked like the company was doing its part to make things right.

Paul and I went into the room and broke the news to Michael Hayes and the *one* other writer who was in the room. The other three people* were writer's assistants, including Ed Koskey, who would soon be promoted to writer and eventually become the longest-tenured and most liked (despite being a Phillies fan) writer in WWE history.

Vince McMahon then entered and brought in Vince Russo, introducing him formally to the team. I had met Russo only once, when I interviewed for the job years back. He didn't remember me, but he did know Paul and Michael, and he treated us all warmly. Bruce Prichard was working remotely from Houston, and we eventually updated him by phone.

---

*Complete with names and faces!

Vince left, and we proceeded to hear Russo out as he pitched his ideas. We were all on our best behavior and Russo was, too. He wasn't like Alec Baldwin in *Glengarry Glen Ross*, putting us mortals in our place. He was energetic, approachable, and passionate about his ideas, the main one being a long, intricate story line involving Shane McMahon and...Eric Bischoff.

This was the first (of many) times we'd all be very confused. Before the brand extension started we inquired about a number of WCW talents, with Eric at the top of the list. Why wouldn't we? Eric was the guy who, as head of rival WCW, took WWE to the brink of ruin, with *WCW Nitro* famously beating *WWE Raw* in the ratings eighty-three weeks in a row. In addition, he was a great on-air character, as he encompassed just the right blend of fiction and reality. Like Vince McMahon, he started as an on-screen announcer who the "smart" audiences knew was actually running the show. To me this is different from a writer absolutely no one knows putting themselves on TV. We all wanted Eric to join WWE but were told that he wasn't interested in coming in. (Later we learned the offer put out to him was on the low side.) When we pressed and inquired a second time we were told point-blank that he (along with most of WCW's top stars) was not coming.

So aside from his main story line revolving around a guy we were told wasn't available (though, as WWE fans know, he eventually would be) the story itself—again, in my opinion—was convoluted. As Russo outlined his story he told us:

"Everyone knows, as a shoot, about the personal heat between Eric and Shane."

They do? I mean I assume there's some professional-level animosity between the two based on the very nature of them trying to put each other out of business, but the stuff Russo was talking about epitomized the best and worst of him. There were some parts of the story that I thought were genuinely clever and fun. Other parts were so far inside that even I didn't know what he was talking about.

"Swerves"—taking an expected outcome and doing the opposite—and "shoots"—incorporating real life into the story line—were two of Vince Russo's favorite weapons. When done right they can be magical. The problem at WCW was they happened so often they began to lose their impact. Oftentimes you'd see someone in character, then later in that show they're out of character talking about their character (aka "shooting"), and eventually you didn't know what the hell you were watching. At least I didn't.

Imagine you're watching *Breaking Bad*, and it's the tense scene with Walt and Hank in the garage. Suddenly Walt walks off, sits down, refers to himself as "Bryan Cranston," and starts talking about how personally he didn't think Hank should've discovered Walt's secret while sitting on the toilet. Then he walks back into the scene with Hank and says, "Dean, I mean this as an absolute 'shoot,' tread lightly . . . bro." If that happened, you'd probably want to throw yourself in a bath of hydrofluoric acid.

I could see that dangerous mix rearing its ugly head in this Shane-Eric pitch but despite being extremely tempted to ask questions, Paul and I heeded the words of *Don't ask how something can NOT work*. We laid it all out and put it on the dry-erase board in the office. Leadership by example!

Next, we shifted our attention to the WWE Championship. I'd like to clear up a rumor that arose a few years back—that Vince Russo upon returning wanted to fire the Undertaker. I have no recollection of him ever saying that. What he did want to do was strip the Undertaker, who was Champion at the time, of the WWE title and have a tournament to crown a new one.

This gave us all pause because it was the exact same thing that was done on *WCW Nitro* in April 2000, when Russo made his debut as a full on-screen character. Similar to the WCW episode, there wasn't a defined on-screen reason as to *why* we'd be stripping Taker of the title.

Instead, Russo explained that Taker's a legend but he's not hip and cool. Russo then went on about how his son and his friends all talk about this "RVD." That was who we should make champion. Rob Van Dam, the breakout star from ECW, had an undeniable coolness factor, and while most of us didn't object to the idea of RVD becoming champ, stripping the Undertaker of the title and mapping out a tournament just because a test audience of three teenagers at a CD Warehouse thought it'd be neat did not necessarily seem like the wisest move.

But again, we complied and started creating brackets and matchups. As we did, Russo, looking at our talent roster, had a moment of inspiration.

"Bro, have you guys ever done Chris Jericho vs. Triple H?"

"Motherfucker that was literally the main event of this year's *WrestleMania!*" Michael Hayes replied (minus the "motherfucker," but his tone seemed to indicate he was thinking it). Either way, we all found it strange . . . even if you haven't been watching the show, if you're coming on to essentially lead the team, shouldn't you at least be slightly familiar with it?

From there we talked about a number of things, including Russo's desire to bring back Chyna* and reform DX.

"We can do it. We bring back Chyner. Road Dawg's almost out of prison. We gotta reform DX!"

We continued laying out any and all ideas on the table. Then the day was over and Russo left, flying home and scheduled to meet us on the road for TV. Once he left, we all felt a sense of accomplishment. We conducted the meeting with no squabbling, no personal insults, no cursing . . . Michael Hayes didn't even fart loudly to voice his displeasure, as was his custom. None of that. We'd conducted ourselves as professionals and accepted the new normal.

It was now time to recap our meeting to Vince McMahon. In Vince Russo's numerous accounts of this, we all "buried him behind his back." Why? Because, according to him, we had no choice. None of us had what it took to lead WWE to any level of success, and deep down we all knew that once Russo was hired, there would be no need for us. The truth is Russo's argument, much like his WCW shows—see if you can pick up on a common theme here—didn't make any sense.

---

* Or, as he called her, "Chyner."

Putting aside the fact that Heyman was already an integral on-screen character as the manager of Brock Lesnar, Michael Hayes was one of WWE's top backstage producers, and I had the support of much of WWE's top talent, the truth was that Vince McMahon was *never* going to fire an entire writing staff and let one writer be in charge again. Why? Because the last time he did that he got burned and saw his two-person writing staff abruptly leave the company and go to the competition. If *anyone* should realize that, it should be Vince Russo, whose shocking departure established that practice in the first place. Why would Vince McMahon ever put himself in that position again? Would he get into a hardcore match with his own daughter a week before her actual wedding? Sure. Pull down his pants in the ring on live TV and have grown men literally kiss his ass? Why not? Get caught without an entire writing staff when there's hours upon hours of television to produce each week? No chance in hell.

We laid out what we discussed with Russo as Vince took it all in. We presented it unbiased. If anything, after working on it all day, we were actually excited about seeing what Vince thought.

It didn't take long to find out. As we wrapped it all up a look came across Vince's face. We knew that look. Vince hated it . . . all of it. I know Russo has said he laid out the entire story line to Vince before he started and Vince loved it. Well, if you think Vince can't personally love an idea one day and then do an about-face forty-eight hours later you might not know him as well as you think.

While the idea of Bischoff in WWE had a lot of intrigue, Vince found the potential Shane-Bischoff story line as appealing as a monthlong diet of Taco Bell. In addition, he went semiballistic when he heard we were going to strip the Undertaker of the title for no particular reason and then have a tournament to crown RVD. He also was in no mood to reassemble DX and wasn't exactly pleased to see Triple H vs. Jericho as one of the tournament matches. Vince knew Russo hadn't been watching, but he was really put off by the fact Russo hadn't done the bare minimum of research. For those of you reading this book to gain insight on what it might take to join the WWE writing team, knowing the main event of the *WrestleMania* that had just taken place months earlier would be considered a plus!

Vince then asked us point-blank what we thought, and we gave him our honest answer—there was a lot of stuff that *could* be potentially cool here, but there was also a lot of inside stuff and WCW rehash that didn't work. If Eric Bischoff were coming, we could certainly dig into a Shane-Eric story line. We had no problem with building to a potential RVD Championship, even though none of us liked stripping Taker and having a random tournament. If we wanted to reform DX (despite Triple H being the biggest heel in the company at that point with designs of forming his own brand-new group) then break out the glow sticks and let's do it. Those were our thoughts, so our feeling was *Just tell us what you want to do and we'll get behind it and make it work.*

Vince sat in silence as he contemplated what he was going to say next. For the first and possibly only time I can recall in my sixteen years in the company, Vince apologized.

"This isn't going to work…I'm sorry I brought that asshole back."

Shortly thereafter we learned Russo was out. In order to save face after making a big announcement and letting the word get out, Vince was going to keep him on as a consultant. It would be my job to call him each week, get his ideas, then pass them along to the team. The calls were always professional, and I actually looked forward to getting Russo's input. Again, he's an extremely creative guy.

Ultimately, it didn't last more than two weeks. Russo left to take a job at Jeff Jarrett's wrestling company, TNA, where it didn't take long before he once again became a writer / on-air character. I guess some birds aren't meant to be caged.

But in the end, despite the cries that the writers spoke ill of him in order to save their jobs, that Stephanie and Triple H each conspired against him so as to not lose any power, and that Vince himself caved to pressure, I'd like to give my version of why Vince Russo's return didn't work out.

Vince McMahon does what Vince McMahon wants to do. And he didn't want to do this. To put it another way:

- The McMahons didn't screw Russo.
- The writers didn't screw Russo.
- Russo screwed Russo.

Now that's a swerve.

CHAPTER 10

Vince: Life Lessons and Survival Tips

After experiencing the whirlwind that was the 2002 Vince Russo regime, it would be fair to sum up the writing team's feelings like this:

Vince McMahon—the cause of and solution to all our problems.

That totally original joke (not at all ripped off from *The Simpsons*) has been felt at one time or another by everyone at WWE. It's impossible to feel otherwise. Vince *is* the company. Over the years I'm sure you've heard most of the common stories and rumors—everything you see on TV runs through him, he's the first to arrive, last to leave, he hates sneezing and sleeping since that means you're not in complete control of your body and that is therefore a sign of weakness, he eats super healthy, he works out like crazy, and he despises giraffes on general principle, since he feels an animal that big should not resign itself to eating just plants. As Han Solo would say:

"It's true, all of it."

There is no one more passionate about WWE than Vince McMahon. It would be quite easy for him to have passed the baton by now and called it a career, but he's not going to do that. Not now, not ever. And it's not because he doesn't trust others to do the job, it's because he truly enjoys it. For those wanting Vince to step aside, the biggest obstacle, in my opinion, was never WCW or the federal government, it was and always will be Clint Eastwood. If Clint can be directing, acting, and even scoring full-length feature films into his nineties, you better believe Vince McMahon can be instructing Bianca Belair how to skip and twirl her braid in his midseventies. (I don't know if he's ever done that, but I'm enjoying the visual.)

Those who work closest with Vince—like I did for over a decade—tend to look at him as more than just a boss. He becomes a sage, a mentor, a really jacked Yoda, dispensing not just lessons on how to write his show but on life in general. Here's a few I've accrued over a sixteen-year period.

LESSON #1: LEARN TO LIKE A CERTAIN TYPE OF . . . SANDWICH

There's a common misperception that Vince loves surrounding himself with yes-men—that Vince hates to be challenged. This is completely untrue. In fact, Vince despises spineless yes-people (he considers them the giraffes of humans), and they typically don't last long in positions of power. Vince likes to be challenged; it just depends on how you do it.

One of the traps young writers fall into when they first start working in WWE is making friends with a talent and then trying to push them to the moon. This almost always backfires, and the talent you're trying to push is the one who suffers. I remember befriending Al Snow early in my tenure. Al's a really nice, down-to-earth guy and very approachable. Al's also a realist. He knew Vince didn't see him as a top guy and knew Vince wasn't a big fan of his in general.

"What kind of name is 'Al Snow'? That is the worst name for a wrestler I've ever heard of in my life."*

I heard Vince say that out loud, with literally no one asking or even bringing up Al's name in a conversation. He just happened to be thinking it. Of course, that didn't stop me from championing Al early on. I made it my mission to change Vince's mind about Al Snow, on one car trip pitching "Al Snow vs. Jeff Hardy" so many times Vince would not have been convicted of manslaughter had he thrown me out of the SUV. Every time Al Snow won a match, I felt like I had won. This constant assault on the

---

*Vince had no issues with "Bastion Booger," "Husky Harris," or "Mr. Ass."

senses involving all things Al Snow (who wanted to get an occasional win to have credibility but in no way urged me to bring up his name every five seconds) only served as a detriment to his and my cause.

It was only after I stopped constantly pushing for Al to win matches and concentrated on getting him over in other ways (mainly through crazy vignettes with Steve Blackman) that I finally made some progress. As it turns out, being the unofficial spokesperson for Al Snow was just the beginning of my unique form of Vince irritation.

During my first *WrestleMania* weekend (*WrestleMania 2000*), in Vince's hotel suite, I found myself constantly arguing with him. The funny thing is I have absolutely no recollection of what we were arguing about. None.* But after one particularly contentious *WrestleMania 2000* meeting, I went back to my hotel room full of piss and vinegar. Who did Vince think he was telling me my ideas were wrong? I've been the one watching and consuming the product for years! When was the last time he paid for a ticket? I'm a twenty-six-year-old lifelong fan—who *better* to have insight of what other fans are looking for? Then it just hit me. Ho-ly shit. I had been in the business for a total of five months and was arguing with Vince freaking McMahon about *WrestleMania*! This is like a writer joining *Saturday Night Live* and telling Lorne Michaels how he should do Weekend Update, or a child telling Frankenberry how to be a mascot for a cereal that gives you uncontrollable diarrhea. The experts are experts for a reason!

I left my hotel room, marched straight back to Vince's, and knocked on his door. He answered and I immediately apologized. I didn't do it out of fear of losing my job. I did it because it was the right thing to do. Vince told me he appreciated that. He loved to be challenged and that everything was fine.

About a week later I was summoned to executive producer Kevin Dunn's office (the only time that had ever happened) who essentially told me everything was in fact not fine.

---

*Free advice to current and future WWE writers: It may feel like what you're arguing about is a matter of life or death. Trust me . . . it isn't.

Again, Vince does like to be challenged, but you need to be smart in how you do it and not let your passion and ego get in the way of being a professional. Did Vince himself always lead with professionalism? No, but it's *his* company. He doesn't have to. Vince has a revolting but on-point catchphrase when it comes to working, especially in creative:

"Sometimes you need to learn to eat a shit sandwich and like the taste of it."

That is to say sometimes you're not going to like how something shakes out, but you need to accept it. If you feel strongly about something you should speak up, you should give it your best shot, but if it doesn't work out, so be it. Doesn't mean you're a yes-man; it's just reality. You're not going to win every argument, you're not going to like every result, you're not going to always get what you want. If you want to get everything you want, simply work your way to the point where you then own the actual company. Once that happens you better believe the Al Snow comeback tour that nobody (not even Al at this point) is asking for will be in full effect.

Lesson #2: To sell or not to sell

"Selling," in wrestling, is the act of visually expressing the pain and physicality of a move. Selling is essential for getting over with an audience, especially as a babyface. In the real world, selling—letting your true feelings show, especially when dealing with something negative—can be a mixed bag. Which is especially tough because selling is a very human instinct, whereas "eating shit and liking the taste of it" is not.* It's one way Vince tests you—throwing adversity your way and seeing how you register, or "sell," it. I should point out, the selling I'm referring to is for common, everyday workplace occurrences. Truly horrific things that also happen to be criminal offenses should absolutely be "sold" and dealt with.

This version of the "no sell" is more about having an idea you're

---

*Other than in the deepest, darkest recesses of Pornhub.

fighting for get flat-out rejected (be it as a writer or a performer). If you don't get your way and pout, officially known as having the "boo boo face," you gain a reputation and everything becomes an uphill battle.

No one was worse at this than Jim Ross, for years Vince's number one commentator and head of WWE Talent Relations (and the best to do both in WWE history). JR knows this, as he's documented it in two very successful autobiographies. The more he "sold," the more he showed his disgust over an angle or a decision that would change his live-event bookings, the more likely he was to be wearing a sailor suit on a Halloween episode of *Smackdown*.*

Executive producer Kevin Dunn, on the other hand, was a master at no-selling everything Vince threw his way. Sure, he'd have his share of disagreements and arguments, but as far as being baited into showing raw, unhinged emotion? Not a chance. Not surprisingly, he's in his fifth decade with the company.

One time, in a rare instance where we were all hanging out in Vegas after a show, Vince handed Kevin $1,000 as we passed a blackjack table and said, "Here, see what you can do with this."

The first hand Kevin had was lousy and he busted pretty quick. The next hand he was dealt a 20. The dealer proceeded to deal himself a 7, an 8, and a 6, for 21. Something like that would've haunted me for months no matter how rich I was. I would've probably been thrown out of the casino for yelling the loudest obscenity ever recorded. Vince and Kevin laughed about it and left. Sure, it helps to be preposterously loaded, but still...

In general, the more you don't sell (again the small stuff!), the harder it is to let your emotions get the better of you. It's a good tip in life to try to reign it in on the little things and not go off the handle, but again, it's not natural. We're not robots, we're emotional beings. Our visceral responses to things are often difficult to completely mask. So whenever I'm faced with something adverse, especially when there are people watching, a

---

*Okay, that one might've been my idea—sorry, JR!

little Vince pops on my shoulder and says, "Dammit Brian, don't sell." This usually happens waaaay after I have sold a great deal.

LESSON #3: R-E-S-P-E-C-T, OR "WHAT NOT TO DO ON A CORPORATE AIRPLANE"

Sometimes it seems that most of the angles on WWE TV are about someone disrespecting someone else.* It's something we can all relate to. Vince is big on respect, too, not just for him but for the company in general. WWE is in a never-ending battle to make legitimate strides in the entertainment world—to be taken seriously. I think it's in a much better place as far as respect from the entertainment industry now than in the days of the Attitude Era. The sponsorships, television deals, and ancillary streams of revenue WWE brings in today wouldn't be possible in the days of "Diss the Diva" from the Diva Search competition of 2005 where the improvised phrase... ahem... "cum-burping gutter slut" made its way onto live television. The response backstage by wrestlers who had been previously chastised for saying the word *bitch* was quite the spectacle. At least we didn't turn it into a T-shirt.

Vince is very old-school when it comes to respect. One of the rules of the road is you cannot sleep in a car as it's a sign of disrespect to the person driving. They have to stay awake and are providing you with safety, so the least you can do is stay awake with them. Similarly, you can't sleep on Vince's corporate plane unless Vince falls asleep first.

I made the mistake of falling asleep on the plane my first month in the company. Vince saw this, got up from his chair, got within an inch of my face and screamed my name, as loud as he could, waking me up and scaring the shit out of me.** Also, in an attempt to not get airsick, I took

---

*Hell yeah, I'm including my fine idea when Booker T felt disrespected after losing out on a Japanese shampoo commercial to Edge. Something that egregious can *only* be settled at *WrestleMania*!

**Yes, I most definitely "sold" and now I find myself unable to sleep on planes... ever.

a Dramamine before a flight, and while I didn't throw up, I *did* fall asleep in the production meeting (at the head table facing everyone).

Granted, that's not as bad as the one time on a flight when an employee who shall go nameless was complaining about having to pee, asking me every two minutes to ask the pilot how much longer until we landed. This was before the actual WWE corporate jet, and we were in a much smaller plane with no bathroom. In fact, there was one seat up front where you could take the cover off and convert it into a toilet if you really had to go...in full view of everyone. Why it was designed this way, I don't know, as it seemed like a lose-lose for everyone involved.

This employee made the mistake of telling a plane full of people, many of whom had taken actual brutal in-ring bumps, "There's no greater pain than the pain of having to pee." Ultimately this employee couldn't wait and asked (or more accurately "told") the person who occupied the "toilet seat" to move to the back—Linda McMahon. As the plane began to land and the nameless employee dropped their pants to sit down (standing would've been a disaster of unspeakable proportions) Vince literally dove to the back of the plane so as not to be anywhere near ensuing urination. I've never seen him move so fast in my life. Amazingly the pee-er in question is still with the company and, suffice to say, has never lived this moment down. Out of respect, he will remain nameless...

Okay, it was Michael Cole.

Which reminds me:

LESSON #3.5: IT'S A GOOD IDEA TO WAIT TO USE THE BATHROOM IN THE ARENA, BUT *DON'T* USE THE ONE IN VINCE'S PRIVATE OFFICE AND THEN FIND YOURSELF LOCKED IN FROM THE INSIDE, UNABLE TO GET OUT, AS THE PRODUCTION MEETING YOU'RE SUPPOSED TO BE LEADING IS STARTING

Yes, that happened. I'm not proud.

Lesson #4: Don't work yourself into a shoot

I was the master of finding out how little things I didn't even intend to be disrespectful could in fact be very disrespectful. When you're on Vince's plane and in his employ, you're supposed to be sociable. Vince neither likes nor comprehends introverts, which didn't do me any favors. As soon as we would enter his plane after a long day and night of producing live television, the last thing I wanted to do was to talk more wrestling. We had just spent the past fifteen hours talking wrestling, and I'd recharge by putting on a pair of headphones and either watching a movie on my portable DVD player, listening to my iPod, or doing a crossword puzzle. In fact, I got the reputation of being a big crossword fanatic, even though I had never done them until boarding the WWE corporate jet. Michael Hayes would nudge me and say, "Hey, we're talking about Nunzio's match," and I'd just say, "Sorry, I'm closed." The problem is, unless you're actually paying for the plane, the crew, the food and drink, and the fuel, you are most definitely "open."

One time I made the critical mistake of donning the headphones while the Undertaker was on the plane. As I was obliviously listening to Weezer and acing the *USA Today* crossword (who's cooler than me), little did I know I was incurring the wrath of both Vince and the Deadman. Vince's wrath I could deal with, as it happened nearly every week, not so much in regards to Undertaker.

When the plane landed I was told Undertaker was very put off by my "standoffish attitude." I had my moment with Undertaker in Wrestlers Court, and while we weren't close I thought at least we were cool. But now I had really messed things up. You do not want the Undertaker on your bad side. First off, he's just an awesome guy, but beyond that he's the locker room leader. I had heard stories about how guys back in the day, particularly the Ultimate Warrior, got on Andre the Giant's bad side and could never get off it. I didn't want to be *that* guy, especially over something as stupid as listening to "Hash Pipe" while figuring out a four-letter word for "Broadway play involving felines."

The proper thing to have done (aside from taking part in the plane conversation in the first place) was to have just found the Undertaker and apologized, but I did what they call in the business "working yourself into a shoot." Michael Hayes had laid it on pretty thick about how the Undertaker truly felt disrespected, and Vince didn't disagree. I had the privilege of sitting on a private plane with the Undertaker, potentially picking his brain and talking shop, and I chose to go off in my own world. The truth was that night the atmosphere on the plane was pretty loose, with red wine flowing and a good time being had by most. It was almost like a party atmosphere, and like most parties, I preferred to RSVP "maybe" then just stay home.

As I walked the halls of the arena the following day I had it in my head Undertaker was seriously upset. As if this "incident" could actually weigh on his mind for more than five seconds. While there probably was some feeling of "what was that about," the idea of Taker being extremely angry was more in my mind and not real (a "work") but I treated it as extremely real ("a shoot"). I had visions of him calling me out in front of everyone and getting labeled a disrespectful brat who deserved universal scorn and derision. Once that happened, I played out a scenario in my mind where I'd say something offensive and sarcastic and then he'd deck me. This is, I should point out, insane. I have no idea what I was thinking. Again, this was somewhat early in my WWE career, and knowing the type of person Mark Calaway is, the mere thought of him doing this is absurd. But at the time I got myself whipped into such a frenzy, I legitimately thought it was going to happen.

I was left with no choice. I made up my mind, right then and there— before something like that could happen, I needed to kick the Undertaker in the balls. It was my only chance to save any face if we got in a fight. Yes, there would be ramifications and it would probably be the end of my WWE career, but it was the only way out of this and my only chance to avoid getting publicly humiliated. I couldn't beat Taker in an actual fight, but I could surprise him by kicking him in the balls and then running as fast as I can. This seemed like a perfectly acceptable option.

I tried avoiding Undertaker all day, but invariably our paths would cross. When they did, thankfully, a moment of sanity came over me and I did what I should've done in the first place—I apologized. I went on about knowing how pissed off he was and how at the end of the day I just like to recharge and...Taker cut me off as a smile came across his face.

"Hold on. You thought I was legitimately pissed?"

"Yeah, Michael said—"

"Nah man, we're cool. Believe me, if I was pissed...you would know it."

I felt extremely relieved and extremely stupid at the same time. Though I probably never would've had the guts to actually go through with it, I'm glad I never attempted to physically assault the Undertaker.* If this was Vince's lesson about proper plane etiquette and a life lesson of not "working yourself into a shoot," then it definitely worked. From then on, whenever I entered Vince's private plane, I would still put my headphones on but not immediately. I would take part in the general conversation about how the night went until deciding enough time had passed. And while Undertaker's win streak at *WrestleMania* eventually ended, my streak of "Days being grateful I was never stupid enough to kick the Deadman in the balls" lives on.

LESSON #5: THE TRUE DEFINITION OF INTELLIGENCE

One of the many Vinceisms that always stuck with me was his feelings on intelligence. Being book smart didn't mean you actually *were* smart. "It's not about how much you know but how you apply that knowledge." If you know all the biological and chemical reasons why eating a diet of cotton candy can cause tooth decay, weight gain, and diabetes but you choose to eat it anyway, then you're really not that smart even if your SAT scores say otherwise.

So how would I apply a decade-plus's worth of life lessons from Vince once I found myself out in the real world? I'd find out soon enough at the

---

*Though it would've been quite a discussion point in my year-end performance review with Stephanie.

table read for the pilot episode of *Ballers*, when I squared off against an unlikely adversary—Mark Wahlberg.

This was in December 2014, and while I was still working as a creative consultant for WWE part-time, I was also working part time for Seven Bucks Productions, and we were about to have the cast read the pilot of our first scripted television show—HBO's *Ballers*.

A table read is when all the cast, writers, producers and network executives meet in a room and literally read the script out loud. Mark Wahlberg was an executive producer on the show, and as everyone was milling about, someone introduced me to Mark. He didn't really make eye contact and had a rather soft handshake, two things I wouldn't have given a second thought to pre-WWE, but since they are the first things Vince looks for in a person, I noticed it immediately. That in itself was no big deal—I mean, who was I? Maybe I didn't warrant eye contact and handshake firmness. It was certainly nothing worth reacting to. But then something happened.

Dwayne had gone to the bathroom, and I turned my head and saw him reenter the conference room. Mark then tried to make eye contact with Dwayne. Since our pleasantries were over and done with, I started walking away. But as I did, out of the corner of my eye, I could see Mark Wahlberg make a motion with his hands. I'm not 100 percent sure but I could've sworn he was making a "shooing" motion at me, as he approached his friend and *Pain and Gain* costar.

Suffice to say, inside I was livid. First off, I *liked* Mark Wahlberg. I remember "putting him over" to anyone who would listen after what I thought was a genuinely hilarious performance in *I Heart Huckabees*. Also, I started internally reneging on all that "who was I to deserve eye contact" talk. I'll tell you who I am...I was...the one-time seventh most powerful person in wrestling according, to some subscription-based online wrestling newsletter, dammit! I wrote main-event angles for *WrestleMania*! I survived the XFL *and* Wrestlers Court! You think I'm going to stand being "shooed" by the star of the eighth best *Planet of the Apes* movie?

In the heat of the moment, I abandoned Vince's life lessons. I "sold," glaring at Wahlberg the entire table read (which he fortunately did not pick up on and if he did would certainly not have cared). And I definitely worked myself into a shoot—that is to say, created an entire blood feud entirely in my head.

After the read, I went back to my hotel room, steaming, and saying to myself, *I bet you anything Wahlberg's a bad guy.* I turned on my computer and Googled "Mark Wahlberg dick." Word to the wise: Don't do this, as you will be besieged by an assortment of *Boogie Nights* photos. As I was sitting alone in my hotel room, looking at Mark Wahlberg's prosthetic* genitals, I decided to finally listen to my inner Vince and simply "eat shit and like the taste of it."

Vince made peace with guys who've bad-mouthed him, held him up for money, even testified against him in court, far worse affronts than a brief shooing. Doing what's "best for business" wasn't just a McMahon television catchphrase, it was a way of life.

So I didn't go through with any revenge fantasies I had concocted on the ride back to the hotel, but a few days later I did tell Dwayne the story, and he laughed.

"Aw, man you should've told me about that immediately! I could've had some fun with that. Mark's a good dude. He really is. But eeeeevery now and then you see some of that old-school Boston come out."

Fair enough, I thought. He shooed me just like the Mets shooed the Red Sox out of a World Series trophy back in '86.

Boom! How do you like *them* apples?!

Wait, that's Matt Damon.

Either way, the next time I see Mark Wahlberg I will shake his hand (firmly) and not cause a scene due to an incident he has no memory of. And for that I have Vince McMahon to thank.

Of course, when it comes down to it, all these pearls of wisdom could be lost at a moment's notice. When you suddenly find yourself involved

---

*I think?

in the creation of a story line where all rules and conventional wisdom go out the window. When things snowball so catastrophically no amount of shit eating, no selling or respect can get you out of it. That's what happened in 2002, when one woman single-handedly upended the boundaries of reason and good taste. Her name was Katie.

CHAPTER 11

Katie Vick Is Dead

Seinfeld's "The Contest." *The Simpsons*' "Marge vs. the Monorail." *The Sopranos*' "Pine Barrens." When do the writers of those shows know they're making something classic? Do they have an inkling when they're creating something that will be quoted verbatim decades later? People no doubt wonder the same thing about certain WWE story lines, but with a slight twist: "When did you first realize you were creating something that will go down in history for its unparalleled awfulness?"

"How on earth did you think this was going to work?"

"Is it possible to have you retroactively drug tested?"

Ask any fan of this post–Attitude Era what story line embodies those questions and two words will emerge above all others: "Katie Vick."

It's October 2002, a few months after *Raw* and *Smackdown* were split into two separate shows and rosters. Again, the brand extension was always supposed to be taking two steps back in order to take three forward, but right now we were still in our "step back" phase. *Smackdown* was emerging as the "wrestling" show, whereas *Raw* needed to have that "live, anything can happen, outrageous" feel. That meant we on *Raw* had more leeway to take chances that culminated in a fun show concept—"Raw Roulette" from Las Vegas. It was an excuse to have a bunch of "gimmick" matches from the serious (Steel Cage Match) to comedic (Vegas Showgirl Match in which Goldust and William Regal crushed it) to the pay-per-view worthy, in this case a four-way Tables, Ladders and Chairs match for the tag team titles. This was hotshotting (defined as putting potential

121

money-making attractions on free television in the hopes of popping a big rating) at its finest, but we were excited about the show as we reviewed it during our Saturday afternoon conference call with Vince.

Vince liked the creativity and the stipulations, but something was missing. Just before the call ended, he pointed out there really was no big overall story. No cliffhanger.

I can't say he didn't have a point. We had put so much energy into coming up with creative ways to have fun with the roulette wheel, we weren't looking at the big picture. It definitely felt like a standalone show. Then Vince dropped the hammer.

"What if, after Kane wins the TLC, Triple H comes to the stage and steals his moment? What if he tells Kane he knows his secret? What if Triple H says, 'Kane . . . you're a murderer!'"

Silence on our end . . . and then enthusiasm! I was down! In all honesty, it sounded like a pretty compelling hook. Kane's character was becoming more human during this time, and the audience was feeling empathy for him. Accusing him of murder could send the monster spiraling back into a void he vowed never to return to. It sounded like Vince had been cooking this up for a while, and all of us were excited to hear what was going through his head.

"And what happens next? Where do we go from there?" I asked.

"How the hell should I know? You guys are the writers. Figure it out," Vince replied.

With that, Vince hung up, and the mood from those left on the call went from intrigue to dread. I didn't consider myself a seasoned Hollywood veteran by any means, but I did know in order to break a major story like this, especially one that will unfold over the course of several weeks if not longer, you need to map it out, make sure it made sense and was compelling. We needed the one thing we didn't have, which was time. Okay, no reason to panic. We can do this. We had about forty-eight hours before the words "You're a murderer" would leave Triple H's lips on live television. Let's figure this out. Starting with "Who exactly did Kane allegedly murder?"

In our subsequent follow-ups with Vince over the weekend, it wasn't enough to simply accuse Kane of murder, we needed a name. We had a young talent named Scott Vick ready to debut soon, so we decided to sneak the name "Vick" in there. At least we could possibly debut someone new into a major story line. Vince also wanted something that sounded pure and innocent, so we landed on "Katie" as the first name.* The problem with the Scott Vick idea was that when the higher-ups eventually saw Scott wrestle, they deemed him to be too green and his inclusion too risky to include in a main-event angle like this. So real-life Scott was out, dead, fictional Katie was in.

Throughout the night in Vegas, I was hounded with questions from Triple H:

"Why are we doing this?"

"Do you people have any idea where this is going?"

"Does anyone else find this really fucking stupid?"

Suffice to say, Triple H was not a fan of this angle, and unlike our disagreements in the past, this time I really had no counter. Resistance was not only futile, it was dangerous. Often when Vince has an idea he feels strongly about, the more pushback he gets the more resolute he becomes. You're fighting against his gut, and Vince's gut has a pretty impressive track record. It helped him amass enough money to buy the company from his father, stick a fork in WCW and all other competitors, beat the federal government in court, introduce the world to not one but multiple Doink the Clowns, and now that gut was going to have Triple H accuse Kane of murder on live television.

So Triple H delivered those words to a shocked Kane and a bewildered *Raw* audience. Little did he know it was only going to get worse from there. (Actually, he probably had a pretty good clue.)

With *Raw* over we had a week to make sense out of all this and we

---

*I Googled "Katie Vick" and found there's a real-life pediatric dentist in Alabama named Katie Vick, so if Dr. Vick happens to be reading this...on behalf of the 2002 WWE creative team..."our bad."

needed to start with Kane. Kane's normally a great character to write for, and I often had fun using movies as inspiration. Kane's speech in group therapy with Daniel Bryan, which I wrote with Matt McCarthy, was inspired by Dr. Evil in group therapy, one of my favorite comedic monologues. I put up a fight and won out to have Kane and Shane sit down in a restaurant and have a tense but civil conversation à la Pacino and De Niro in *Heat*. And Glenn Jacobs, the man who plays Kane, is one of the most professional people you'll ever meet and a great actor, too. That's what made this whole experience so difficult. Before Triple H could take a sledgehammer to his skull, we were taking one to his character. Kane was to admit on live television that his high school girlfriend Katie died in a car accident while he was driving. Kane...aka the Big Red Monster... aka the Devil's Favorite Demon...had a high school girlfriend...

Let's back up a bit.

Kane's backstory was that of a classic horror monster—his brother the Undertaker burned his house down when Kane was a child, killing his parents and leaving him physically and mentally scarred. Paul Bearer (revealed to be Kane's actual father) then raised Kane in a mental asylum, unbeknownst to his (half) brother, until unleashing him on the Undertaker live on pay-per-view. Crazy as it sounds, it all tracks. Kane wore a mask to hide his burns and communicated by speaking into a mechanical voice box, which was rare as he barely spoke at all. It was one of the most talked-about character launches ever. Kane's intricate backstory *worked*. He was the personification of twisted evil.

Despite my bringing up Kane's backstory in the writers meetings, Vince didn't really see it as a deterrent. As the "Hollywood" guy, I probably should've been more adamant, insisting that a scarred mute monster secretly living in a mental institution probably would not have gone to high school, period, much less been out partying with his girlfriend who he accidentally killed due to poor weather and his inability to drive a stick shift. I'm not up to speed on Leatherface's backstory, but I'm pretty sure he didn't kill his girlfriend using tainted eggs while trying to make her a Denver omelet. And Kane now needed to explain all of this in front of an arena of confused French-Canadians in Montreal, home of that week's *Raw*, as well as a world-wide audience. Stephanie McMahon was the unlucky victim assigned to write this promo (with heavy input from Vince) and she walked around backstage like Téa Leoni in *Deep Impact*, standing on the beach right before the asteroid hit, resigned to her fate.

Glenn, the ultimate pro's pro, normally never seemed rattled when having to deliver a promo. This was the man who withstood multiple false starts to his WWE character, having infamously played the evil dentist, Dr. Isaac Yankem (DDS), and what would be commonly referred to as "fake Diesel," when he stepped into the role after Kevin Nash left for WCW. (WWE had momentarily lost its mind, thinking fans wouldn't notice or care.) He could normally withstand anything. This was the exception.

It was the longest promo his character ever cut, saying words his character would normally never say. You could almost see his soul exit his body as he explained how an animal jumped out in front of them as he was driving Katie home from a party.* It was brutal. The crowd who started by chanting "WHAT" was just silent in the end, and not "edge of your seat waiting to hear what he'll say next silent," more like "we need to reevaluate our life choices" silent. By the time Triple H came out talking about how Kane's semen was found at the accident scene (Vince had a strange obsession with Kane's semen, though to be fair, who doesn't), we on the writing team knew we could take comfort in knowing at least it couldn't get any worse.

As usual, we were wrong.

Look, no one bats 1.000. Vince in general has a pretty good track record. I remember watching him in awe as he dictated the entire debut of the *Nexus* off the top of his head, an angle universally lauded for its boldness and originality. Unfortunately, that would be years later. In this particular writers meeting, he was talking about Triple H's next step.

---

*This was presumably when Paul Bearer let him out of the mental institution for good behavior.

Triple H would "embarrass" Kane by dressing up as the Big Red Monster himself, entering a real funeral home, and simulating sex with a mannequin (ostensibly dead Katie) in a casket.

Here's the thing, though—who exactly is getting embarrassed in this scenario? When the action designed to embarrass the opponent is far more embarrassing than the original act itself, is the recipient of the embarrassment really that embarrassed? Again, this should've been brought up on the spot. Someone should've said, "This is insane. Not only are we killing the mystique of one of our greatest characters, but we're doing this in literally the most tasteless way possible." No one did, myself included. We could've regrouped and said we *need* to come up with something better and try to force Vince to change his mind. We could've pulled an all-nighter with Stephen King, Jordan Peele, and the ghost of Alfred Hitchcock, it wouldn't have made a difference.

Vince knew exactly what he wanted from this scene and started acting it out in the writers room. The man had passion, you had to give him that. As Vince was wrapping up this pitch of faux-fornication, I witnessed something I had never seen before—Vince was in the midst of a giggle fit.

"And at the end..." Vince said, tears practically rolling down his cheek, "he reaches down, pulls out some goop from Katie's head, flings it towards the camera and says, 'I just fucked your brains out.'"

I looked over to fellow writer Ed Koskey and whispered, "Call the police."

Okay, I actually just sat there with a horrified frozen smile...It's easy to say *now* that we should've been more adamant about not going down this path. At the time, while none of us can honestly say we thought this was good, we also universally thought there was no going back. The marching order was to see this through. This was either going to go down as the most shocking buzzworthy segment in WWE history, or it would be an angle so disastrous just the mere mention of Katie Vick two decades later would have people solemnly recall where they were when they experienced it like our parents did after JFK was assassinated.

What happened next has been well documented. Bruce Prichard

and Vince took a camera crew to an actual funeral home with an actual funeral in progress across the hall. While Triple H and Bruce made a last-ditch effort to save face by wanting to perform the vignette over-the-top and comedic, Vince wanted it done as serious as possible. In the end it was a moot argument. Would you rather die by hanging or lethal injection? Debate it all you want, the end result will still be the same. Still, in this case, over-the-top would probably have been the lesser of two evils. At least the audience would've known WWE (the company) knew this was plain ridiculous. Instead, Triple H (against his will but a company man through and through), violated that mannequin with the gravitas of Daniel Day-Lewis addressing Congress in *Lincoln*.

When the segment aired, the entire arena in Nashville watched in stunned disbelief. Well almost, stunned disbelief. There was one person sitting in the crowd, laughing like a madman—yours truly. I wasn't laughing at the scene (though I was watching it for the first time like everyone else). I wasn't even closely watching the scene. I was mainly watching the people watching the scene. The look of confusion mixed with disgust and bewilderment, combined with the hopelessness we all felt as writers, made me burst out like Robert De Niro at the movie theater in *Cape Fear*. By the time the following week rolled around and Kane's friend the Hurricane was getting his "revenge" on a fake Triple H by staging a scene in a hospital where objects were being pulled out of Triple H's ass (sigh), the tide had finally turned. Even Vince at this point knew we needed to end this as soon as humanly possible.

Maybe all of this had something to do with the angle airing and the WWE stock in turn hitting its lowest point ever.

Things weren't much better over on *Smackdown*. Also tasked with embedding a shocking soap opera–style twist, Paul Heyman and Brock Lesnar introduced the world to "Tracy," a woman who claimed to have had a three-month affair with the Undertaker while he was married. She slapped him and even called him "Mark," eighteen years before doing that on TV was cool. The audience didn't go for this one either, and it's mainly forgotten now. Having a character simulate sex with a corpse dressed in a cheerleader outfit tends to overshadow whatever other stories you have going on.

By the time we got to the pay-per-view, Vince was ready to move on to the next thing. To signal to the audience we had recognized the error of our ways and were going to try to lighten up, I pitched a quick cold open where Undertaker is sitting forlorn in his locker room when he's joined by Kane. Kane takes a breath and simply says, "So...how was your week?"

Sure, the actual pay-per-view matches still needed to happen, but from the perspective of the writing team it was finally over. A low-key, understated end to perhaps the most tasteless, outrageous angle in the history of sports entertainment.

Unlike poor Katie herself, at least we lived to tell the tale and no one tried to have sex with us (though that was likely to happen either way).

CHAPTER 12

Does Funny Equal Money?

The debate to have the Katie Vick funeral home scene play serious or tongue-in-cheek was probably a flawed argument to begin with, as it should never have even gotten to that point. (Cut to the family whose actual funeral was taking place as we shot the vignette nodding vigorously.) But it does lead to a bigger question that's been argued among wrestling circles since the beginning of time:

"Does 'funny' equal 'money'?"

When I started in WWE, I was told point-blank by many people that funny does not in fact equal money. Meaning—comedy angles and characters can occasionally be a nice diversion, but nobody will ever buy a ticket to see it. Or more specifically, "Keep your 'comedy' the fuck out of our wrestling ring." It's a classic old-school mentality—in its essence, wrestling comes down to getting people to pay to see one person kick another's person's ass. Start including too much "ha-ha" (as wrestlers and *only* wrestlers call it) and in theory the issue no longer comes across as serious, thus nobody buys a ticket to see it unfold, thus funny does not in fact equal money.

Think of any fight you've ever had in your life, physical or verbal. When you're truly pissed at someone, do you ever think about making jokes (aside from heavy sarcasm that hopefully crushes the other person's will to live)? In wrestling, you might be able to sprinkle in a little humor as a babyface or a lower-card talent, if it has some edge to it. But if you're a heel, especially a top heel, how can you get people to hate you if you're making them laugh? Polluting wrestling with comedy, at least in the main-event scene, essentially weakens the product. If the performers aren't taking what they're doing seriously, how can the audience?

And that's just with *good* comedy. Bad comedy in wrestling, which occurs far more often, can be even more disastrous.

Those are the arguments that were told to me numerous times. It's still a popular complaint by a lot of old-school wrestling people—wrestling was fine until Vince started hiring these damn "comedy writers" who ruined the business. Ironic that the main proponent of such thinking, legendary manager Jim Cornette, got in trouble a few years back for telling an unfunny, cringeworthy joke some have called racist on air.*

Look, I get it. Nobody wants to make the business itself into a joke. And while there are places for comedy spots in certain matches, once the bell rings the action for the most part should remain serious. It's really all a matter of degree. According to Apple Movies, *Die Hard*, *Lethal Weapon*, and *Guardians of the Galaxy* are all classified as action films, but each contain genuine laugh-out-loud moments.** I think the same principle applies to WWE when it comes to comedy, though it's not always an easy process.

WWE is a weird place when it comes to comedy. Vince McMahon himself may have—well, let's call it a "unique" sense of humor. One of the first things he told me was "There's nothing funnier than someone stepping in dogshit. If I could do a whole show on people stepping in dogshit, I would."

At first, I thought he was joking. Years later I can confirm—he wasn't.

But what Vince finds funny isn't so much the act of stepping in dogshit itself (though make no mistake, he does find that hilarious) as it is to see

---

*Sorry, it wasn't a "racist" joke, according to Jim. It was just an innocent heavily recycled "starvation joke," which is totally cool!

**In *Guardians* the most consistently funny character is Drax, played by former World Champion Dave Bautista, whose WWE persona was almost always super serious. He debuted as an angry, mute Deacon!

someone, mainly a rich asshole, get taken down a peg. An uptight snob who's now just as screwed as the rest of us. I'm willing to bet Vince loves Rodney Dangerfield in *Caddyshack*. In many ways Vince *was* wrestling's version of Rodney's Al Czervik, a wild card with a "unique" personality, upending the old boys club, shocking the establishment, and throwing a big party while declaring, "We're all going to get laid!"*

I actually took more pride in the serious story lines I helped write as opposed to the comedic ones. Shawn Michaels vs. Chris Jericho, the Kurt Angle, Stephanie McMahon, Triple H love triangle, and Batista's slow break from Triple H and Evolution being among my personal favorites. There really is nothing better than a long-term money-drawing story line with an amazing payoff (and yes, I realize most would argue the love triangle didn't have a good payoff, but that's a story for someone else's book).

"We don't do 'comedy,' we do humor," I was told early on. At first I didn't know what that meant, but after a while, I decoded it. The Mr. McMahon character, especially in his heyday, was absolutely hilarious, but he was never outwardly *trying* to be funny. The famous scene with Mr. McMahon in the hospital being visited by Mankind, Yurple the Clown, and eventually a bedpan-wielding Steve Austin was the perfect example of that. Everyone, even Mick, was playing it straight. Within the context of Mankind's character, he absolutely would pull out a sock to entertain Mr. McMahon, not as a joke but thinking it would genuinely help. That's why it was brilliant and prompted me to dress as Corporate Mankind for Halloween that year at a party with a not so surprising 22–1 male-to-female ratio.

Typically, when WWE is not trying to be funny it can be hilarious. When they are, let's just say it's a mixed bag. When dogshit isn't readily available, WWE's comedic go-tos usually involve goofy sound effects and very broad facial expressions. A show like *Arrested Development* would leave Vince stone-faced, shaking his head, wondering what the hell he's watching. Suffice to say, I loved *Arrested Development*.

---

*If that wasn't screamed backstage after the first *WrestleMania*, I'd be shocked.

That being said, Vince's number one goal is always to entertain the audience, and as long as they're responding, he'll typically give you a big leash to make something work, even if it goes against conventional wrestling wisdom. The biggest example of that would be your Olympic hero—Kurt Angle.

Kurt debuted on WWE TV right around the same time I joined the company, in November 1999. The vignettes to bring him in were an example of Vince at his best. Vince was astute enough to know that bringing a legit Olympic gold medalist in as a Hulk Hogan clone was not going to work in this era. Instead, he had Kurt debut as a holier-than-thou goody-goody who practiced the three Is (Intensity, Integrity, and Intelligence) and was billed as "the most celebrated REAL Athlete in the WWF"—which probably got him more heat with the boys backstage than with the fans.

When I saw that Kurt, stripped of all his inhuman athletic ability, was basically like me—a well-meaning nerd in a backstage world he knew nothing about, I knew I had to work with the guy. Kurt had never been an entertainer before, but for reasons known only to him, he decided to put his trust in me. Like a wrestler-wrestler relationship in the ring, trust is key for a wrestler-writer relationship. If a wrestler thinks you're just blindly parroting Vince's words, then it's never going to work. I was lucky in that when I started, there was a lot more leeway for writers at the time. Entire promos or backstage segments never had to go through an approval process. Once the premise was locked in, we just went out and did it. We caught hell afterward if the vignette didn't work (the most dreaded thing one could possibly hear backstage was "Vince wants to see you at Gorilla"), but there was a rush and creative freedom in just going out and trying something.

For a lot of people on WWE Creative, writing for a wrestler is like a form of wish fulfillment. You can come up with all the things you wish you could say to other people but can't. I couldn't get away with insulting, say, Big Show's haircut, but the Rock could. I couldn't insult an arena full of drunk, angry Red Sox fans in Boston for losing the '86 World Series, but Edge and Christian could. I certainly couldn't say highly insulting, flat-out disrespectful things to the man who signed my paychecks, but the Rock, Chris Jericho, John Cena, and plenty of others could. I'll admit it— there were times when I got upset with Vince, I just bit my tongue and had a character express what I was feeling live on the air. It was a warped but *very* effective form of therapy.

Kurt Angle was a dream come true—he was up for anything, had incredible comedic instincts, and was a legit badass. When he said he can make you tap out, he's 100 percent telling the truth. The key with Kurt was taking a page from the Mr. McMahon character—play it straight. This principle worked no matter how ridiculous the situation. Kurt could be passing out condoms in Penn State on a worldwide crusade for abstinence, awkwardly trash-talking Rey Mysterio ("You're a boy in a man's world, and I'm a man who loves to play with boys"), or wearing a ridiculous wig/headgear combination after getting his head shaved. No matter the circumstance, his character was usually never *trying* to be funny, which was why it always worked.* (I realize this is an extraordinarily basic rule in comedy, but not so much in the world of wrestling.) Most of Kurt's humor came from accidentally saying something offensive because he didn't know any better. Every insult he made to the crowd, either bashing their sports team, city, or local celebrity (deepest apologizes to the estate of Mr. Rogers), was rooted in something real—you don't boo an Olympic gold medalist and you sure as hell don't tell him, "You suck."

Vince always let us go out and do our thing, but there were a lot of concerns from other top talent and producers that Kurt was being a little too comedic and that "funny doesn't equal money." I remember getting into the same arguments about Edge and Christian during this time, but it was worse with Kurt, since he basically entered the scene as a main eventer.

My counterargument, even if I didn't always convey it in the clearest, most mature fashion,** was this: Once you're no longer a kid and you

---

* Shawn Michaels's theme song parody aside.

** Okay, I *never* conveyed it in the clearest, most mature fashion.

realize wrestling is work, you have to have funny/entertaining aspects to it. Otherwise, it's too earnest and has the potential to get repetitive and stale really quick. I know that sounds blasphemous to some people, but it was always the case with me and my friends, and I'm pretty sure we weren't anomalies. I thought it was especially true in the era of WWE churning out countless hours of TV a week. Not everything can nor should be life and death. When Kurt's music hit, as an audience member you knew you were in for something fun promo wise and something amazing in the ring.

Truthfully, the ones shaking their heads after another goofy Kurt moment weren't exactly wrong. If a character like Kurt's didn't grow and he remained who he was in 1999–2001 forever, he'd be dead in the water. It's all about how the character evolves. By the time Kurt was headlining WWE's ECW show, he was still entertaining but much more of a badass and I think the experience he gained from wearing a tiny cowboy hat with Steve Austin and spilling milk onto Undertaker's motorcycle helped him broaden his range and ultimately grow to become confident in whatever role he was given.

I was lucky to work with some very talented people over the years at WWE and on what I considered to be some genuinely funny moments, starting with Al Snow and Steve Blackman (a man physically incapable of smiling), Edge and Christian, Booker T and Goldust, the vastly under-rated William Regal, Santino Marella, Vickie Guerrero, Chris Jericho, Big Show, and the Rock (among many others) but throughout my time at WWE, the question of "Does Funny Equal Money" still remained. I would think looking at it through today's prism and seeing the success of talents like Big E, Zelina Vega, and Maxwell Jacob Friedman in AEW, who combine comedy and seriousness into their personas and ring work, maybe the answer is a solid "Yes, if done right."

Fortunately for me, I didn't have to wait two decades to get an answer. It was answered for me in the form of a real-life altercation on the streets of New York City.

In 2003 I was walking home carrying two bags of groceries. As was my custom, I had my headphones on, listening to songs on a giant portable

CD player so as not to accidentally start a conversation with a stranger.* It started pouring, but luckily I was only two blocks away from my apartment. All of a sudden, a guy riding a bicycle (on the sidewalk, mind you) sideswiped me, bumping into my elbow and nearly twisting me around 180 degrees. With my headphones on, and not really understanding how loud my voice was, I audibly screamed "What the *FUCK*?!!"

The bicycle immediately stopped, and the angry rider got off and headed straight for me. We proceeded to have the following exchange:

"You calling *me* a fuck?!"

"No! I said, 'What the fuck,' which is totally different."

"I know you just called me a fuck."

"You sideswiped *me*. So I said, 'What the fuck,' which is more of a reaction than an epith—"

Before I could continue the guy headbutted me. Just flat-out rammed his head into my face. In response, I didn't make a joke, but I was so shocked/nervous/bewildered I just started laughing.

"Did you just headbutt my *face*?"

The stranger (now assailant) just looked at me quizzically. "Yeah man, I'm packing. Don't you know I'm packing?"

I had lived such a sheltered life I actually thought he meant he was going on a trip and was late to start packing.

"I didn't know you were packing. How should I know you were packing?"

It should be noted not a single soul on this busy Third Avenue sidewalk stopped to intervene, which, as every true New Yorker knows, is perfectly normal and acceptable.

With that, the man got back on his bike and started pedaling away. My urge to always be right then got the best of me as I shouted:

"For the record, there is a difference between saying 'What the fuck' and calling someone a fuck!"

---

*I'll wear earbuds on the streets and especially in the subways even if I'm not actually listening to anything. It makes life a lot easier.

I saw him turn his head, almost in bafflement that this conversation was continuing as he thankfully decided to ride off. I have to admit, after the initial shock wore off, I was not in the mood for comedy. I went up to my apartment and then did what any rational-thinking person would do at that moment: I called my friend who just so happened to be an Olympic gold medalist. Kurt picked up and listened to my hysterical rant, then calmly told me what I needed to do:

"You have to go after him."

"What?"

"Get out, see if he's still there and confront him. He disrespected you on *your* turf."

"Dammit, Kurt, you're *right*!"

I should just point out the obvious—there is no part of this story that makes any sense. Under normal circumstances I would tell Kurt he was crazy, plus at this point I started to understand what was meant by "packing," but I was so souped up on adrenaline I didn't care. I marched out the door of my apartment* and went outside. Having seen the headbutter already start to pedal off earlier, I had a pretty good feeling that he wasn't out there lingering, but I walked out into the street, took a long hard look in both directions, and gave a satisfied *That's what I thought* nod.

That rush of testosterone. That feeling of *I don't care what happens, I'm having a confrontation and I'm going to like it!*

That got me more in the space of what a wrestler should be feeling heading into a match, not taking practice bumps in the ring. It was proof that when push comes to shove, in the heat of battle, it's not comedy that one feels when itching for a fight, it's raw emotion and bloodlust!

So maybe I had been wrong all this time.

With that, I got ready to tackle that week's script with a different mindset than I ever had before. And I did! It was probably the most "serious" *Raw* script I had ever written. Then, about a week later I wrote a vignette with Goldust dressed as the Crocodile Hunter.

---

*After putting away my perishables—I'm not a caveperson.

Funny may or may not equal money, but in the end, another axiom ultimately prevailed—don't try to be someone you're not. I was not going to turn into some tough guy just because some bicycle-riding lunatic with a poor sense of linguistics decided to headbutt me, but I did see the importance of realizing that there's a time and place for everything, and when you truly want to beat the holy hell out of someone, comedy shouldn't come into play. So thank you to Kurt Angle for ramping me up that night, and if the person who headbutted a guy in the pouring rain on Third Avenue and Twenty-Seventh Street in 2003 is reading this:

Seriously man . . . what the fuck?

CHAPTER 13

... *What the Rock Is Cooking*

O f course, the entire "Does funny equal money" debate could've been settled with a definitive yes, based on a simple two-word answer: the Rock.

The Rock deftly combined comedy and action in a way that made people want to pay to see it. A backstage Rock promo from 2000 is really not that different from a *Jumanji* movie today—it's all about taking the audience on a fun, entertaining, unpredictable ride. It goes back to one of Vince McMahon's favorite expressions:

"A match is a promo; a promo is a match."

Meaning a promo, no different than a match, needs to tell a story. Ideally, you catch people's attention right away, then get your message out before ending with "the big finish."

My favorite match as a kid was Roddy Piper vs. Adrian Adonis at *WrestleMania 3.* Steamboat vs. Savage was universally known as the best match on that card, Hogan vs. Andre the most historic, but for a Roddy Piper fan, believing this was in fact going to be his retirement match, all I wanted that night was to see Roddy win.

The match started off hot as Piper threw Adonis and his manager, Jimmy Hart, around the ring as the crowd went nuts, then settled into the story as Adrian got his heat. Roddy was on the cusp of losing before it ramped into the big finish with Piper applying the sleeper, winning the match, and cutting Adrian's hair. Okay, technically Brutus Beefcake cut Adrian's hair for some reason, but the point is, the match had a great start, told its story, then ended in a huge, memorable way. It's a basic formula that's successful for a reason, and it was one Rock and I always tried to follow when putting together a promo.

That's why whether it was having Jonathan Coachman do the Charleston, making Lilian Garcia admit her hidden love for him, or finding new ways to make fun of the Big Show's chokeslam (grateful for Paul Wight's sense of humor), we'd always try to start a promo in a way that no one could see coming (after the initial "Finally…"). But even the most laid-out promos don't always go according to plan.

In a backstage environment, a promo is easier to control. For one thing, in the rare instance where the Rock momentarily forgot what he was going to say, all he had to do was dramatically pause and the fans would start coming with the "Rock-y, Rock-y" chant. This provided valuable time for him to collect his thoughts and get back on track.

Live, out in the ring, there are other variables. Sometimes the crowd would get so loud the wrestlers literally couldn't hear each other. A super-hot crowd is not the *worst* problem—in fact, it's pretty much the goal of every performer—but it can cause some issues.

In Chicago, traditionally the hottest crowd in the country (sorry, NYC), we had a promo segment with the unusual alignment of Stephanie McMahon, Rhyno, and Booker T in the ring with the Rock and Chris Jericho (another guy who loved to collaborate and could think on his feet as well as anyone) up on the stage. This was designed to build up Rock and Booker T's story, and featured Rock insulting Booker's intelligence via a verbal flashback to Booker T in grade school:

" 'What's two plus two?' 'Thomas Jefferson!' "

Rock then started to compare Shane McMahon and Booker:

"The punk-ass sucka and the silver-spooned mutha—"

Stephanie was supposed to cut Rock off before he could finish the sentence, but it was so loud Steph couldn't hear. She started screaming, "That's enough!" but was a second too late as Rock had no choice but to unleash the full "muthafucka" on live television. Not an ideal situation, but to use another of Vince McMahon's favorite sayings:

"Nothing bad can ever happen on live TV."

Even if it's a mistake it can become a memorable spectacle. In all my years working with the Rock, we never had a full-blown disaster. But in 2011, when the Rock returned to Madison Square Garden to team with John Cena against Miz and R-Truth, we came pretty close.

MSG was a special place for both of us and the greatest arena in the world (sorry, Chicago). For Rock, it was where he made his official televised WWE debut in 1996. It was also where he sat in the crowd as a kid watching his grandfather, High Chief Peter Maivia, and his father, "Soulman" Rocky Johnson. I obviously didn't have those deep roots, but along with Nassau Coliseum, it was my hometown arena. It was where I watched Andre the Giant wrestle as a kid, the Shawn Michaels vs. Razor Ramon *WrestleMania X* ladder match as a young adult and countless Knicks losses as both. We wanted to make sure the Rock's return to MSG and his promo commemorating the occasion was something truly special.

Sitting in the refurbished Knicks locker room that was doubling as Rock's dressing room that night, we put together the bones of a live backstage promo. There was plenty for Rock to talk about, the only question was: What was going to be the big finish?

Always up for a song, Rock had the idea of singing Frank Sinatra's "New York, New York." Not only singing it but getting the entire crowd singing along. As we practiced the promo backstage, for whatever reason Rock was having a hard time remembering one part. The whole "And find I'm A-number one, top of the list, king of the hill, A-number one" section. Whenever we got to that part Rock would bump up against it and forget the order. This being the song that played at Yankee Stadium whenever the Yankees won, I had tried to avoid "New York, New York" whenever possible, so I didn't really know the words, either.

Going with the song was a big risk. Rock singing "New York, New York" at MSG live and messing up the words would not sit well with the NYC crowd. So what did we do? What we always did—created a safety net. For years I had written key words in a Sharpie on a piece of paper and stood by the cameraman as Rock did a live backstage promo. Rock's promos were significantly longer than most, so it was helpful to have a visual reminder of how the promo was supposed to go. He usually didn't need it, but if he did it was there, and with the Rock typically wearing sunglasses backstage, it would never look like he was reading.

On this occasion, due to the length of the promo, I had multiple pieces of paper, the most important one being the lyrics to the tricky part of the song. I stood with the paper positioned underneath the camera as the Rock (no sunglasses in this one) prepared to go live.

As Rock got into the promo, I found it going even better than antici-pated, with the MSG crowd showing a lot of love. When it got to the song, everyone started singing along, arms waving like it was the monthly MSG Billy Joel concert. Then, we got to *that* part. As I flipped to the last page which contained the order of the lyrics, I thought I saw Rock give the slight-est hesitation as he started singing but thankfully he ended up nailing it.

After a rousing "If you smelllll what the Rock is cooking," I took a sigh of relief. Mission accomplished! Everyone standing around backstage started clapping as Rock motioned my way. Not knowing any better, I strode confidently forward.

"Do you realize what you just did?" he asked.

Helped nail another successful promo? I thought to myself, slightly con-fused with his tone. Did this *not* just go perfectly?

It was then when Rock told me to look down. The piece of paper with the lyrics written in Sharpie, ensuring he wouldn't stumble on the one part of the promo that was giving him fits, was facing the wrong direc-tion! I had proudly, assuredly, held up the paper and without realizing it, had the paper facing myself as Rock was set to sing live. Rock managed to get through it unscathed, but I can only imagine what he was think-ing when the idiot standing next to the cameraman obliviously held up a blank sheet of paper in his moment of need while nodding confidently.

There's no telling what would've happened if he'd messed up the lines. He very well could've stopped the live promo and called me into the shot reaming me out in front of the millions. Maybe he messes up the lyrics, the crowd boos, he turns heel, and the entire dynamic in his program with Cena changes. Maybe some Disney executive sees this and gets second thoughts about casting him in *Moana* (yeah . . . probably not). Thankfully it never came to that, and now I triple-check before holding up a paper for a Rock promo and sweat profusely whenever I hear "New York, New York."

* * *

If there's a show on television that can draw direct comparisons to WWE, it's *Saturday Night Live*. Aside from the obvious live show element, there's the iconic catchphrases, the brutal schedules, the hierarchy of main-event, midcard, and newer talent, the people online complaining when a star from the outside comes in and steals the thunder of the cast who's there every week, and of course the legendary creator who oversees everything.

SNL was always a favorite show of mine, and Rock has always said Hollywood first started taking notice of him in March 2000 when he hosted *SNL* for the first time. Having just started at WWE, I wasn't at that show, but WWE writer Tommy Blacha, fresh off of writing for *Late Night with Conan O'Brien*, was. He regaled me with stories of producing Vince McMahon and Lorne Michaels in the cold open. I was a little jealous. And while I was lucky enough to sit in the stands and watch as Rock hosted for the third time in 2009,* I never really had any actual *SNL* interaction until the cast of *MacGruber* hosted *Raw* in 2010.

Will Forte and Kristin Wiig came on to guest-host in character (along with Ryan Phillippe) as well as *MacGruber* writer / director / Lonely Island member Jorma Taccone.** The *SNL* crew was pretty surprised to learn we typically only used one camera with no editing for backstage scenes. We also didn't have any cue cards or teleprompters for the actors. In addition,

---

*At one point he looked up into the stands, smiled, and gave me a loving wink, which was cool but odd. I later found out I was sitting next to his then-girlfriend and future wife, Lauren, so the wink *might* have been for her. There's no way to be sure.

**Consider this foreshadowing to the upcoming chapter about the infamous Guest Host Era. You've been warned.

we'd often shoot *during* the show where a vignette could be busted any-time due to a loud crowd pop, a pyro explosion, or Michael Hayes yelling "Fuck me running" at no one in particular. *SNL* is typically performed in front of an adoring audience of less than three hundred people. WWE is performed in front of a sometimes friendly, sometimes hostile, occasion-ally inebriated crowd of thousands. Also on *SNL*, if the audience is bored, they don't start chanting "WHAT" after every sentence. So this would be a slightly different environment from what the *SNL* crew were used to.

I had written the big MacGruber in-ring promo earlier in the week and was relieved when Will and Jorma told me they liked it not just for the sake of the show but also because I was a huge fan of theirs. That was the good news. The bad news was that the show itself had all sorts of last-minute changes; travel difficulties with the *Raw* crew from overseas resulted in a ton of rewrites, including an opening Triple H–CM Punk promo that went long and clocked in at twenty minutes. That's not ideal when you have a twenty-minute promo scheduled for segment three.

Still the bit was fun, the *SNL* people were great, and we all hung out at a party downtown after the show where Chris Jericho thought Terrell Owens, aka "TO," was famous rapper "Ney-O" and was pissed off when TO didn't want to talk music with him.*

I thought this would be my one and only *SNL* excursion until the Rock was asked to host for a fourth time in March 2015. At this point I was splitting my time between WWE and Seven Bucks Productions, so when Rock asked me to come along with him to *SNL* for the week and asked me if I had any sketch ideas, I was excited but hesitant.

It's pretty well known that *SNL* doesn't really like outsiders, espe-cially friends of the hosts, coming in and attempting to write material. As someone who's received countless pitches from friends,** agents, even wrestlers' parents who felt their progeny should be champion (cough,

---

*As detailed in the best-selling Chris Jericho book *Undisputed: How to Become the World Champion in 1,372 Easy Steps*, available now on amazon.com.

**I had to let my friend Stu down gently when I told him we were *not* doing his idea where a wrestler acquired the power of telekinesis.

Christian, cough), I completely get the mindset of "let the professionals do their jobs." The last thing I wanted to do was become "that" guy who walks in and tries to tell *SNL* people how to do their show.

At the same time Rock said to show him any and all ideas. So I wrote a bunch of ideas down, including one which involved two wrestlers cutting a backstage promo on each other with one of them getting way too personal. The note I wrote as an example was "He's got <u>herpes!</u>" (Underlining herpes makes it funnier.)

Rock saw its potential and shared the idea with the *SNL* writing team, who mostly responded with polite nods. I'm well familiar with what a polite nod means in that circumstance: *Thanks but no thanks, and please never make eye contact with us again.*

But in deference to Rock, the writers took a shot at it, and the sketch made it to the table read on Wednesday when Lorne Michaels, the host, cast, and writers sit around a table and read fifty or so sketches to see which ones will make the cut for that week. This version of the "WWE Promo" sketch was a little different from what we had pitched. It was a little weirder, with the wrestler going off on random tangents and making non sequitur analogies. It was funny, but not funny enough to make it to the next round of cuts. I thought that was the end of it, but Rock went to bat for the idea one last time. I was sitting in his dressing room with Hiram Garcia* when we were told we were needed in the *SNL* writers room.

This was a pretty big deal. I can honestly say in sixteen years I was never once nervous in a WWE writers room, but now I was reverting back to my natural introverted form. The SNL writers room, overlooking legendary Studio 8H, was the ultimate dream to be sitting in for any fan of comedy, much less one who'd watched *SNL* religiously since junior

---

*Current president of Seven Bucks, über-talented producer of all Rock's movies, author of a book highlighting Rock's career in pictures. He's known Rock since they were both teenagers at the University of Miami. He, too, is a diehard Canes fan, proving no one's perfect.

high. We sat down and were asked to repitch the idea. I momentarily froze, but thankfully Hiram, who never really watched *SNL* and was intimidated by nothing, got the ball rolling.

He laid out the concept, and the writers now seemed to get what we were going for. After the initial tension was lifted, I joined in and we were all throwing around jokes and concepts. It went from being nerve-wracking to actually being fun. We talked about the one wrestler, Koko Watchout (Rock), revealing extremely personal things about the other wrestler, Trashyard Mutt (Bobby Moynihan, who's an actual wrestling fan in addition to being an incredible performer). Koko would reveal Mutt's aforementioned herpes, his perverted internet history, and the fact that Mutt has a daughter he's never met. *SNL* writer Rob Klein had the idea of linking the daughter Mutt never knew to the picture of the girl he was "spankin it to" (who turned out to be Koko catfishing him). It really was a brilliant way to tie everything together, and I left the room feeling pretty good. This might actually become a reality. Now all I had to do was one minor thing... write a version of the Rock's *WrestleMania* promo segment.

WrestleMania 31 was to go on the night following Rock's *SNL*. On the one hand it was perfect timing—Rock was hosting *SNL* in NYC, so no one thought he'd be able to make it to *WrestleMania* which was in Santa Clara, California. On the other hand, I knew we weren't going to have time to truly work on the promo until after *SNL* was over. We had the general concept approved (a promo segment with Stephanie and Triple H, with Ronda Rousey getting involved) but that was basically it. I wasn't even sure if Vince had told Triple H (who had a huge match scheduled against Sting) that he was going to be in it.

It was during the filming of the *SNL* Fast and Furious / Bambi piece that I decided to get started on writing the WWE promo. Filmed television shoots (unlike the one-take WWE shoots) could be pretty lengthy, plus it was absolutely freezing, so I decided to go into the house *SNL* had rented out to give the *Mania* promo a shot. That turned out to be a mistake.

Right next door was the room where the *SNL* cast (minus Bobby and some others) was hanging out between takes. As I tried to write, I heard them not exactly "bashing" the WWE skit, but not really loving it. I think the phrase I heard was "What is up with that WWE thing?" Someone had said it was just something that Dwayne and his guys had pushed, and there was a general feeling that it wouldn't make it past dress rehearsal. Again, nothing really malicious, and if I were an *SNL* cast member and not a WWE fan, I'd probably feel similarly. At the same time, the good feelings I had walking out of the *SNL* writers room had now completely evaporated, and I proceeded to write the worst *WrestleMania* promo in existence. We try to be judicious when it comes to Rock's catchphrases. I think in this version I used pretty much all of them in the first three minutes, which is an indication of having nothing original to say.

At that point I was convinced the WWE skit wasn't going to make it on air, and I tried to overcompensate by throwing out any line I could to Rock to see if he'd like it and suggest it for the show. My pride was getting the better of me. I would probably never get a chance at *SNL* again. I *had* to contribute something, but the more I pitched the worse it got with every joke or line reeking of desperation.

In my mind, I went from the brilliant writer who conquered the *SNL* writing room to the world's biggest hack and the *SNL* cast hating me (in reality, most had no idea who I was). As the show got closer to air and everyone else's energy was off the charts, I walked around like Cameron in *Ferris Bueller's Day Off* after his dad's Ferrari crashed into the ravine.

By Saturday night I had accepted my fate. As most *SNL* fans know, the show is actually performed twice on show night. Once earlier in the evening for a live audience dress rehearsal, after which Lorne Michaels meets with the host and the top writers to arrange the sketch order and make their cuts. The dress rehearsal run sheet had the listing of the sketches for the night. From what I understood, the lower down on the page your sketch was, the more likely it would get cut barring a reversal of fortune. The WWE Promo sketch was listed ninth of the ten live in-studio sketches, and at that point I was convinced more than ever it would never air.

From Rock's dressing room I sat, still in a fog. None of the last-second jokes I threw out to him registered, and it looked like this was going to be a great night for Rock (the show itself was loaded) but a bitter disappointment for me personally. I took pictures of the dress rehearsal performance so at least I could show people how close I came to actually contributing something. But then an interesting thing happened as the sketch was being performed—the audience responded...loudly. Maybe the dress crowd were disproportionately wrestling fans, or maybe, just maybe, it was funny. In that moment, I allowed myself to think, *This thing has a chance.*

Dress rehearsal ended, and Rock went to meet with Lorne and the writers to decide what was actually going to be on the show. I've heard about how nerve-wracking this can be for *SNL* writers and performers. The fate of the sketch they've worked on all week, if not longer, being decided in a matter of minutes as you wait helplessly. Before Rock came back to the dressing room a new, updated run sheet for the actual show was dropped off. I looked at the spot where the WWE sketch was before, and it was gone!

"Son of a bitch—after all that, they still cut it!"

That gut-punch feeling once again returned. But then, as I scanned up the run sheet, I saw it. *Ho-ly crap!* Not only did it make the show, it had been moved up to the coveted "first live sketch after the monologue" spot. Better yet, the audience responded even louder for the actual show version. Rock and Bobby played it perfectly, with Rock having to cover his face with his forearm to stop himself from laughing on camera multiple times.

I had contributed something to *SNL* lore, and suddenly like Marty McFly did when George finally kissed Lorraine (it's an '80s movie reference kind of chapter), I sprung back to life as Hiram and I high-fived.

All the stress of the week had magically evaporated. Rock, gracious as ever, was telling everyone where the idea came from (not to take away anything from the *SNL* writers who did an incredible job actually writing the sketch), and that self-doubt which had been building and building all week was suddenly no more. We strode into the *SNL* after-party like conquering heroes. I even got the nerve to strike up a conversation with cast member Vanessa Bayer to tell her my appreciation for her Jacob the Bar-Mitzvah Boy when I heard a voice screaming:

"Brian! We're fucking leaving! Let's go!"

It was Michael Cole! Not the longtime WWE announcer, but one of Rock's security guys who has the same name. Apparently in my moment of celebration, I neglected to see literally everyone in our party exit the restaurant and pack into SUVs to ride to the airport and fly cross-country. *WrestleMania* was tomorrow (technically, later that day) and I had forgotten all about it.

We got on the plane at around 4:30 a.m. still high on adrenaline. Ronda Rousey, who was in the audience at *SNL*, was also on the flight, and now we could finally talk about the *WrestleMania* promo. I downed a large energy drink and we got cracking....

...for about ten minutes, and then everyone fell asleep.

I couldn't fall asleep if I wanted to, so I put together what I could, based on our brief discussion, and then sat on the plane for the next three hours, unable to blink.

After landing, checking into the hotel and getting about two hours of sleep, we headed to Levi's Stadium, home of *WrestleMania 31*. This was where the majority of the promo was really going to get done, as I hadn't yet gone over anything with Stephanie and Hunter, let alone Vince.

People don't realize how "on the fly" things can get in WWE, even on the biggest show of the year. The prior year at *WrestleMania XXX* in New Orleans, we did a huge surprise opening promo segment with the Rock, Stone Cold Steve Austin, and Hulk Hogan. Vince, concerned about the segment leaking online, gave Hogan limited information, telling him only about his part. We gave Hulk his opening promo and told him to just go with the flow with whoever came out to interrupt, until the very end when he'd hit his catchphrase. Hogan legitimately had no idea Rock and Austin were coming out. Vince had initially told both Austin and Rock they were coming out last, so that had to be sorted. Apparently at some point that night it was decided the Undertaker's 21–0 *WrestleMania* undefeated streak was coming to an end.

Point being, despite all the build-up and best-laid plans, *WrestleMania* can get pretty chaotic. Back at Levi's Stadium, I got with Stephanie and Hunter. They liked our framework, as did Vince. I took down Stephanie's thoughts and then went to go put everything together into one cohesive script.* Keep in mind *WrestleMania* had already started at this point, but now I was actually happy it was a four-hour-plus-long show.

Rock had a huge private dressing room area and was out of the room going over the segment's physicality with Triple H and Ronda, so I'd be able to work in silence... that is, until Ronda Rousey's MMA friends (otherwise known, with Ronda, as the "Four Horsewomen") came in. They were understandably very excited about the evening, and it put me in a dilemma. How do I politely tell three of the toughest women on the planet who can easily break my legs to kindly shut the hell up so I can work? Even on two hours' sleep, I wasn't crazy enough to find out.

I watched on the monitor as Triple H beat Sting, in part because the initial plan was to have a Rock/Ronda vs. Triple H / Stephanie match the following year. Ultimately, Rock had a conflict with his movie schedule, so Kurt Angle ended up replacing him, and the four had what many considered the best match of the night. After that, Triple H showered, changed, and joined myself, Stephanie, Rock, and Ronda in the dressing room, With less than thirty minutes until the segment started (in front of 77,000 people), we finally discussed the promo as a group.

It was a simple structure—Triple H and Stephanie announce the attendance, take credit for it, and cut a heel promo on the fans when Rock comes out. Rock defends the people and insults Triple H and Stephanie. Stephanie then slaps him and tells him to leave the ring, knowing Rock won't hit a woman. That's when Rock exits, walks up to Ronda in the crowd, brings her into the ring, and then fireworks ensue. After everyone

---

*I don't think Stephanie gets enough credit when it comes to her promo skills. She can go toe-to-toe with anyone on the roster and can improvise with the best of them. I'm sure the internet wrestling community will calmly agree in silence and totally not start several angry threads on Reddit.

ran through it, the only thing we still needed was the line Rock would say to Stephanie that prompts Stephanie to slap him.

I kept pushing for an exchange where Stephanie would talk about how Rock and his entire family were only stars because of her family, and how the Johnsons would be nothing without the McMahons. This would lead to Rock telling Stephanie that, with all this talk about McMahons and Johnsons, the truth was "you wouldn't be in power if it weren't for Vince McMahon's Johnson."

When in doubt, keep things classy.

It was now minutes before the segment started, and we were all standing behind the curtain at *WrestleMania*'s Gorilla Position. Rock wasn't feeling that line, possibly because it was a little unfair to Steph. She had always been accused by fans of just being handed her job without having earned it, even though that wasn't the case.* We started throwing out alts until Steph actually spoke up, advocating for the "Johnson" line and saying she liked it. Rock agreed, and literally seconds later Steph and Hunter were on their way to the ring.

I watched from the crowd as the segment played out to perfection. It was like it had been planned out for weeks, as opposed to mere minutes before it started. Everything went even better than expected and I never had a stress-free *WrestleMania* night with the Rock ever again...

...until the following year, when we secretly tried (and failed) to break a Guinness World Record for loudest crowd-decibel level in a promo with Bray Wyatt that had legit Guinness reps on the floor, outside the ring, with whatever they measure sound with.

The *SNL/WrestleMania* weekend was the most intense, emotional, nerve-wracking, yet triumphant two days of my life. As the Rock's music hit and he acknowledged the crowd, I leaned back, took a big exhale, and savored the moment.

Little did I know there would be one more experience that night, which in the grand scheme of things meant the most of all.

---

*Okay, *now* they can start that Reddit!

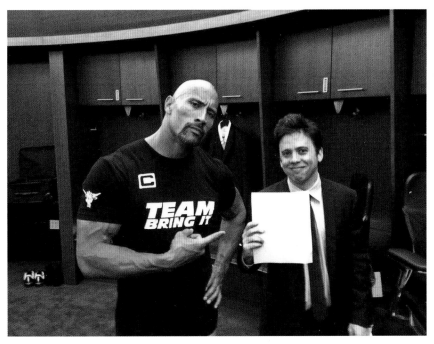

If you're going to hold up the lyrics to "New York, New York" for someone to sing on live pay-per-view, with millions of people watching worldwide, always make sure they're facing in the right direction. (*Author collection*)

You haven't truly made it until you see a sign calling for your firing at Madison Square Garden. Thanks to my sister (*middle*) and cousin (*left*) for taking a picture with this monster afterward. (*Author collection*)

At a *WrestleMania* after-party with John Cena, Shane McMahon, and Liz "Oooooh Chavo" Pena. In hindsight I probably shouldn't have told John he was going to lose to Kevin Federline right before the picture was snapped. (*Author collection*)

Greatest birthday gift ever: the beer-soaked shirt worn by Roddy Piper at *WrestleMania 23* when he screamed "Bullshit!" and Vince almost chucked his headset at me backstage. Totally worth it. (*Author collection*)

The two Piper dolls I had as a kid: one for Piper's Pit, the other wearing the title belt after beating Hulk Hogan in my basement for the 1000th time. (*Author collection*)

Hanging with LL Cool J at *Smackdown* in 2002, during my ill-advised "dye part of my hair blue" period. It would get worse before it got better. (*WWE*)

My WWE television debut at *Smackdown* in 2001, playing "Befuddled waiter whose vest doesn't fit." (*WWE*)

Hanging on the field at Shea Stadium with Taz, wearing the biggest smile ever captured of him in his entire WWE tenure! (*WWE*)

From Reddit, so can't argue with any of this. (*Reddit*)

Most people don't know this, but if the Rock doesn't like your promo, he *will* hit you with a left hook when you're least expecting it. (*WWE*)

At WWE HQ for the "Sheamus deposition" vignettes, as David Otunga attempts to ban the Brogue Kick. Considered by many to be the 87th most popular story line of 2012! (*WWE*)

Watching Syracuse win the national title in 2003 in Vince's office. I believe Vince had $50 on Kansas. (*WWE*)

It's always intense backstage at Gorilla Position. The lighting, making Vince look like Satan, is totally unintentional (I think). (*WWE*)

Being awarded "Writer of the Year" by Trish Stratus (I was not allowed to keep the tiara). (*WWE*)

Backstage with Stacy Keibler, trying to convince everyone we're the same height. (*Author collection*)

Raw script from my final show at WWE. I'll always appreciate the little tribute the writers gave me in that week's title. (*Author collection*)

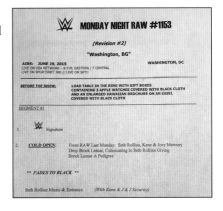

Behind the Scenes on NBC's *Young Rock*. As someone who watched MTV every day for hours waiting for the classic WWE "Land of a 1000 Dances" music video, this was a very big deal. (*Courtesy of NBC*)

From sitting in the stands at *WrestleMania XI* with a home-made Mantaur sign to actually getting Mantaur himself on an episode of *Young Rock*, written by me, Dwayne, and Hiram: my proudest accomplishment (really!). (*Courtesy of NBC*)

CHAPTER 14

Roddy

Growing up, there was one story my uncle, Howard Gewirtz, had seemingly worked into a number of shows he wrote on:

Main character encounters his hero from childhood, often a celebrity who's down on his luck, and he must somehow help him turn his life around.

This happened on *Wings*, *Taxi*, probably on *Down and Out in Beverly Hills* the sitcom (hey, they can't all be winners), and it was pitched when we were both working on NBC's *Jenny*. It was always a fun story line, but I remember calling out my uncle on the fact that as often as he'd gone to that well, something like that rarely, if ever, happens in real life.

Cut to six years later. I'm working for WWE, and who should enter my life? A somewhat down-on-his-luck, childhood idol of mine— Rowdy Roddy Piper. Maybe I was wrong and this does happen to people semiregularly.

A little context—as mentioned several times, Roddy Piper was the reason I became a wrestling fan. Watching him in action against Hulk Hogan on MTV on *The War to Settle the Score* was what got me hooked as an eleven-year-old, and my fandom only grew from there.

I was "that" kid. I had the Roddy Piper poster proudly displayed in my bedroom. I wore out my "Hot Rod" T-shirt to the point where I had to buy a second. After I saw Piper take on Adrian Adonis (with Andre the Giant as the special guest referee) on Long Island, I bought an eight-by-ten picture of Piper for five bucks from a guy in the parking lot afterward (and I still have it). Despite my fear of any movie that looks remotely scary, I saw *They Live* in the theater opening night. I had not one but two Roddy Piper LJN action figures. One intact with his shirt and kilt on so he could host Piper's Pits in my basement, and one (after I discovered you could take a coin and scrape off the T-shirt so the figure was bare-chested) for when he "wrestled." I always displayed the shirtless Piper with a Championship Belt even though he didn't actually have one. Didn't matter. In my world Piper was Champion.

Why would a seemingly well-adjusted kid root for someone so reprehensible? Simple—for all his atrocities in the ring, Piper was two things I wanted to be—funny and fearless. Always talking shit and doing so right to his opponent's face. If I liked the people he was antagonizing maybe I'd feel differently, but I always found Roddy far more interesting than the "good guys," including Hulk Hogan. Maybe it's a Long Island thing. They're notorious for cheering for the heels, and they cheered Roddy so loudly when he fought Mr. T in a boxing match at *WrestleMania 2* it practically turned him babyface that night. I was at just the right age where I was discovering the joys of being a smart-ass, and Piper was the patron saint of smart-assery.

In March 2003 I was now the twenty-nine-year-old head writer of *Raw* but was back to acting like an eleven-year-old fanboy when the idea was pitched to have Roddy do a run-in during the Hulk Hogan vs. Mr. McMahon match at *WrestleMania 19*. I know it wasn't a unanimous decision among the higher-ups, but when it was finally confirmed, I was practically hyperventilating. As the date approached, I realized there was only one problem: As the head writer, I represented everything Piper hated about the current state of the business.

Roddy was as old-school as they come. I didn't know it watching him in the WWF in the '80s, but he had been working all over for years in territories like Mexico, Portland, Los Angeles, North Carolina, and his native Canada, just to name a few. Everywhere he went he got himself over. The very notion of a writer handing him a script was ridiculous and also insulting. Who the hell was I to tell Roddy Piper what to say?

And sure, you can make the same argument for guys like Ric Flair, Hulk Hogan, and a host of other legends from that era, but I didn't have that personal attachment the same way I did with Roddy. He was my guy, and I sure as hell didn't want to screw this up and piss him off.

Fortunately, I had one weapon in my back pocket to help make sure I'd at least have a chance at getting off on the right foot—Bruce Prichard. Bruce, who had been at WWE forever and had done just about everything: from backstage producer, to Talent Relations, to former '80s heel icon Brother Love, was good friends with Roddy. (He was the one who pitched the Roddy run-in to begin with.)

Bruce knew how huge a fan I was and was nice enough to put in a good word for me before Piper arrived at Safeco Field the day of the show for *WrestleMania 19*. This was Roddy's return to WWE for the first time in years, having made the jump to WCW during the Monday Night Wars. Piper had a pretty heated relationship with then WCW head writer Vince Russo and had a naturally skeptical view of wrestling writers to begin with, but Bruce "put me over" beforehand, explaining how much I liked and respected both him and the wrestling business in general. Bruce being Bruce, he also smartened Roddy up to how much I didn't like being touched, so when Bruce introduced me to Roddy the first thing he did after I extended my hand was hug / pat me down like he was looking for concealed drugs.* Normally something like this done in full view of the locker room would be embarrassing, but I couldn't have been happier. There's no good way to say, "The eleven-year-old in me loved to get inappropriately touched by Roddy Piper," but you get the idea.

Roddy's run-in during the actual *Mania* match was electric, with the fans going nuts when he revealed himself. Sure enough, shortly after *WrestleMania*, WWE signed Roddy to a contract. I went from meeting him to actually getting to work with him! Okay, so maybe Roddy wasn't exactly "down on his luck" like the subjects of my uncle's sitcoms, but he was far from his peak, having last been seen by a nationwide wrestling

---

*And after the stories I've heard about wrestlers in the '80s, maybe he was.

audience years before and having accumulated many injuries and surgeries in the time since. Plus, he wasn't exactly in top physical condition.

I immediately assigned myself as the writer of the first Piper's Pit segment (on WWE TV) in fourteen years. His guest would be none other than Mr. McMahon. Vince infamously had a love-hate relationship with Roddy. Yes, they respected each other, but as I can attest from being alone in a room with each of them, they drove each other nuts. It's probably because they're so similar—legit tough guys who had tumultuous childhoods and learned from an early age not to take crap from anyone. They're both alphas who are experts at spotting a phony from a mile away. Plus, each can make a legitimate *You wouldn't be nearly as successful as you are were it not for me* claim and not be lying.

Bruce tried to warn me working with Roddy would be a challenge. Roddy wasn't the type to take a piece of paper, read it, and say "Okey-doke." He would hear your suggestion and then smile and say, "Yeaaaaah, but what if we did something like this..." Which normally is fine.

You *want* Roddy to be Roddy, and you want him in the driver's seat as much as possible. On the other hand, you're not working for Roddy, you're working for Vince, who *knows* you idolize Piper and is very specific when giving his marching orders:

"Make sure Roddy says *this* and *only* this. Don't let him start to ramble. It's your job to make sure he stays on point." That was Vince's direction every time I was working on a Piper's Pit. However, on that first Piper's Pit, the concept of being "on point" went out the window almost immediately.

It was as close as we ever came to an old-school promo, where Vince and Roddy outlined what they were going to say (insult each other and then agree they both hate Hulk Hogan) but let it fly in the ring. Since it was a *Smackdown*, we had the benefit of editing in case anything went too far. But when it came time for the segment, years of love-hate frustration was let out for the world to see. Vince went on a run about Piper's gut, referring to it as "Piper's Paunch." Roddy then proceeded to outline all of Vince's business failures outside WWE and said the only business he was ever successful in was the one his daddy gave him. This was less than two years after the XFL folded and the WWE Times Square restaurant was no more. He then capped it off by calling Vince "Junior" (in reference to Vince's dad, Vincent J. McMahon), a moniker Vince legit hates.

I was sweating bullets during that promo, hoping it wouldn't go off the rails. For the most part Roddy and Vince were happy with it; afterward they were laughing backstage and proudly recalling their best insults to each other in private.

It was right then and there where I decided maybe being the assigned writer to a Roddy Piper segment wasn't such a great idea. For one thing I didn't want to accidentally insult him by giving him the impression I knew his character better than he did. Plus, he really doesn't have a "character"—what you see is what you get. Second, it would be agonizing if the segment went south and I was the guy responsible in any way for hurting Roddy's tenuous status in the company.

So sure, I'd still work on Roddy's segment when writing the show over the weekend and try to get it into as good a shape as possible by the time we got to Monday night, but as far as working with him on the day of? Better to leave most of the Roddy segments to someone else and experience just the fun parts. It was like being the divorced dad who didn't raise his kids but made sure he was there for the holidays and birthday parties. I loved talking to Roddy backstage and getting a drink at the hotel bar after the show. More important, I wanted him to like me and I didn't want to jeopardize that in any way. So, yes, I was pretty much taking the easy way out.

I was able to make that plan work, as I was usually the one assigning which writer worked on what segment. That wasn't the case for *WrestleMania 21*, for which Stephanie McMahon made the assignments. On the day of the show (an early-starting west coast show, as we were in Los Angeles), she told me I'd be writing the surprise Eugene–Muhammad Hassan–Hulk Hogan segment. Great. Easy. Then she told me I'd *also* be the writer for the heavily advertised Piper's Pit with special guest star Stone Cold Steve Austin.

This sent me into a bit of a panic. For one thing, while our conversations now consisted of more than just one-syllable responses, I wasn't exactly Steve's best friend (more on that next chapter). More pressing, these were two of the greatest talkers in the history of the business who didn't need (nor want) a writer. Yet, it was also the biggest show of the year, timed to the very second, and going into the day the *only* thing we knew was happening in that segment was that at some point Carlito was going to interrupt, talk shit, and get stunned. We literally had nothing else written or even conceived for the rest of the segment. It was a "we'll figure it out day of" situation, and the person in charge of the figuring was me.

After I calmed down, I realized how cool this actually was—working on *WrestleMania* Piper's Pit with two of the greatest of all time. I was determined to make it the best segment possible. I asked Stephanie if she could assign someone else to cover the Hogan segment so I could devote my full attention to this one. She declined. It was actually a huge compliment she wanted me working on both, so I quickly wrote something up for the Eugene-Hogan segment (which admittedly was very basic in setup and execution), then went to find Roddy in catering.

He again greeted me with his TSA-style pat-down (it had become our thing) as I asked him what he wanted to do. He thought about it for a while and then pitched the idea of slapping Steve Austin across the face before Steve could even get a word out. That was Roddy in a nutshell. The quips and verbiage he wasn't concerned with. What he wanted to do was figure out the biggest "holy shit" moment possible. Then Roddy pitched the idea of Steve slapping him right back. I loved it. The question was, would Steve?

We found Steve and the three of us sat down at a table in catering to hash it all out. In this case, my instinct was to let these guys work their thoughts out and be there to make sure it was outlined on paper so Vince could approve it. I would offer some suggestions in terms of direction and structure, maybe an occasional line, but there was no way in hell I was going to start suggesting huge passages of dialogue or sweeping changes.

I let it be known to Steve rather quickly that this was their show. As long as I had the basic outline—Piper talks about being back at *WrestleMania*, questions who the biggest rebel in WWE history was, introduces Steve, slap, slap, tensions rising, alpha dogs not giving up any ground, and Carlito interrupts, commence stunning—then that was all we needed.

Because of the stress of the day, it's one of those moments I didn't really appreciate while it was happening, but thinking about it now—sitting at a table with Steve and Roddy (we didn't meet with Carlito until later) and putting this segment together was a moment any wrestling fan would dream of. It's definitely in my top three of "Holy shit, I can't believe I was involved in this" promos, with Rock and Hogan's face-off in Chicago and Bret Hart's return with Shawn Michaels being the others.*

I met with Vince afterward. He liked what was laid out but gave me two strict directives—(1) make sure the segment doesn't go over its allotted time, and (2) make sure Roddy doesn't curse. I imparted those two things to Roddy, who assured me neither would happen. Then I took my position on headset backstage at Gorilla Position and said a silent prayer as Roddy's music hit and he stepped through the curtain.

I'll admit, I had goose bumps. Roddy soaked in the crowd, and I got a little emotional when he thanked the fans for getting him inducted in the WWE Hall of Fame the night before. That fuzzy feeling was broken up as I heard Vince in my headset snap, "Jesus Christ, Brian, when is he going to get into it?" Thankfully, Roddy soon did get into it. He was actually in vintage Piper form, and everything was going great. Then Roddy asked the crowd: Who was the biggest rebel in the history of WWE? The fans, anticipating who was coming out, started chanting "Austin"—to which Roddy, live on the biggest show of the year, with literally the *only* specific note being not to curse, looked to the crowd and responded:

"Bullshit!"

I saw Vince rise from his chair as he screamed, "Did you know he was going to say that?!"

---

*CM Punk's promo with Jared from Subway, not so much.

"No, I had no idea—"

"Fuck!" Vince screamed, violating his own "no cursing" rule, as he slammed his headset down. I said the same thing to myself. There were tons of television executives, sponsors, potential sponsors, and celebrities in attendance. Vince wanted to show everyone that WWE had moved beyond the raunchy content they were criticized for in the past, and here's Roddy yelling "Bullshit!" in the middle of the ring on the biggest show of the year.

In hindsight, over fifteen years later, you can't help but laugh, but at the time it was a very tense scene. (For me, at least. Roddy, as far as I could tell, was having the time of his life.) The rest of the segment went off fine, but Vince wanted me to have a long talk with Roddy about the swearing once he came back.

It's every Piper fan's dream to privately scold him for his choice of language—and now I got to live it out!

Roddy was pretty elated as he stepped through the curtain. He reeked of beer, having drunk a couple cans and also having been doused by several more from Austin at the end of the segment, but he could see I didn't share in his joy.

"Pretty good, huh? What's the matter, kid?"

I asked him to follow me out of Gorilla.

"Yeah, the thing is Roddy, you know how I told you how Vince specifically didn't want you to curse? You kind of...screamed 'Bullshit.'"

I don't know if he was working me or not but it honestly seemed Roddy had forgotten all about it. Then he gave a pause and said:

"Yeaaah, but is 'bullshit' really considered a curse word?"

I was pretty sure it was, probably top five, but what was the point in arguing semantics? Roddy was happy, Austin was happy, and Vince had bigger things to worry about, like anointing two new stars that night in John Cena and Batista. I still to this day don't know if Roddy planned to say it or if it just slipped out in the heat of the moment. What I do know is that months later, that summer, we were back in LA for *Raw* the week of my birthday. I decided to have a little get-together and invited Roddy to come, since he was living in LA at the time.

When Piper walked into the restaurant, a wave of nostalgia hit me. Roddy Piper, whose VHS tape *Rowdy Roddy Piper's Greatest Hits* I had watched more than *Star Wars*, was showing up to *my* birthday party. Not only that, he came bearing a gift—the beer-soaked "Hot Rod" shirt he wore at *WrestleMania 21*. He signed it, added, "Your MY hero" and also added "That's Bullshit" as a little nod to the kerfuffle from that day.* I have the shirt shadowboxed hanging on a wall in my apartment.

Roddy continued his love-hate relationship with Vince, getting fired and being brought back on multiple occasions. He did many more segments, some more memorable than others, but when he was on and the material was good, it was like he never lost a step. I beamed with pride about a Piper's Pit I worked on with him with John Cena and Wade Barrett. I broke my own rule of working with Roddy on something heavily scripted, but Roddy went out and nailed it. Even Vince remarked how impressed he was.

On the flip side, I smacked myself in the head for coming up with a concept on a Viewer's Choice *Raw* where fans could vote on one of three potential guests for Piper's Pit. I was working from Stamford on the "Home" writing team at the time and initially thought it was a cool concept, but I should've known better—it was way too much for Roddy to remember three different potential segments in one night.

I don't remember much about it, as I haven't watched it since it aired, but I remember things being a mess and I felt terrible for putting Roddy in that position and not being there to help.

Looking back, I prefer to think of segments like the ones we did with Santino Marella and Jimmy Kimmel's "Cousin Sal," Sal Iacono. Sal was just like me—a wise-ass, heel-loving Mets fan from Long Island who also grew up idolizing Piper. I suppose the one thing more impressive than Roddy showing up to your birthday party would be actually wrestling on *Smackdown* with Roddy in your corner and helping you get the win, as Sal did.

---

*And in case you're wondering, fuck no, I didn't correct him on the use of "your" over "you're." Shame on you for even thinking it.

And that brings me back to the night of *WrestleMania 31*. Sal was there, and I decided to meet up with him at the *WrestleMania 31* after-party.

I usually avoided the *WrestleMania* after-party as it's the worst place for a writer to be—you basically have a lot of drunk wrestlers cornering you and pitching looooong story lines that in all likelihood aren't going to happen. But off the euphoria of the *SNL-WrestleMania* weekend, I decided to go anyway with my friend Liz Pena, who voiced the unmistakable "Ooooh Chavo" from Chavo Guerrero's WWE entrance theme. That was where I saw Roddy, who I don't believe was even on the show outside of Fan Axxess autograph signings over the weekend. He was hanging out at a table with Sal and some of his friends when he saw me and invited me over. After a few minutes, I decided to get some food from the buffet and asked him if he wanted anything. Roddy gave a long pause then said:

"Can you grab me . . . some potatoes?"

It just struck me as such an odd thing, with so many types of food, that Roddy would ask for *only* potatoes.

"Would you like me to grab you anything else? Maybe some . . . meat to go with the potatoes?"

Roddy thought about some more and then said, "Yeah."

So I capped off that whirlwind weekend grabbing my childhood hero an ample serving of potatoes (with meat!). I brought it back and then hung out for a bit. We shared some laughs, talked about the *WrestleMania 31* promo, and then we hugged as we parted ways, with Roddy once again doing his exaggerated "too much touching." I smiled, expecting nothing less.

It was the last time I ever saw him.

Roddy Piper died in his sleep of a heart attack a few months later. Despite conquering Hodgkin's lymphoma in his fifties, Roddy had always said, based on his life as a wrestler, that there was no way he was living past sixty-five. He was sixty-one when he passed away. It hit me pretty hard. It was three days after my birthday, and I couldn't help but stare at the signed T-shirt he had given me nearly ten years earlier. I then grabbed my phone and looked at the last text message he had sent me in December 2014:

"Happy Holidays Brian. Love to your family from mine. Can hardly wait to feel you up in 2015. A kiss on the cheek for now. Love Hot Rod."

I didn't want to focus too much on the sad then and I don't want to now. Roddy lived an incredible life, and I was lucky to be on hand for even a small part of it. In fact, rather than end this chapter on a down note, I'd rather reflect on the positive.

When you're on the creative team, you start to learn pretty early that your opinion and what *you* want to do ultimately doesn't matter. As Vince would always remind us: It's not about what you want, it's about what the audience wants.

The sooner you realize that (and some people never do), the better. You shouldn't write something just because it would make *you* happy. But I freely admit to violating that rule on November 5, 2006.

The pay-per-view was *Cyber Sunday*, and I pitched a match where Ric Flair would team with a legend of the fans' choosing to take on the tag team champions the Spirit Squad, a collection of evil male cheerleaders (as if there's any other kind).

The fans could choose between Dusty Rhodes, Sgt. Slaughter, and Roddy. Even though the *Cyber Sunday* voting results were never rigged and were completely legitimate (that's not sarcasm—Vince was adamant about keeping the integrity of the fan voting even when others argued against it), in my heart I knew Roddy was going to win the vote. That's when I pitched he and Flair actually winning the tag titles. I knew it wouldn't be a long-term thing (they dropped them to Edge and Randy Orton a few weeks later), but seeing Roddy standing backstage with the Championship brought me back to my basement, when as a kid I made sure that shirtless Roddy action figure always had a title belt around his waist.

* * *

Working with Roddy was one of the greatest experiences of my career. It was more than just wish fulfillment / hero worship. It was validation of why working in WWE actually mattered. Because even if the matches are scripted, the connection between fans and their heroes is real. More real than just about any other form of sports or entertainment out there. To say anything less would be, to quote my friend Rowdy Roddy Piper, "bullshit."

CHAPTER 15

It Looked Good on Paper

I n 2003 WWE had a "Goldberg" problem. On the one hand, two years after the much-reviled WCW vs. WWE "Invasion" angle, WCW's top home-grown star was finally signed to a WWE contract. On the other hand, it was a one-year deal with no assurances Goldberg wanted to extend beyond that.

The question became: What do we do with him?

If it was up to Bill Goldberg, the answer was obvious—do what worked in WCW. Have Goldberg run up impressive victory after impressive victory, let his actions do his talking, give the people what they want, and reap the benefits. Vince saw it another way. If Goldberg just beats everyone on the WWE roster then disappears after a year, what exactly was accomplished? Sure, you might score a few big pay-per-view buy rates (like WWE did with the initial "Invasion" pay-per-view before things fell off a cliff in a hurry) but it would mean short-term gains for potential long-term damage.

If Goldberg was the "Goldberg" we all knew and loved, it would certainly get Goldberg over and excite the audience, but we on the writing team were told to think of the bigger picture. What happens when all you have left are his opponents who got their asses kicked? Straight-up beating Goldberg wasn't the answer, either. You're paying top money for a top talent—beat a guy like that (whose entire gimmick was tied into annihilating his opponents), and fans will crap all over it. Moreover, people *liked* seeing Goldberg destroy people. To do otherwise would risk alienating

163

even more fans who already had a sour taste in their mouth after the "Invasion" angle. (Did I mention it was much reviled?) Goldberg needed to be a success, but we needed to be smart about it.

Vince loved Goldberg's intensity and natural charisma but was never truly impressed with what WCW did with him. It's easy to make a guy an unstoppable winning machine when the matches are predetermined, but what about the character? Sure, we had Goldberg beat the Rock in his debut match, eventually become WWE Champion, and even beat Rodney Mack in the White Boy Challenge.*

The question we were charged with answering was: Who *is* Bill Goldberg? Why should the audience care about him? How do we go from making him a snarling, fire-breathing killing machine into a three-dimensional human being? The logic being, if we could make Goldberg into something more than what he was, we'd not only be improving on the WCW version, he might become so enamored with WWE, and the direction of his character, that he'd feel compelled to stay. Even if he didn't, we would at least have delivered far more interesting stories than simply repeating "Goldberg beats everyone."

We were in the writers room meeting with Vince and discussing ways to "humanize" Goldberg, when I offered a suggestion that some have said has done irreparable damage to Goldberg himself, the wrestling business in general, and the planet as a whole:

"What if Goldust met Goldberg and broke the ice by putting his wig on his head?"

Yes. That idea came from yours truly and is a classic example of how some things might look good on paper but are quite the opposite in execution. And yes, I'm aware that many would argue *that* particular idea looked terrible on paper to begin with. As a writer at WWE (and pretty much anywhere), you need to be prepared to have an idea, a story, a joke, or a moment that you consider to be perfect, flop in spectacular fashion.

---

*Yes, that was an actual thing. Probably comes in at about seventeenth on the "things that would never in a million years be allowed on the air today" rankings.

In my defense, I had a tremendously successful track record of having one guy put something on another guy's head. If WWE were college, "Putting stuff on other people's heads" would probably be my major. It started with Al Snow and Steve Blackman, with Al putting various objects from a sombrero to a block of cheese on the head of the man dubbed "the Lethal Weapon."* It was done in an effort to bring out Steve's personality. Did it single-handedly end the Monday Night Wars? No, but they were fun vignettes that did their job—Steve became more entertaining, and the audience always responded to Steve and Al's antics. We had a vignette once on an actual farm with Steve learning how to milk a cow. I had a syringe with milk to squirt in Steve's face off-camera (implied on camera as if the cow did it, defying the laws of physics as Steve was milking downward and the milk sprayed upward). The shot kept getting messed up, and I must've squirted Steve at least six times. Steve kept getting more and more pissed, and it's actually somewhat of a miracle that I and the cow are still alive. But, lo and behold, the next time Steve appeared on *Raw*, he got a pretty loud (positive) reaction from the crowd.

Next was Goldust and Booker T, which was hugely successful for both guys. It was Vince's idea to put them together in a movie-review vignette I mainly wrote, and their chemistry was off the charts. Nothing makes me smile more than seeing Booker T superimposed in *The Scorpion King* holding a sword. It was originally intended as a one-shot deal, but after the vignette aired we knew we had something special. In an effort to get Booker to leave the nWo and become his tag team partner, Goldust would don various disguises and, for reasons that in hindsight don't make any sense, would have Booker dress up as well. Booker T is a ridiculously talented performer to begin with, and he really sunk his teeth into these vignettes. His facial expressions when wearing a lumberjack outfit, brandishing a lightsaber, or (key point here) having Goldust put his wig on his head got a huge audience response. Those vignettes helped humanize Booker T's character as he went from highly entertaining heel to insanely entertaining babyface.

---

*Not a misnomer. I have no doubt he can kill a human in less time than it takes to solve a game of Wordle.

My line of (flawed) thinking was, if that magic could work for Booker T, why not Goldberg? Vince agreed and we were off to the races. Unfortunately, what we didn't realize was, to once again paraphrase Goldberg from that first night in WWE with the Rock, "There's just one problem...I ain't Booker T."

We pretaped the vignette on a *Raw* in Richmond, Virginia, and I explained the logic to Bill before the shot. Bill was still under the impression that we shouldn't try to fix what wasn't broken. He kept telling us: Don't try to change his character, just do what worked in WCW. (I would have felt the exact same way if I were him.) Bill can be admittedly surly at times and didn't have great relationships with the WCW writers,* but on this day, he was in a pretty good mood and decided to give it a try.

We shot the vignette and waited for the pop when the wig was donned.

It never came.

There are few feelings worse than watching an idea go up in smoke like this. We made sure Goldberg gave Goldust a very stern "never do that again" warning before he left, but that was like putting on your seat belt *after* your car drives off a cliff.

The audience did *not* like this...not one bit. The online outrage was even worse.** Once again, it was an attempt by Vince and the creative team to bury WCW and everything that made it great. We might as well have had Goldberg dressed as Shirley Temple singing, "I'm a little teapot."

Afterward, Goldberg didn't throw a fit. On the contrary, he was quite professional, but I could tell his expression was one of *Well, we gave the WWE method a try and I'm never listening to these idiots again.*

It didn't stop us from still trying to make Bill a more rounded character, but at the very least we got the audience's message loud and clear and

---

*Who had ended his famed undefeated streak by having him get zapped with a cattle prod. Now I feel better about this chapter.

**I can't even fathom what the response would have been had today's social media been around.

never attempted Goldberg-Goldust comedy again (or really any Goldberg comedy).

The irony is if you've ever seen Goldberg on ABC's *The Goldbergs*, he's actually quite funny.

I'd like to think maybe deep down, the idea of being a special recurring guest star on a hit sitcom would never have occurred to Bill had it not been for one fateful night in Richmond when, for a total of 2.3 seconds, he donned a platinum-gold wig and, thanks to us, set the business back fifty years. I'd like to think that, but I'd probably be wrong.

In the end, the attempt to make Goldberg a well-rounded character didn't really work. Despite working in several main events and being treated seriously, Bill was done once his contract expired. It was only when WWE brought him back over a decade later, and had him be the dominant killing machine he always wanted to be, did he truly "get over" with the WWE audience. I wasn't there for his return, but I can pretty much picture him meeting with the writing team and saying, "If *any* of you fuckers even think of putting a wig on me, I will legitimately throw you into traffic."

This doubly sucked for me because after being asked by Michael Hayes, "Do Jews celebrate Thanksgiving?" (he was legitimately curious), here I had the opportunity to do right by the man who takes every negative Jewish stereotype and jackhammers it to oblivion. I felt I let every Jewish kid aspiring to rise against their playground tormentors down:

JEWISH KID: Goldberg could beat Austin easily!

GENTILE TORMENTOR: Yeah, well at least Austin never let Goldust put a fucking wig on his head!

JEWISH KID: Damn you, Gewirtz.

Do I think the wig vignette completely undercut an entire character's future and legacy in one fell swoop? No. But it definitely didn't help. Thankfully once it was over we decided to go in a more logical direction—we had Goldberg beat Triple H for the title, and Goldust got electrocuted, which somehow caused him to have Tourette's.

L'Chaim!

* * *

The Goldberg issue could be squarely blamed on me—it was an idea I had and not a good one. But in WWE anything can send an otherwise decent idea off the rails—an actor from Hollywood ill-equipped to deal with the crowd chanting "WHAT" after every sentence, a wrestler taking a nasty bump in a match and then forgetting everything they're supposed to say in a postmatch promo, or three words that still shake Adam Copeland, aka Edge, to his core to this day:

John...Cena...Senior.

We were in the middle of John Cena vs. Edge, a very popular angle featuring two of the hottest stars in their prime. These guys had done everything to each other—Edge became the first man to cash in a Money in the Bank contract (on Cena) and win the WWE title. He and Lita celebrated with a "live sex celebration" the next night on *Raw*, which could be its own chapter called "It Was a Batshit Crazy Idea on Paper," but since that wasn't my brainchild, I'll leave it for someone else's book.

John attacked Edge in the ring, backstage, and in Edge's hotel room, and even threw him into the highly polluted Long Island Sound. The challenge with a story line as hot as Edge-Cena was finding new ways for it to continue. When in doubt, the best way to keep a story from going stale is to get outside the arena and make it personal.

Thus was born the idea for Edge and Lita to invade John Cena's childhood home in West Newbury, Massachusetts, and get into a confrontation with his real-life father. On paper it was a very cool idea—the audience would get some insight into the actual childhood of John Cena and see Edge be a total dick in the process. Adam Copeland in real life is one of the nicest guys you'll ever meet but can play a tremendous dick; whereas Christian, aka Jay Reso, is a tremendous dick in real life who plays a tremendous dick on TV (I mean both as a loving compliment); whereas Lita, aka Amy Dumas, is very cool in real life but can play a tremendous dick on TV, even though I think she'd prefer not to.

Where was I? Oh right, Cena Sr.

Edge and Lita were a real-life couple at this time and were truly hitting their stride. "The Mickey and Mallory of WWE," as Paul Heyman would call them behind the scenes, invoking *Natural Born Killers*. We couldn't have them flat-out murdering people on TV but we *could* have them slap the shit out of John Cena's dad. Edge and Lita were game, liking any idea that did not involve them having a live sex celebration.

We wrote out the vignettes, and Bruce Prichard and I set off to West Newbury, Massachusetts, with Edge and Lita the weekend before *Raw* to shoot them. As I was pitching the idea to Cena himself, I couldn't help but notice a smirk come across his face.

"So you're going to get a taste of Johnny Fabulous, huh? Have fun."

Doing some research online, I came to discover John Cena Sr. was a regular on the New England independent wrestling scene, adopting the persona of "Johnny Fabulous," a larger-than-life manager who'd carry around "Fabo-bucks"—fake money with his picture on it. My first thought was that this was great—he's obviously smart to the business. So what if his wrestling character was a little over-the-top? It's not as if real-life Kane, aka Glenn Jacobs, went around setting people on fire like his on-screen character. Hell, ECW's Sandman would sit backstage doing the *New York Times* crossword puzzle in pen! Johnny Fabulous shouldn't be a problem, I thought. Who wouldn't want to walk around with fake currency with their picture on it if given the chance?

When we entered the Cena homestead, Cena Sr. couldn't have been friendlier and more welcoming. The house itself was big but certainly not extravagant (Cena grew up with four brothers). We went to explore John's room to find a closet full of Mitchell and Ness jerseys like the ones he wore on TV, as well as boxes and boxes of pretty much worthless baseball cards from the late '80s and early '90s (something I could most definitely relate to). In addition, there were baby pictures, old trophies, and, in Cena's bedroom, a mattress on the floor serving as his bed. Plenty of material for Edge and Lita to sink their teeth into.

We shot around the house, and then it came time for the capper—the confrontation with John Sr. In cases like this I tend not to script actual dialogue. Maybe I'll throw out a key line but not the whole scene. Better to give the premise to the talent and let them run with it. With that in mind, Edge and Lita got in John Sr.'s face and verbally ran him down. Now it was time for John Sr. to retort. We had envisioned a very real, grounded reaction—the type of reaction one might have when clearly intimidated but still being a proud parent standing up for your son. So it was a bit of a surprise to hear John Sr. look at Lita and yell:

"Let me tell ya something, chicky-poo! You and your boy toy keep this up, I'm going to send the both of *you* to the *edge*."

Ummm...cut?

Cena Sr. went full Johnny Fabulous. On multiple takes this very well-meaning and extremely likable man turned into a pseudo-1940s gangster, sometimes breaking the fourth wall by looking directly into the camera. On the one hand, it was pretty fantastic. Obviously, John Sr. was a fan of the business and had a passion for it. Personally, I could watch Johnny Fabulous threaten to send Edge "over the moon with a baking spoon" for hours. I don't think John Cena Sr. was bad; I think WWE wasn't ready to embrace his level of awesomeness.

Bruce and I tried to get John Sr. to take it down a notch (or several), but it didn't matter. John Cena Sr. was the genuine article, and what you saw was what you got. And for the record, he sold it like a champ when Edge slapped him (though he might not have had much of a choice). Bruce and I thought he might've been over-the-top, but it's John Cena's *dad*. The man who sired the progeny who carried around a bag of nuts on the off chance that he *might* have an opportunity to make a "deez nuts" joke. So what if he's a bit of a character? Vince would get a big kick out of it. The next day at *Raw*, after Vince watched the edited footage, he rendered his verdict:

"This very well might be the worst thing we've ever done."

Now personally I would disagree—I don't think that was the worst thing we produced that *week*, let alone ever, but Bruce and I both knew arguing would only make it worse. I braced myself to get chewed out when Vince said these magic words:

"I'm very disappointed in you... Bruce."

Vince turned his glare directly at Bruce, who was at a loss for words. At this point I stepped forward and said, "Vince, this was a team effort. If anything, I took the lead on these vignettes and wasn't clear enough in my direction to the talent, so if anyone should bear the brunt of this heat, it should be me."

I'm obviously joking.

Instead I said nothing. Actually, I might've turned to Bruce and shook my head in disappointment as well. How could this seasoned WWE producer let us all down so badly?

Bruce, having suffered every indignity imaginable working with Vince for so many years, did not try to protest. I truly believe if that happened today I would've stepped forward and taken my deserved lumps, but back then I hadn't reached that level of maturity. Once it was decreed that this was all Bruce's fault, in my mind I was making it rain with Fabo-bucks. I did feel bad, though. Bruce had always been there for me, once giving me a legit ear infection at my request so I could get out of going to a company Christmas party.

Instead of tossing the vignette out completely, Vince decided to take out all the sound, edit around John Sr., and have Edge narrate the entire spectacle from the ring. Edge, being the pro he is, managed to make the segment entertaining. But again, what started out as something we were all excited about on paper turned into something we were happy to escape with our employment still intact.

But what are you going to do, Chicky-poo?

* * *

There are some ideas so brilliant they can single-handedly launch a global phenomenon.

"What if he has to protect like... a *baby* Yoda?"

Somewhere within the early creative meetings of *The Mandalorian* someone, somewhere, pitched that idea, and with it came untold millions in merchandise money, Disney Plus subscriptions, and adorable memes.

It might be the most successful idea for a television show ever.

I myself had an idea in 2002 that produced the exact opposite effect. (If you've read up to this point, this shouldn't come as a surprise.)

An idea leading to relationships fractured, money lost, and legacies questioned. An idea that led to the unthinkable: Stone Cold Steve Austin walking out of WWE.

The idea was this:

"What if . . . we had Stone Cold Steve Austin face Brock Lesnar?"

It was a typical *Raw* meeting on the fourth floor of Titan Towers, and we needed a main event. Austin vs. Brock was where my mind went to first. Vince gave a pause, then said, "Damn, that's strong." Oftentimes, we don't know what to make of that. Strong as in "good" strong? Or too strong to do for TV (as opposed to pay-per-view)? It soon became clear it was the former.

Now you don't just give away a match of this magnitude, for the first time ever, between the biggest star and the hottest-rising star in the business. And you certainly don't have the biggest star lose, as was originally the finish, in a match with no buildup in something as underwhelming as a qualifying match for the *King of the Ring* tournament. That would be dumb, reckless, and leaving money on the table.

And while that's a very valid and rational argument, that night we saw it differently. We looked at it as something else—a "freebie." What I mean by that is this:

We were about to move Brock Lesnar to *Smackdown* while Steve was going to remain on *Raw*. This was back when we thought the brand extension (still in its infancy) would actually be held to the strictest of standards. The rationale was it would be *years* before we had this match again and when we did, we'd do it right. It could potentially be a *Wrestle-Mania* main event. When the time was right, we'd give Austin vs. Lesnar the proper buildup, but for now we could get away with it as a huge one-night attraction.

We actually debated the pros and cons of the match for some time. There were those who felt it would be much more special to do this years later for the first time ever. Vince runs hot and cold when it comes to the value of "first time ever." Sometimes it can be a huge selling point, sometimes it's *Who cares?*

Arguably the biggest match in WWE history—Hulk Hogan vs. Andre the Giant at *WrestleMania 3*—was billed as being the first time ever despite them squaring off at Shea Stadium a mere seven years earlier (albeit a totally different version of Hogan and WWE).

Just months earlier on a *Raw* main event the week before the epic Rock vs. Hogan match at *WrestleMania 18* we had Rock and Austin team up against Hogan, Hall, and Nash (the only time Austin and Hogan competed in the same match in WWE). While looking back it feels like way too much to give away (Hogan actually pinned Rock!), it didn't seem to affect the Rock vs. Hogan *WrestleMania* match, which had the most electric atmosphere I've ever witnessed.

During this time when the network was getting antsy, with ratings ebbing due to the split rosters, we felt we could pop a big number on *Raw* and book the match again years later with the same magnitude of a "first time ever" match. In fact, by the time we'd do it, most wouldn't remember this match even happened. Those who did and complained would be watching regardless. Hence, the idea of the match being a "freebie."

The other issue open for debate was how the match would end, aka "the finish." Steve was in a program with Eddie Guerrero at the time, and the idea was to enhance their story line by having Eddie come down and interfere, costing Steve the match. This was hardly a unique circumstance. A few years back, Chris Jericho had interfered in a Triple H match, resulting in the Hunter being pinned by the Brooklyn Brawler. As noted earlier, Triple H was, shall we say, none too happy about it.

Steve himself was no stranger to this concept as he had run down in an epic, historic match on *Raw* years earlier, costing the Rock the title against Mankind. Years later he would run in and cost the Rock a match against the Hurricane. Point being, it wasn't going to be a clean decision. Steve vs. Brock was the Trojan horse to get us deeper into Steve vs. Eddie.

In his attempt to reach out to Steve on the day of the show, Vince changed the finish to a non-finish disqualification, but at that point it was too late. The damage had been done. The biggest star in the company, arguably in the history of the business, had reached his breaking point. A simple idea that came out of my head caused a chain reaction that left millions of people shocked and upset, and sent the company into turmoil. This is not hyperbole. No one was bigger than Stone Cold Steve Austin, and now he was gone. When it was all going down, I didn't feel defiant. I didn't feel ready to argue my case to anyone who would listen. Instead, I just felt guilty.

Some background on my relationship with Steve Austin: I was like everyone else in 1997–1999, watching Stone Cold become the hottest star in the business and loving every second of it. I was glued to the TV, calling my friends when he showed up in the hospital hitting Mr. McMahon with the bedpan and when he poured concrete into McMahon's Corvette. When I got hired by WWE I found the real-life Stone Cold to be intense—a perfectionist. Someone who took his job very seriously, not in a pretentious way but in a way that made you think, *That's why he's number one.*

Before I could actually get to know Stone Cold, something truly shocking happened. As mentioned earlier, after my first week of TV in November of '99, I was informed that Austin needed neck surgery and might never wrestle again. The plan was to take him out later that month at *Survivor Series* in a backstage hit-and-run scene. The identity of the assailant to be figured out later.

When Steve left he was the undisputed number one guy in the business. When he returned full-time nine months later, the landscape of WWE had changed. The Rock was now the top babyface in Steve's absence, and the new writer, the one at Vince's side who looked like he was still in high school was very much a "Rock guy"—a fact that wasn't lost on Steve. In fact, the sight of me and Rock laughing out loud as we worked on a promo in the locker room made Steve's skin crawl.

I almost had a superpower when it came to my ability to piss off Steve. One weekend there was a live event in Atlantic City that I decided to go to last-minute, mainly to hang out afterward with Kurt Angle and gamble. I knew that if you're going to a show, make sure to get there before it starts;

otherwise it would be disrespectful to the performers. In the days before GPS, my friend and I rented a car, proceeded to get lost, and got to the arena just as the show was ending. As we pulled into the parking lot and made our way backstage the only thing I was thinking was *Don't run into Steve*—who, of course, was the *first* person we ran into.

"You're *just* getting here?" Steve asked, shaking his head. For an old-school guy like Steve, some goofy writer bringing his friend backstage was bad enough. To show up after the show had already taken place was flat out blasphemous. (Note: He's correct on all counts.)

It's well-known now, though I didn't know it then, that Steve wasn't in a good place during this time. He was dealing with a lot of issues both with his health and in his personal life. To make matters worse, Vince was relying more on writers than he ever had before. No one wrote Austin's famous "Austin 3:16" promo nor any of the other promos he cut while becoming a top star. Sure, Vince and the creative team came up with the scenarios and angles, but once a mic was put in Stone Cold's hands it was up to Steve to deliver—which he did, better than anyone. But shortly after Austin was written out for his surgery, WWE became a publicly traded company, and the idea of being more like a "legitimate" TV show with professional writers delivering professional scripts to professional performers became the new normal. That meant everyone needed to adapt to this new line of thinking, including Steve.

What could possibly go wrong?

The idea of scripted promos wouldn't be enticing to Steve to begin with, and it sure as hell wasn't going to work with some nerdy "comic book geek"* handing him pages of dialogue.

How do I know this? Well in addition to having a pulse, Steve said so himself in an interview with *WWF Magazine*, telling readers how he'll be damned if he's going to start taking orders from some kid straight out of "sitcom school." (Shout-out to the S. I. Newhouse School of Public

---

*I actually stopped reading comic books in 1985 when my two favorites, the Flash *and* the Mirror Master, were killed in *Crisis on Infinite Earths*, but explaining that to a locker room full of wrestlers did not seem like a good idea.

Communications at Syracuse University, the Harvard of communications schools. Go Orange.)

Despite this, Vince wanted me to establish a relationship with Steve. It didn't have to be as chummy as the ones I had with Rock, Angle, or Edge and Christian, but it should at least be functional. If Steve knew how much time we were putting into making him happy, maybe he'd feel differently about things.

It was during this time every creative meeting would begin with the same question being thrown our way: "How's Stone Cold going to raise hell this week?" It was a fair question but one we came to loathe. We wanted to write something cool for Steve, but the whole process had become rote. If you're raising hell every single week, for years on end, and everyone expects it, are you even raising hell to begin with?

The creative felt forced, and Steve usually hated it. This was doubly frustrating because 80 percent of our Vince time was devoted to Steve, and with Vince often coming up with the creative himself. Normally relaying this creative to Steve was a task that either Bruce, Michael Hayes, or Paul Heyman would deal with directly, since they took turns calling Steve to update him after our meetings. For a while Vince wanted me to do it, and the calls went something like this:

> ME: So, Steve, great news. We're going to have you raise hell this week, stunning the Big Show.
>
> STEVE: Yep.
>
> ME: Then you go into the locker room and hit Eddie Guerrero with a trash can.
>
> STEVE: Uh-huh.
>
> ME: Then Shane interrupts, you kick his ass, beer bash.
>
> STEVE: Yeah.
>
> ME: Then you acquire a time machine, go back to the Cretaceous era, find a Tylosaurus, which is a carnivorous marine reptile, flip him off, and stun him. Any questions?
>
> STEVE: (pause) Nope.

ME: Okay then, bye!

I didn't even get the courtesy of finding out why Steve hated it. He respected Bruce, Michael, and Paul enough to tell them what he thought sucked. With me he just wanted to get the hell off the phone. I had gained a measure of respect from certain talents in the locker room based on my work, but not from Steve. Other than the idea of pairing Steve with Kurt Angle for comedy vignettes when they were both hurt, I hadn't written anything Austin-wise to earn that respect.

Steve is one of the sharpest minds in the business. He knew the "raising hell" formula had become stale, and it was one of the main reasons he decided to turn heel in 2001. Again, we in WWE Creative found the weekly attempts for Steve to "raise hell" just as tiresome as he did. In trying to please Steve, we were inadvertently contributing to the monotony of the Rattlesnake character which in turn was driving a perfectionist like Steve nuts.

Looking back, one could say, *Well, maybe if you guys were more talented you could actually write some compelling shit and it wouldn't have come to this.* Fair argument. I remember us getting out there a number of times with Steve's character in our weekly writers meetings, but in the end it was easier said than done. Vince saw Austin a certain way and didn't want to stray from a formula that made him millions. The only way there would be a radical shift in Austin's character was if Steve initiated it himself, which was why he pushed for and was granted the heel turn. I know it's scoffed at now, but I don't blame Steve. If I were him, I would be looking for anything to sink my teeth into and revive my passion.

But as much as Steve put everything he had into making his heel turn work and creating a truly dynamic character, the audience just didn't want to see it. And it was further muddied when Steve was leading the WCW/ECW Alliance forces, which viewers also flat-out rejected. Pretty soon we were back to the same problem of Steve as a babyface and us having our marching orders to script promos for him.

There was one time in particular Vince wrote a promo for Austin that he wanted him to recite. It was a riff on the old-school idea of a heel being billed from "parts unknown." Vince delivered this "parts unknown" promo off-the-cuff, and I have to say it was pretty compelling. Way deeper and more introspective than a typical WWE promo. I proceeded to hand it to Steve and told him where it came from. Steve looked at it, looked at me, said, "I'm not saying this shit," and walked away.

And that probably would be considered one of our more positive conversations.

The irony in all of this was the last thing I wanted to do was script Steve Austin promos. If it were up to me, I'd let Steve say and do whatever he wanted. Some guys like Kurt Angle and Randy Orton, when he first started, liked their promos scripted. Less for them to worry about as they're working on their matches. If a performer trusts a writer, then it's a "do your thing, get it to me, and then we'll go over it" type of thing. For guys like Steve, who again has the best instincts in the business and never needed a written promo in his life, the very idea of a "writer" represented everything wrong with where wrestling was heading.

I wanted to say *Steve, I agree with you! Steve, we care! Steve, I will never hand you a piece of paper again! Please like me!* But doing that would have just made things worse. In wrestling it's better to be labeled an "idiot outsider" than a "desperate kiss-ass" (though not by much).

So Steve's frustrations, along with everything else going on in his life, were determining factors when he heard he was facing Brock Lesnar with no buildup on a *Raw* and then losing on top of it. That was the last straw. If that was how the company saw him after he single-handedly made them a mint of money and led them to a decisive win in the Monday Night Wars, then screw all of them—starting with the writer from sitcom school. (Shout-out to Syracuse University, currently tied for fifty-ninth in the 2022 *US News and World Report* college rankings. Take *that*, Rutgers!)

To Vince's credit, he never buried me or made me a scapegoat for Austin's frustrations, which I've always appreciated. There were many factors that led to Steve's displeasure; my existence was just one of them. Which was why, in hindsight, maybe the Austin vs. Brock match wasn't such a terrible idea. I believe the writing was on the wall—if that match had never been proposed, it would have been only a matter of time before another idea or decision would've resulted in the same thing happening. It was just a bad situation all the way around.

I should point out Steve has publicly expressed remorse over his reaction to the Brock match multiple times. He calls it the biggest mistake of his career and even expressed deep regret during his WWE Hall of Fame induction speech. Thankfully for me, Steve lives very much in the moment and doesn't hold a grudge. Nowadays when our paths cross, it's a much more pleasant experience.

To describe Steve now as being in a way better place would be a vast understatement. To see Steve backstage, as I did on the *Raw* twenty-fifth anniversary show in Brooklyn, is to see a man content, happy, even *smiling*. He had one of the greatest careers in the history of the business, and he's now doing projects he loves and being a living, breathing American Institution.* And while I'll probably never be on his Christmas card list, I think the fact that I was at WWE for as long as I was eventually led Steve to gaining some level of respect for me. Now when I see him backstage at a show, he'll get a big grin on his face and say, "Hey kid, how you doing?" We'll engage in some pleasant small talk, and then I'll exit on a high before I accidentally say something stupid (which, like a Stone Cold Stunner, can occur suddenly and without warning). It truly is great to see Steve living his best life.

The funny thing is, all these years I was so concerned over the Austin end of the "Austin vs. Brock" match, I rarely ever thought about it from Brock's perspective. Did he, too, feel it was a huge mistake? Did he resent me and the writers for even suggesting it? Did he even care, or was it just another match to him?

I never bothered to find out. In fact, I usually tended to avoid Brock Lesnar, who almost always worked with Paul Heyman. I stayed in my lane and generally kept my distance until *WrestleMania 30*.

I was backstage, having submitted the outline for the Hulk Hogan–Steve

---

*I now set my washing machine cycle to "cold" without having any idea whether I should simply because Steve said to do so once in a Tide commercial.

Austin–Rock opening segment, when I saw Brock talking with Under-taker, Paul, and Michael Hayes. Holding my laptop in one hand, I ambled over and said hello, shaking hands with Taker and Paul and "nabes" (a Freebird thing) with Michael.

Then I extended my hand to Brock, who just looked at me menacingly for what was probably eight seconds but felt like forty-five minutes. Imag-ine the "How am I funny?" scene from *Goodfellas*. Now imagine instead of Joe Pesci intimidating you, it's Brock freaking Lesnar.

My mind raced with many thoughts, mainly, *What has Paul been telling Brock about me that will make him want to end my life?* Normally I wasn't physically intimidated by other wrestlers because in the back of my mind I figured: What are they really going to do? But Brock was different. Brock was in the "this place needs me a lot more than I need them" space, and if he wanted to put me in a coma, Paul would swear on his life that I merely tripped and crashed into Brock's fist (and didn't even have the decency to apologize).

Fortunately, Brock broke out into a big smile and started laughing, returning the shake, thus ending the scariest moment of my life (and I've had my brakes go out on my car while going downhill in a snowstorm).

I went to Rock's dressing room in a daze, thinking that would be the craziest thing to happen that day, when Rock turned to me and said, "Hey did you hear Brock's beating Taker?"

Holy shit. The Undertaker's twenty-one-match winning streak at *WrestleMania* was coming to an end. This was a record I personally felt should've remained unblemished forever. And I wasn't alone. That one decision divided an entire fan base, robbed certain fans of their inno-cence, and resulted in Undertaker being loaded into an ambulance after suffering real-life injuries during the match and Vince actually leaving *WrestleMania* midshow to be with him.

But even if you do feel the Undertaker's streak ending was a bad idea both on paper and in execution, take solace in the fact that it could have been worse. At least no one proposed Goldust coming down after the match and putting a wig on his head.

CHAPTER 16

Summerfest! Tales from the Guest Host Era

U sually, a single idea that looks good or bad on paper is self-contained for that particular show. WWE moves at such a fast pace, with multiple three- and two-hour shows, fifty-two weeks a year with no repeats, it's rare for an idea to have implications that will affect literally every aspect of the show for months on end. It's even rarer when that idea eventually involves David Hasselhoff, Ozzy Osbourne, Al Sharpton, and Bob Barker.

But it happened for over a full year, and it originated from an extremely unlikely source. Like all ideas that would eventually spiral out of control, it started with the best intentions.

In 2009, we on the creative team and pretty much everyone watching WWE became tired of the evil heel authority figure. It was great during the Attitude Era when Vince McMahon in WWE and Eric Bischoff in WCW weaved real-life expertly into story lines. The concept got a fresh coat of paint when Triple H and Stephanie (aka the McMahon-Helmsley era) took the reins. This was then followed by the regimes of William Regal, Eric Bischoff again (this time on *Raw*), Paul Heyman, Kurt Angle, and Vickie Guerrero, all making life miserable for the babyfaces. And while there were some fan-friendly characters mixed in (notably Teddy Long and Mick Foley) for the most part this trope stood firm:

Said babyface would come out to cut a promo, a heel would confront him, the heel authority figure—dubbed "General Manager" with the arrival of Bischoff—would come out, the babyface would insult the GM, and the GM would put the babyface in an unfavorable predicament.

Of course, it didn't always go down like that, but it certainly felt that way. It wasn't as if these situations or characters were bad. The heels in charge generated a tremendous amount of heat and individually were very talented and effective. But in the big picture the whole concept became very predictable. Fans got tired of watching these segments just as the creative team got tired of writing them.

Our attempt to shake up the formula ended disastrously when we (okay, me) proposed having Mike Adamle become the *Raw* GM. Mike, an incredibly nice guy, was brought in to be a new announcer and lost the fans almost immediately when on-air, live on pay-per-view, he called Jeff Hardy "Jeff Harvey." Fans instantly lose respect for someone when they botch a well-known name. Despite being a former NFL player, host of *American Gladiators*, and someone who could probably kick the ass of many fans his junior, people looked at the character of "Mike Adamle" and fairly or not saw . . . well . . . kind of a bumbling idiot.

Meanwhile, in real life, WWE Creative had at that point gone through quite a few executive vice presidents brought in to manage the team, but many were so in over their heads and clueless about WWE that they were quickly let go. One notable exec tried to endear himself to the writing team on his first day and made a choice one might deem questionable. One night we were all walking to our cars in the freezing cold. Ed Koskey commented on how he likes it when it's so cold he can see his own breath. The exec, who, again, we knew for *one day*, commented:

"You like cold? Then you'll love my wife's pussy."

Awkward lingering silence . . . and he was gone within a few months.*

That was the dynamic I was looking for when I proposed Adamle as GM. We'd seen our share of babyface and heel authority figures. So what if we had someone who was just clueless and a tad bit offensive? Not

---

* But his legacy and that of his wife lives on!

a heel, necessarily, but just someone who was completely in over their head, which could lead to unpredictable and chaotic events. I told Vince it was in the spirit of Michael Scott from *The Office*. Now of course I know Vince had not regularly watched a sitcom since *Sanford and Son*, but he knew of its popularity enough to give it a shot.

The problem was—brace yourself because this is a revelation—Mike Adamle is not as good a comedic actor as Steve Carell.

Okay, so we knew that going in, but in our haste to change the dynamic we set Mike up for failure. We gave him way too much material, including large passages of exposition that, not being a trained actor, he couldn't memorize (he eventually read his promos off a clipboard). We also put him in situations that Steve Carell might've had fun with but was giving Mike nothing but agita. This was totally on us. Mike has, as Liam Neeson would say, a "particular set of skills," and we were not playing into any of them.

We ended the Mike Adamle experiment pretty quickly and came up with a Plan B. What if we had a different person in charge every week?

Originally the idea would be a different WWE Legend each week comes in and has control over the show. You could have a babyface, a heel, a wildcard tweener character. It would be unpredictable, and the fans would enjoy seeing a returning favorite each week.

Vince liked that idea, and as we were trying to figure out the legend for a particular episode, Stephanie said six words that would change everything and turn my life into a waking nightmare:

"What if we had a celebrity?"

Okay, *that* in and of itself didn't make my life a waking nightmare; it was what Vince said in response:

"What if we had a celebrity *every* week?"

Vince's eyes lit up as he saw this as a big opportunity to get mainstream publicity. And why not? Some of the biggest angles in WWE history came from celebrities such as Mr. T, Cyndi Lauper, Mike Tyson, and yes, Donald Trump.

Imagine the magic we could create every week. Well we didn't have to imagine it; Vince wanted us to start the rotating celebrity guest hosts immediately. He said he wanted it to be "like *Saturday Night Live*, only better."

All of us knew that under no circumstances was this going to be better than *Saturday Night Live*. Look, Vince has a lot of superpowers, but his comedy is an acquired taste. If you want to look at a comedy skit written exclusively by Vince, YouTube "Derrick Bateman World's Strongest Man Perfume."

It's . . . breathtaking.

The idea of a celebrity guest host, as we'd come to call it, might have seemed fun on the surface (or not at all), but it opened up a load of headaches.

It meant dealing with publicists, managers, agents, hangers-on, and occasionally the actual celebrity. Most of them had no clue what the WWE dynamic was. We'd work with them on the proposed creative, going back and forth for days, then pitch said creative to Vince, who would change most of it, then have to go back to the celebs team and talking them off the ledge. And once the celebrity stuff was squared away, *then* we had to write the actual show.

At first it actually went smoothly. Seth Green was the first celebrity to guest-host, and he was a huge WWE fan. He was used sparingly, and the night ended in a feel-good moment with the diminutive Seth* raising his arms in victory with John Cena. So far, so good.

Trouble began with Jeremy Piven, who came to host *Raw* to promote his new movie *The Goods: Live Hard, Sell Hard*. We had talked to Jeremy's team, who told us he wanted an extravagant entrance with a big flowing pink robe, among other things. We took his team's notes, integrated them into the script, and after a back-and-forth, eventually got begrudging approval from Vince. Then I got a call from the head of WWE's Celebrity Relations, VP Kristin Prouty.

---

*I can call him that since, at five eight, I'm of average height, according to a 1963 issue of *Reader's Digest*.

"Brian, Jeremy got the script and there's a problem. He hates every-thing. Especially the part of him coming out in a pink robe."

I completely lost it as I relayed to Kristin how we were told that was all *his* idea! I just pitched the crap out of the idea to get Vince's approval, and now he doesn't even want to do it?

Fortunately for us, also appearing on *Raw* was Dr. Ken Jeong. Dr. Ken was Jeremy's costar in the movie and was a huge wrestling fan. He's also one of the nicest and funniest guys on the face of the planet, which always helps.

I met with Ken and Jeremy's team the night before, and we came up with an idea that I really liked. Jeremy and Ken would actually turn heel on John Cena. It would wind up with them both doing physicality in the ring. Usually, celebs of this type promoting a movie were all smiles and sucking up to the crowd, so this was really different. Ken would even serve as Jeremy's annoying hype man and make the crowd sick of him, to the point of it being a relief when Cena threw him over the top rope. Vince approved the new last-minute creative, and I thought we had really made some impressive chicken salad. Then two things happened:

First Jeremy, in his opening promo, pulled an Adamle and called *Sum-merSlam* "Summerfest." The crowd crapped all over him after that, and not in a "we can't wait to see this heel get his comeuppance" kind of way but in a "we now officially declare every celebrity who steps foot in this ring full of shit until the end of time" kind of way.

Then Dr. Ken landed on his head. It was gutsy enough to make him-self so irritating and hateable, but Ken had also agreed to be thrown out of the ring and onto a bunch of wrestlers. In rehearsals he was assured it would be perfectly safe and the wrestlers would catch him. In reality, while he was technically caught, the back of his skull landed hard on the mat.*

As he was being attended to backstage, getting stitches *in his head*, I paced the hallways backstage wondering what Ken's reaction would be.

---

*YouTube that after your second viewing of "World's Strongest Man Perfume."

I felt terrible he got hurt, and I also knew if he was pissed it wouldn't be long until every celebrity in Hollywood would think WWE was unsafe. Instead, Ken burst through the trainer's room full of adrenaline. He wore his stitches like a badge of honor and was so gracious he actually started apologizing to *me*. He said the whole experience was thrilling, which is truly saying something coming from a guy who jumped naked out of a car trunk in *The Hangover.*

Ken took his botched bump like a true, seasoned pro and, in effect, saved the celebrity guest host angle. So fans of the well-received shows starring Shaquille O'Neal, Pee-Wee Herman, and Ozzy and Sharon Osbourne can thank him. Fans irate about the shows starring Al Sharpton, NASCAR drivers Kyle Busch and Joey Logano, Kathie Lee and Hoda, well...I'm sure Ken, if confronted, would apologize for those shows, too, despite having literally nothing to do with them. That's just the type of guy he is.

* * *

Few celebrities fit the mold of what a guest host should be more than Mike Tyson. In 1998, Tyson getting into a scuffle with Stone Cold Steve Austin on *Raw* was a seminal moment every wrestling fan talked about. Some people think it was the pivotal moment when WWE officially became the must-watch programming over WCW. Throughout his entire career Tyson carried this aura of unpredictability. You saw him and felt that anything could happen. His angle with Austin and DX worked so well because you believed it. This wasn't just a random celebrity coming on to promote a project, this was a lifelong fan who might truly be "the baddest man on the planet." When he said of Lennox Lewis, "I want to eat his children," you nodded along and said, "Yeah, that checks out."

A lot had changed in Mike Tyson's life between 1998 and when he guest-hosted *Raw* in 2010. He had long since retired from boxing, found religion, gained mainstream comedic praise for his role in *The Hangover*, and become a devoted family man. He might not be the Tyson of circa 1998, but all of us in the writers room were genuinely excited about the prospect of him coming to host.

I was one of those kids of the '80s who played *Mike Tyson's Punch-Out* religiously after school, a fact I gushingly told him, probably becoming the three millionth Gen-Xer to do so. My entire family (parents, aunt, uncle, cousins) would regularly gather for two things during that time—extremely long Passover Seders and extremely short Mike Tyson pay-per-views.

I didn't know what to expect when going over that night's creative with Mike, but he was very laid-back and liked everything we had. He was there to have fun and let some of his children (who were also big fans) be backstage among their heroes. We often had the celebrities working with the tag team of Chris Jericho and Big Show, mainly because both were seasoned pros who had genuine acting chops, and this was no exception. We had a major angle laid out where Tyson befriends and ultimately turns on Chris Jericho, resulting in Tyson knocking Chris out. We rehearsed it in the afternoon and all went well. It was honestly one of the smoothest days in celebrity guest host history. Then about an hour before showtime, we encountered...wait for it...just one problem.

We lost Tyson.

His family didn't know where he was. None of the stage managers knew where he was. Vince didn't know where he was, and the clock was ticking. We had a pretty big night for Tyson planned—an opening promo segment with then WWE Champion Sheamus, Randy Orton and John Cena, vignettes with DX (Tyson was last seen on WWE TV knocking out Shawn Michaels at *WrestleMania 14*) plus a main event tag match of DX vs. Tyson and Jericho. Mike Freaking Tyson was competing in a match on *Raw*, and less than an hour before showtime we had no idea where he was.

It was all hands on deck as all the writers fanned out to look for Tyson. The hour before showtime is always the busiest backstage. Vignettes are being shot, promo segments and matches are being fine-tuned, with plenty of last-minute changes that need to be relayed to the production truck. In short, it's a madhouse. For that reason, I was relieved when one of the writers approached me saying they found him.

Apparently, Mike wanted to, as Rock would say, "smoke one of those funny cigarettes," and he didn't want to do it in his dressing room with his family.

O-o-o-okay, forgetting momentarily that he was supposed to be punching out Jericho later, my next question was "Where is he?"

"I didn't know where else to take him."

"Again, where is he?!"

We approached the writers room as the reply came: "In the writers room."

I opened the door to see Mike Tyson sitting up on a table, funny cigarette in hand, legs dangling over the table's edge, like John Candy atop the fish tank at the end of *Splash*.

"Hey, you don't mind if I do this in here, do you?"

"Um...sure, no problem, Mike Tyson."

What else could I say? I wasn't about to get into an argument with the man. Honestly, I was just relieved we found him as writers scrambled to their walkie-talkies and let everyone know the crisis was averted. As he went to leave, I thanked him for signing a boxing glove for me earlier in the day. This led to one of the greatest moments in celebrity guest host history, thanks to a new writer named Erik.

Erik was one of the Hollywood writers we had brought in. He had an impressive IMDb page and seemed to be a fan of WWE as well. His problem was adjusting to life on the road. Some people are ideal fits for the weekly road experience that is WWE—Erik was the opposite of that. While very affable and a good guy, he just wasn't made for the road. He was older and had an almost magical ability to get injured doing things one normally doesn't get injured doing, most notably pulling his back trying to yank his luggage out of a rental car. At one point we had to get him one of those motorized Rascal scooters to ride around in backstage, which certainly caused *no* unwanted attention. Athletically he made me look like Bo Jackson.

Upon seeing me with my prized new autographed glove, Erik reached into his bag and pulled out a pristine, old-school '80s wrestling magazine.

On the cover was Iron Mike and Hulk Hogan in what the magazine deemed a "Superstar Dream Match."

This was the moment he had been waiting for. He had that magazine in his basement for twenty-five years, and now he was going to get Tyson to sign it.

"Excuse me, Mr. Tyson, I happen to have something I would love to get—"

The second Tyson saw the magazine his eyes lit up.

"Omigod, the magazine with me and Hogan! I've been looking for this for years! You don't mind if I keep this, do you? Okay, bye!"

Tyson grabbed the magazine and happily walked out of the room as Erik's face dropped, his Sharpie dangling from his hand. A part of me felt bad for Erik. Another, far larger part, thought that was one of the funniest things I had ever seen in my life. So funny that I forgot to find Jericho to tell him that the punch he'd be receiving from Mike Tyson on live television was coming during a somewhat "altered" state.

Fortunately, Tyson executed the segment just fine. The spot with Chris looked great and was totally safe.* All in all, it was a memorable night.

And yes, Erik quit the company a few weeks later. But hey, at least he had the wherewithal to give Mike Tyson his magazine and avoid being permanently confined to that Rascal, so overall, a win-win for everyone.

* * *

Excitement about an upcoming guest host depended on who you were. Vince and Michael Hayes in particular were very excited about Cheech and Chong.** There were a few closet Trekkies on the crew who let their excitement be known about William Shatner hosting. I was very excited about Jesse Ventura coming on to host because I always wanted to hear Vince and Jesse do commentary together one more time. It was the first thing I wrote into that show, and I was elated when Vince agreed to don the tux and actually do it.

---

*I'm assuming.
**Nothing like 1970s drug humor on a PG-rated show where you can't say "hell."

But across the board *everyone* was excited when they heard we got Bob Barker.

We all had pangs of nostalgia for Bob Barker. He's a true legend who had performed on television for over fifty years. To put that in perspective: When Bob first hosted *Truth or Consequences* in 1956, Vince McMahon was eleven!

As a kid, two major benefits from getting sick were getting to miss school and being able to watch *The Price Is Right*—and not necessarily in that order. I was such a huge fan of the show, the first spec script I ever wrote back in college was a *Simpsons* episode where Homer goes on *The Price Is Right*. The note from my professor was "maybe lean into more *Simpsons* style humor and less *Price Is Right* jokes."

Suffice to say I was super excited. I went all out when writing that week's script with a replica *Price Is Right* Contestants Row, having legendary ring announcer Howard Finkel tell wrestlers to "come on down," incorporating prizes into the matches, and, of course, making sure we had the classic "skinny microphone."

Bob Barker was there to basically do two things—promote his new autobiography, *Priceless Memories*, and get the word out about his Animal Rights charity. Selling the book was easy, as the WWE production team would make sure it was represented in graphics, on the Titantron, and physical copies strewn throughout the backstage set. The charity part was a little trickier; Vince decided to move the backstage vignette promoting the charity into a WWE.com feature. Maybe he figured Bob, at eighty-six, wouldn't know the difference.

In anticipation of Bob Barker, I made sure to read his entire book within the week, poring over it on the 7 train to Citi Field and missing the Mets turn a double play because I was reading about "Plinko."

At this point of the Guest Host Era, the writers would usually meet with the celeb the night before the show. We were a little iffy how the crowd in Chicago would treat Bob. Chicago, as previously mentioned, is typically one of the best and loudest crowds, but they're WWE fans there for a WWE show. They might love Bob, but they also might boo him out of the building. For perspective, this was only one month after "Summer-fest." I bristled at the idea of fifteen thousand fans in unison chanting and clapping along to "Fuck-You Barker."

We sent the script over to Bob and his people and never heard any-thing, but I still made sure to get out to Chicago a day early. Granted, that might've been influenced by the fact that White Sox catcher A. J. Pierzynski was going to cameo on the show and left me free White Sox tickets. I went with my friend Jessie Ward, a WWE stage manager,* to the game, and since I still hadn't heard from Bob, we spent the day walk-ing around Chicago and engaging in a healthy dose of day-drinking. The day was winding down when, while at an outdoor music and craft festival, sufficiently inebriated, I got a call from writer Dave Kapoor.

"Hey maaaaan. I just got a call from Bob Barker's manager. Bob wants to meet. Like right now. And he doesn't seem happy."

Uh-oh.

I raced back to the hotel, trying to sober up, and met Dave in the lobby as we headed up to Bob Barker's hotel suite to meet him. His man-ager, Henry, a very nice man wearing a suit, who somehow looked and most likely was older than Bob, let us in as we awaited the legend.

I thought I might be still suffering the effects of alcohol when I saw Bob enter in a robe and silk pajamas. I'm assuming that had to be a clas-sic Hollywood '50s power move. "Wanna make 'em take notice? Show up in a meeting in a robe and silk pajamas. It's how Bogart landed *The Maltese Falcon*." Bob was cordial but did not seem pleased. For one thing he wanted to know where the vignette was mentioning his charity. Dave tried to placate as only he can.

"Oh, we have that in there, sir. See, at the bottom of the last page for 'WWE—After the Bell' we have the whole vignette..."

Bob slapped the shit out of him.

---

*And former contestant on MTV's *Tough Enough 2*. She was also, at my behest, the on-screen stage manager in the scene with Goldberg and Goldust, etching her place in WWE immortality.

I'm kidding, but it wouldn't have surprised me if he did. Instead, he said calmly but sternly:

"That's for the internet. I don't want it just for the internet, I want it on the show!"

So much for thinking Bob wouldn't notice. Normally at this point a writer would say, "Well, I know Vince liked it here, but let me make the suggestion to him and I'll let you know if it changes."

Again, it might've been the drinking, it might've been the need to impress, it might've been the power of the pajamas, but instead of saying that I simply replied:

"You got it, Bob. It's back in the show!"

Bob seemed satisfied as we started to go over the script meticulously. Every note Bob had, I simply said, "Done." For one thing, they were actually good suggestions, and unlike when Vince infamously instructed the Slammy Awards guest host Dennis Miller how to do stand-up comedy, I was not about to tell Bob Barker, of all people, how a *Price Is Right* sketch should go.

We then got to the vignette where Bob was supposed to karate-chop Chavo Guerrero. With his book fresh in my memory, I asked him if this was inspired by the martial arts training he did with Chuck Norris.

"Oh, you read *Priceless Memories*?"

I did indeed! And as I seamlessly segued into a story from his days as a fighter pilot for the U.S. Navy reserve, I could see his businesslike exterior begin to soften. "Say, would you boys like some white wine? Henry, let's get them some glasses."

From there it was a party! Dave Kapoor and I drinking wine with Bob Barker, who was now showing off karate moves in his silk pajamas. We talked about his time in television, as a naval aviator, and, of course, *Happy Gilmore*. I told him about my *Simpsons* spec I wrote at Syracuse, and he ended the night with a boisterous "Go Orange!"

Years earlier, after a *Raw* in LA, I found myself with my college friends hanging out at the Rainbow Bar on Sunset Boulevard. At the table next to us were Jericho, X-Pac, the Godfather, the band Cypress Hill, and various actresses from adult films. Despite any heat I had at the time, my friends and I were invited to join the table, and by the end of the evening, wrestlers, pornstars, and Cypress Hill were chanting my name in unison in an attempt to peer-pressure me into taking a hit of what was then an illegal substance for the first time in my life, which I did—I know, such a rebel.

I bring that up because cool as that night was, "karate fighting, silk pajama wearing, wine drinking Bob Barker night" was way cooler.

As we exited his suite, Dave and I were giggling like a couple of schoolkids. Now all we had to do was execute the actual show. I lucked out when Vince approved Bob's changes. That was all well and good, but how would the live crowd respond? How would Bob do in an environment that even he had never experienced before? They don't shout "WHAT" in the *Price Is Right* studio audience when someone's bidding on a toaster.*

The opening "come on down" segment hinged on a confrontation with Bob and Chris Jericho (again it was almost always Jericho). Chris was a super-serious heel at the time, and it took some convincing to get him to go for the idea of coming out bare chested, in his gear, with the classic *Price Is Right* name tag taped to his chest. Ultimately, he went along with it, the key selling point being that it might be comedy to everyone else but to your character it's deadly serious. The more serious you are, the better it will be.

Not only did Chris and Bob crush it, but the crowd absolutely *loved* it. Leave it to Chicago to show Bob Barker the respect he deserved. They grew up with the man, and when they saw the effort WWE was putting in to make his guest appearance everything it could be, they rode the nostalgia wave and embraced it. Even with this atmosphere, live television, in front of fifteen thousand screaming fans, Bob would not break a sweat. He even started improvising and threatened to take Jericho "over his knee." In a little over ten years, WWE went from Mike Tyson getting shoved by Steve Austin to Bob Barker threatening Chris Jericho with a spanking—but it worked.

---

*Have I mentioned how much I hate the "WHAT" chant?

It was, in my opinion, easily the best show of the Guest Host Era. And the fans agreed, eventually awarding Bob a Slammy award in the fan voting for "Best Guest Host," which is listed on his Wikipedia page alongside his nineteen Emmys. If we had ended the guest host experiment after the Bob Barker show, I'm sure it would've been seen as a nice diversion and an interesting footnote in WWE history.

Instead, it went on for another full *year*.

One of the main problems was that we gave the celebrities the powers of an actual GM with the ability to make matches and stipulations. It was a major disconnect as far as the audience was concerned, and those two things—"celebrity guest" and "decision maker"—should've been separate. Again, we wanted to replace the heel authority figure, but we should've realized way sooner that this was not the way to do it. Vince reached his breaking point when David Hasselhoff was in the ring declaring the main event of *SummerSlam*. Not only did the audience not buy it, but like with Mike Adamle, it required the guest host to memorize a ton of clunky exposition. Maybe the heel authority figure wasn't the issue so much as an authority figure, period.

Eventually we course-corrected and made it so that the celebrities didn't have any actual power within the story lines. We changed their title from "Guest Host" to "Guest Star." It created some fun shows and memorable moments (the shows with Pee-Wee Herman, Hugh Jackman, and the Muppets come to mind) but ultimately the concept went on for way too long. By the time we mercifully got to the cast of the Three Stooges (in character), this gimmick was met with a mixture of boos and indifference (despite huge WWE fan and ultratalented Will Sasso playing Curly). So Vince finally put a stop to it and the celebs were phased out, except for special occasions.

As far as having an authority figure, we were right back to where we started. We didn't want to go back to the stock heel, but there weren't any strong babyface choices, either. We hadn't yet reached the point of simply saying, *Why have an authority figure at all?* so we decided to go another route.

What if we had a General Manager and no one knew who it was?

CHAPTER 17

The Crazy Eyes

I n short, the answer was no. That's what I said to friends who asked, "Did you ever consider putting yourself on the show?" There's a long history of writers—or, as they were known before the mid-'90s, "bookers"—putting themselves on television. The results have usually ended in resentment, at best (especially if you were a wrestler serving as booker making yourself Champion), and disaster at worst (if you were a writer making yourself Champion, which, again, actually happened in WCW).

Look, when it comes to a writer deciding to put themselves on TV, I get it. I don't agree with it, but I can see the appeal. If fame was your thing, putting yourself on the air was a surefire way of getting it. When I started at WWE in 1999 there was no YouTube, Facebook, TikTok, Tout (for extreme WWE loyalists), nor any form of social media. The only reality TV at the time was either *Cops* or MTV's *The Real World*, two shows unaffiliated with wrestling but did showcase plenty of unhinged lunatics running around with their shirts off.

During the Monday Night Wars, Vince McMahon and Eric Bischoff would step from behind the curtain and put themselves on TV to great success. Of course, they weren't typical writers. As announcers they were already known on-air entities, and anyone with a cursory knowledge of the wrestling business understood their real-life roles and the real-life power they wielded.

Wrestling writers, on the other hand? No one knows who you are if you're doing your job right. Some people believe movies are a director's medium and that scripted television is a writer's medium. Well, even though WWE is scripted, wrestling is and has always been a performer's medium. Does great writing contribute to its success? Of course. Can a terribly written segment or angle bring a show down? I can personally attest—absolutely. But unlike most other forms of scripted television, where you get days to memorize your lines and often multiple takes to get them right, WWE is based on the performer's ability to make fans lose their minds through a combination of skill and sheer force of personality. There's undoubtedly an "it" factor in wrestling. You know it when you see it.*

Vince always believed in the concept of "that's my guy/girl." Meaning, even if you know it's all scripted, as a fan you sit back and suspend disbelief when your favorite performer comes on-screen. That's how I watched Roddy Piper as a kid and Owen Hart as a young adult. Sure, I (eventually) knew it wasn't real, but when those guys came on, it didn't matter. I didn't want to just see them perform, I wanted to see them *win*, because they were my guys.

Everybody wants to be "the guy," but there are challenges. In order to "get over" you need to be on TV. There's a finite allotment of minutes each week and an ever-growing number of people on the talent roster. For a talent starting out and trying to establish themselves, winning and losing matches isn't nearly as important as television exposure. Time is a precious commodity, so imagine if you're a new talent, putting your body on the line every day in hopes of breaking through, getting so close to appearing in that one spot on television that would make all the back-breaking days, months, and years of physical brutality all worth it, only to witness some writer who probably couldn't beat up a reasonably sized seventh grader hog that moment instead.

I felt putting yourself in that position, as former WWE writers Vince

---

*Note: Literally every wrestler alive thinks they have "it." Many do. Many more do not.

Russo and Ed Ferrera did in WCW, was a big mistake and a no-win situation. If you're terrible, you're wasting the audience's time and you risk them tuning out. If you're actually good at it, then you're still taking valuable airtime from someone who could be in that spot, whose livelihood depends on being in that spot, and could actually be drawing money.

When I first entered WWE, I'll admit it, I thought, *Wow, maybe I can sneak in under the radar as a backstage interviewer, get involved in an angle, become a manager like Bobby Heenan, get a verse in the eventual remake of the classic WWF "Land of 1,000 Dances" music video, and become attractive to women wrestling fans with extremely low standards.* Those daydreams evaporated pretty quickly once I saw the reality of what it was like to work backstage. As the new "Hollywood guy," I already had megaheat as it was; becoming a character on the air when so many people didn't think they were on the air enough would've been a death sentence.

So as tempting as it was, I dropped the idea of putting myself on the air relatively quickly. Those people you see in suits walking in the background of various shots backstage that seemingly have no place being backstage at a wrestling show? They're usually writers, and I even avoided that.

That's not to say you can't get away with an occasional one-off.

One time (post–Wrestlers Court) when producing *Sunday Night Heat* with Kurt Angle at the old WWF New York restaurant in Times Square, we shot a series of vignettes with Kurt on the street. This was during the time I had dyed my hair blue in attempt to seem NYC hip,* so I put myself in a shot for the sole purpose of setting Kurt up so he can say, "What's your story? Did a Smurf take a dump on your head?" WWE conveniently forgot to submit that episode for Emmy consideration.

Then there was the time Michael Hayes volunteered me to play the waiter in a bunch of skits with Dean Malenko, Terri Runnels, and Perry Saturn. I didn't want to do it, but I was told by the Chairman himself I

---

*It didn't work.

was to do it, and despite my reservations and serving Perry a bowl of mustard and a side order of crayons* I managed to get through it.

The only other time I put myself on the air was again as a waiter (for the purposes of continuity I'd like to think it was the same character), this time with Santino Marella and Ron Simmons. The local actor we had hired was so incoherent, I didn't know what else to do. I turned to Arn Anderson, the producer on location with me, and asked for advice. He replied as only Arn can:

"I don't think you've got a choice. Shitcan the mumbly son of a bitch and strap on the apron."

So that was basically what I did. I couldn't bear to watch it when it aired. I hate all imagery of myself and I am mortified this book has a picture section, but as with the previous stint of "perplexed waiter," it did give me an appreciation for what the talent went through. Wrestling is hard enough even if you never had to actually act and memorize lines. I would often marvel at how the performers did it. It was mind-blowing to watch them memorize promos that would get changed literally moments before they stepped through the curtain. They'd also need to act in backstage vignettes (often several) and, oh yeah, on top of that they'd occasionally have to wrestle.

What both cameos made clear to me was that writers should remain behind the scenes. Unfortunately, that rule was broken on my watch in 2007 by a new writer: Dave Kapoor, the man I shared my life-changing Bob Barker evening with. It's not hyperbole to say Dave is one of the most likable people in the history of the company. They say you should fill the writers room with a "good hang" and Dave epitomizes that. Earnest, friendly, with a big California accent, Dave will do anything asked with no hesitation. That came back to haunt him when the seven-foot-tall Great Khali needed a new manager and Dave (who happens to speak Khali's Punjabi language) was asked by Vince to step in.

---

*To recap: Perry's character had a head injury, spoke in non sequiturs, and became physically attracted to a mop in a story line that would not be remotely attempted today.

First Dave, now dubbed "Ranjin Singh," was accompanying Khali to the ring and saying a line or two like "The Great Khali says you should all bask in his greatness." Next thing you know, Khali goes from monster heel to fun-loving, dancing babyface,* and Dave's hosting the "Khali Kiss Cam." Next, he's in a tuxedo dancing with Khali onstage singing "Putting on the Ritz" in an ode to *Young Frankenstein*. Next, he's in an actual tag team match, shirtless, running around the ring getting hit by Fit Finlay with a shillelagh.

The whole thing became surreal. I remember when traveling to *Raw* with Dave, we were waiting for our bags at the airport when a woman asked me to take a picture of her and "Ranjin." That's not unusual in and of itself, but then the woman *insisted* that Dave hold her baby. Then she wanted a picture with *just* Dave and the baby.

When you appear on WWE TV, random people start handing you babies! That kid is going to have so many questions when he grows up.

Dave never let his sudden on-air fame get to his head. He might've been so well-liked he amazingly didn't even have any heat backstage (at least as far as I knew). But the problem with his escalating role reared its ugly head when he was scheduled to take a bump off the side of the massive Elimination Chamber structure live on a pay-per-view. He did it fine on a crash pad earlier in the day, but when the moment of truth came—surprise!—the guy with no training whatsoever landed wrong and messed up his knee to the point of needing surgery. As an added bonus, the online wrestling media reported he wasn't really hurt, and it was all part of the show. Dave's knee is still screwed up to this day.

Which all confirms my original belief that writers really should not be a regular fixture on WWE television. Despite the cascade of letters flooding the WWE offices demanding the return of my "waiter" character, I

---

*There's an alarming number of monster heels in WWE who eventually turn into dancing babyfaces for no particular reason. It happened to Matt Bloom twice! He went from Prince Albert to the Hip Hop Hippo, and years later evil Lord Tensai to fun-loving, dancing Lord Tensai.

had managed to never actually appear in the ring or perform live. That all changed one night in September of 2010.

With the *Raw* Guest Host Era mercifully coming to an end, we had started a story line where there'd be an anonymous *Raw* General Manager. This mysterious being would send in key decisions via email, which announcer Michael Cole would then read live on the air. The email sound effect would reverberate throughout the arena and always get a reaction. Michael Cole simply walking to the computer (which had its own setup at ringside) and reading the GM's emails eventually forced our hand to turn Michael Cole heel. The sound effect and announcements were that irritating.

One day, to spice things up, I suggested having the GM actually be able to speak for himself live in the ring. We'd modulate his voice so he could remain anonymous and could create some buzz by advertising the Anonymous GM as the special guest on Edge's Cutting Edge talk show segment. What I had envisioned was having the production truck manufacture a Stephen Hawking–like voice. We could prerecord the entire GM's promo and have it play out with Edge asking the GM Computer questions and someone in the truck hitting a button so the GM could respond.

There was one major problem with this: Vince didn't know who Stephen Hawking was, and he didn't think the audience would know, either. I frantically tried to explain how he was one of the smartest men in the universe whose computer-assisted voice had been world-renowned for decades and would instantly be recognizable. No sale.

As it got later in the day, Vince had a simple solution—have someone live backstage in Gorilla Position who just speaks into a live mic and does a robot voice (a shining tribute to the Hawking legacy). After some back-and-forth he did concede to having the production truck alter the mic to make it sound more robotic, but he was adamant that it would be easier to interact with Edge if there was a live person to go back and forth with.

Vince definitely had a point, but the bigger question was who was going to be the voice.

"You came up with the damn idea, *you* do it!" Vince replied as he walked away to attend to far more important matters.

It was my second worst nightmare come true (the first would've been if I actually had to go out to the ring in front of people). I tried to find anyone else who wanted to do it, but it was a universal hard pass. Incredibly, no one wanted to sit backstage and do a robot voice live on the air for a promo segment that hadn't even been fully written yet. It was only a few hours before the show started. This train wreck was going to fall on me. I started to understand the look wrestlers would give me when I presented them with a promo or vignette that appeared somewhat idiotic.

I went over the promo with Edge backstage. The GM, via the computer, would be a guest of Edge's talk-show segment, The Cutting Edge, where after a tense exchange he'd tell Edge he had a match against John Cena. Then after the match, when it appeared as if Edge won, the GM would correctly point out Cena's foot was under the bottom rope, meaning the match must continue. Then Cena would get a "quick one" (an unexpected roll-up victory) over Edge, who would become incensed and proceed to destroy the computer.

Time goes by pretty fast when you're in a full-blown panic. I was a nervous wreck all day, and now the moment of truth had finally arrived. I was seated next to Vince backstage at Gorilla Position as Edge's music hit. I was handed a mic during the commercial break and was told a red light on means the mic is hot, so don't mumble things like *What the fuck am I doing?* I was told the light would come on as soon as Edge's music hit. So naturally if I didn't already have enough to worry about as soon as Edge strode to the ring I looked down at the mic and...nothing. The light wasn't turned on. In fact, the mic was dead. I might as well have been holding a carrot.

As Edge started cutting his promo, I turned to the audio technician who had handed me the mic and mouthed (just in case I was wrong), *THE MIC...IS...DEAD.* The technician proceeded to do the one thing, the *only* thing, I hoped he would not do—he shrugged his shoulders as if to say, *What do you want me to do?*

Now Edge is cutting his promo, setting up the Anonymous GM. Backstage Vince was looking on in amusement as I'm motioning frantically to be handed a mic that actually worked! Miraculously, I was handed a new working mic literally seconds before Edge finally asked the GM his first question.

"Why are you such a spineless coward?"

Okay, here goes nothing. . . .

"Why are *you* such a moron?"

I heard my altered voice for the first time as I spoke, transmitted to the live audience and broadcast across the world. It did not sound anything like Stephen Hawking. If anything, it sounded like a mixture of Johnny 5 from *Short Circuit* and Cartman's "Awesome-O" from *South Park*. Only . . . more terrible.

Edge agreed, because he improvised in response: "First of all, that's the worst voice *ever.*"

Fortunately, the more we got into it (I had the benefit to read directly from the script, something 99.9 percent of those cutting a promo on *Raw* did not have), the more comfortable I got. By the time I got to asking Edge "Why do you despise me so?" I couldn't believe it. I was actually kind of enjoying this!

Once we did our thing where the match was restarted and Cena went over, it was now time to execute an action that had never been done in a wrestling ring before—beat the holy crap out of a talking computer. As Edge approached the laptop and I read my line about him losing fair and square, I actually got so comfortable I started improvising myself.

"Don't look at me like that," I threw out as the crowd actually popped! "You've got the crazy eyes"—a line I stole from *The Life Aquatic with Steve Zissou*. (WWE in general does not plagiarize Wes Anderson movies nearly enough.)

Then Edge started destroying the computer. I've got to hand it to Edge—he went to *town* on that thing. Completely annihilating it. It was almost as if he was getting his real-life frustrations out of being put in this angle to begin with. I think in the heat of the moment I actually started "selling," saying "Ow, ow" as Edge slammed a chair into the computer repeatedly, but either the mic was cut at that point or they eventually edited that out (I don't remember).

Vince seemed to be pleased with the mayhem. Whether he truly didn't think twice of assigning me this role, or if he actually meant to teach me a lesson on the highs and lows of performing on live TV, in his typical Vince way, he had been right all along. I gave the mic back to the shoulder-shrugging audio technician. I was no longer angry at him; now I was just relieved this guy hadn't decided to become an airline pilot or a heart surgeon. I then found Edge, who was smiling from ear to ear, and we shared a good laugh over just how ridiculous the whole experience was.

Like the bump I took when we were snowed in years ago and my other pretaped appearances, this once again gave me a greater appreciation for what it means to be an actual WWE performer. It's one of the reasons I can hardly blame a wrestler for not sticking to a script verbatim. If *I* was feeling it while backstage doing a pseudo-robot voice, I can only imagine what it must feel like for the wrestlers standing in the ring in front of thousands of extremely vocal fans. I truly hope the whole concept of memorizing full-blown scripts goes the way of the Anonymous GM and simply disappears.

Speaking of which, one final note on the Anonymous GM: A lot has been made of who the GM was actually supposed to be. Originally it wasn't important. Vince didn't really care who it was, as it was more of a storytelling device. We'd figure it out eventually. We had employed the same mindset in the "Who ran over Stone Cold" angle in 1999, and that didn't really work, either.

During this time Vince was having the talent attend "promo class" which was a meeting in the morning before *Raw* and *Smackdown* where he gave all the wrestlers insights into the psychology of cutting a good promo. I've got to say it was pretty fascinating watching Vince in this element, where he could just be a teacher. I thought he was extremely insightful, and you could tell he enjoyed dispensing his decades of wisdom. Of course, none of these things really meant much if the talent had to recite a script word for word off the page, as was the current policy, but that's another story.

During these classes Vince would randomly call on talent to cut a promo to the room. One day, he wanted an emotional promo and he called on Dylan Postl, aka Hornswoggle, America's favorite leprechaun, to deliver it.

Hornswoggle had mainly been a comedic character, so it was shocking to hear Dylan cut this passionate moving promo about growing up a little person, getting made fun of as a kid, and getting teased at airports to this day. The promo blew everyone away. No one had seen this side of Dylan before and it gave me an idea.

That week in the office I postulated, "What if the Anonymous GM was Hornswoggle?" Now before you can say—"Like the horribly ill-conceived 'What if Mr. McMahon's illegitimate bastard son was Hornswoggle' angle that crashed and burned the previous year?" I'd respond yes! But also, no!

This would be different because it would not be the fun-loving leprechaun Hornswoggle. What if we used the same promo Dylan cut in promo class to reveal that he had only been playacting the role of Hornswoggle? His real name was Ernie Manfredini and while he was making all your stupid kids laugh as the smiling dancing leprechaun who bites people on the ass, he was really making life miserable for all your favorite superstars? I started cutting the promo in the room in my best "New Joisy" Danny DeVito accent. "Ernie" would take all the anger Dylan felt in real life and put it into this promo. The best way to describe it to people was to compare it to Baby Herman from *Roger Rabbit*, only way more malevolent.

I was looking forward to seeing this play out and if Dylan could pull it off. After cutting the promo to the shocked audience, the idea was for Hornswoggle to become a cigar-chomping lowlife heel, justifiably angry at the fans for making fun of him. Having a little person portraying a leprechaun who acts like a child was one of the most cringeworthy stereotypical things one could do—so let's turn it on its ear! Let's make Dylan into our Peter Dinklage!

At this point I was on the "home team" for the writing staff, meaning I stayed in the office in Stamford to get ahead on story lines and the following week's scripts. On the day of the show Dave Kapoor called me from the road, to let me know how the promo was going.

"Hey maaaan, I just came out of rehearsal."

"Oh cool, how'd Dylan do?"

"Fucking terrible!"

Dave went on to explain that it just wasn't working. Maybe Dylan wasn't ready to ditch his Hornswoggle persona, or maybe the script didn't capture what he was truly feeling. Maybe (as I would later learn) it was the fact that we tried to have him affect an accent out of nowhere in addition to memorizing a ten-minute monologue all in a matter of hours. Whatever the case, it just wasn't meant to be.

Dylan's an extremely talented performer and great guy, but for whatever reason this was just not clicking. I asked Dave what we were going to do. Do we just kill the segment and come up with something else? Do we make the previous match go two segments instead of one to replace this one?

Dave paused then responded: "Nah, we're still doing the segment, but once we reveal it's Hornswoggle, we're just going to have Dylan come out from under the ring and start biting people on the ass."*

Not surprisingly the crowd shat all over it. It was so bad that when we brought the anonymous *Raw* GM back a few years later for a cameo, Vince gave announcers instructions to not even acknowledge it had ever been Hornswoggle. Most (if not all) of the heat came back to me which was fine but it masked the bigger issue. It almost seemed once again that planning a major angle out in advance, like a secret General Manager, as opposed to immediately putting it on TV with no plan on how to get out of it would've been more beneficial. Then again, you don't have to be Stephen Hawking or even remotely sound like him to know that.

---

*I'm sure that was Plan B on *Game of Thrones* had Dinklage botched the Tyrion Lannister courtroom speech.

CHAPTER 18

The Fun Files

I never expected to actually have fun portraying the talking *Raw* GM computer. "Fun" while working on the WWE writing team is a very subjective thing.

Many a former fan turned WWE writer will lament the lack of "fun" in doing a job that on the surface should be teeming with it. I think that has more to do with the monster schedule than anything else: on the road two or three days a week, driving hundreds of miles between towns, coming into the office and working for hours and then waiting even more hours for meetings to actually start. For a place that seems like a WWE fan's dream job it sometimes resembles the first act of *Joe Versus the Volcano* in terms of sheer monotony.* Make no mistake—you're not there to have fun, you're doing a job (an actual job, not "losing a wrestling match" job)—but there is fun to be had. Sometimes it comes naturally, sometimes you need to make it yourself.

* * *

"I rode up and down these very roads with Terry and Buddy, drinking, fighting, and selling out every arena in the state, so, *no*, I am not going to ruin that legacy by stopping for a fucking Frosty."

As you might guess by now, that mini-rant was brought to you by Michael Hayes as the *Raw* writing team (myself, Michael, Ed Koskey, Dave Kapoor, and Chris DeJoseph) were doing a "live event loop." Three

---

* Second *Joe Versus the Volcano* reference in the book—can we go for three?

times a year we'd go to the non-televised shows to check them out—see how the crowd was reacting, how the talent was performing, what was clicking and what wasn't, because clearly there wasn't enough wrestling in our lives. Michael would drive, as he didn't trust us,* and he always made it clear—no stopping.

Thankfully, our whining eventually got him to break his rule and stop...for a fucking Frosty. Not only did he pull into the Wendy's drive-thru, but he couldn't resist getting one himself. Seeing this legend ruin his legacy by sipping on a Frosty with the rest of us overgrown children put a smile on my face as much as any successful promo or story line.

* * *

You take your fun where you can get it, even if on the surface it seems a little shady. As previously mentioned, back in college I would always participate in *Royal Rumble* pools. Thirty people picked one number out of a hat (sometimes fifteen people picking two), and if your number won the *Rumble*, you won the pot (usually $10 each, for $300). You'd think joining the company that produced the *Rumble* and knowing who'd win would preclude me from participating in these things with my college friends. You'd be wrong.

As long as nothing I was doing was changing the actual *Rumble*, I thought, why bother stopping? I'd purposely not look at the order of who was coming out just so I could sit in the stands while the *Rumble* was taking place and hope the winner corresponded to my number. Again, this isn't an NBA Tim Donaghy kind of thing where I would change the *Rumble* to suit my needs. These numbers were picked minutes before the show started, and even I knew better than to jeopardize my job in order to win $300 in a pool with my moronic friends. Still, there is nothing more fun than the *Royal Rumble*, and having stakes makes it even more fun. I'd even get other writers and on rare occasions the wrestlers themselves to participate. I'll never forget the look on Al Snow's face during the 2000 *Rumble* right as he was headed to Gorilla.

---

*Justified, as I had twice failed my driver's test in high school and passed it on the third try with my parking brake on the entire time.

"Al, I got you your number . . . it's 20."

"Dammit," Al responded.

"What's the matter?"

"That's my *actual* number! Ten bucks down the drain."

While the idea of Al going rogue to pocket $300 is intriguing—and would make a great sequel to *Uncut Gems*—that fortunately didn't come to fruition. Once the *Royal Rumble* is booked and the match begins, the outcome remains locked in and airtight.

Except on one occasion when it didn't . . .

* * *

In 2005 while the *Royal Rumble* match was taking place, Ed Koskey and I parked ourselves in Vince McMahon's office to watch the show. Normally I'd watch from the crowd, but this year I was hungry and Vince's office (abandoned during the actual show since Vince is directing traffic in Gorilla) was a great place to watch as it always had steaks brought in earlier in the day from local restaurants. It would be quiet, peaceful, plus there was a monitor with headsets we could put on to hear all the communication to the production truck. The only risk was Vince suddenly bursting in if he had to leave Gorilla to use the bathroom, but it was a chance we were willing to take.*

Of course most wrestling fans know what happened—John Cena and Dave Batista went over the top rope and landed at the same time. As I listened on headset to the panic and confusion emanating backstage, Vince's music hit. He stormed to the ring and then weirdly sat down. Turns out while getting in the ring he tore both of his quads live on pay-per-view. I personally would've been screaming like . . . a person who tore both his quads . . . but Vince to his credit didn't sell it. In fact, you wouldn't have known anything was wrong had he not been sitting oddly in the ring, arms folded, legs outstretched directing traffic. If anything,

---

*I understand now this has been course corrected and there's always security standing outside his office so people like me and Ed don't use it for a personal Ruth's Chris.

he looked more pissed than in pain, angry at his quads for not holding up their end of the bargain.

The *Rumble* itself ended with Batista winning as planned—what wasn't planned was Vince needing surgery and missing the WWE's first-ever trip to Japan for *Raw* and *Smackdown*. I had tried getting out of this trip several times, as I hated leaving the country under any circumstances, but Stephanie was adamant that I go. In hindsight it was a good thing, as with Vince out getting surgery, Stephanie was now in charge, and could use her team at full strength.

Much like taking on the role of the talking *Raw* GM computer, I found something I dreaded to be a tremendous amount of fun.

It didn't start out that way. In my infinite wisdom I decided my first night in Japan that I would take the writing team out to an extravagant Japanese dinner. My restaurant of choice? The Denny's connected to our hotel in the Tokyo Dome. I am not the most adventurous eater. As Ed Koskey would say, "flavor" is my enemy. In this case, my decision backfired spectacularly. All I'll say is Japanese Denny's is not the same as American Denny's and leave it at that. My experience was akin to Albert Brooks sampling Rip Torn's food in *Defending Your Life*.

The next night, after a successful *Raw*, I decided to lead the writing team to a dinner more befitting the Japanese experience—the Tokyo Hard Rock Café. To our surprise, already there were Shane and Stephanie McMahon. Not wanting to wait for a table, we went over, said hello, and took seats at the table, very much uninvited. Shane and Steph greeted us and promptly left. After surviving the day running TV without Vince for the first time, I wouldn't have been shocked if the "Magical Mystery Mojitos" had been flowing freely.

What transpired next was nothing short of amazing. Apparently this scene was witnessed by a large group of Japanese WWE fans, too polite and respectful to interrupt Shane and Steph's dinner (unlike us).

A group of about six fans mustered up the courage to approach us and asked if we knew the McMahons, to which we replied, "Of course we do, we work for WWE." At that there was an audible gasp. I mentioned we had been to Stephanie and Hunter's wedding a few years back and they swooned like a pack of 1950s teenage girls meeting Elvis.

This was in sharp contrast to whenever the writers would enter or leave an arena in the United States. Fans would usually greet us with "Hey look! It's fucking nobody!" These fans in Japan waited for us to finish our meal, then asked if they could take us out for the evening.

We proceeded to embark on a whirlwind odyssey of Japanese night-life. They paid for the drinks and cabs, asking for nothing in return other than if we knew certain wrestlers.

"Do you know ... Edge?"

"Yeah, we once went to Dave & Buster's and played laser tag."

"Oooooooooooh ..."

At one point they took us to the hip club district Roppongi to a bar known as Gas Panic. In the past I used to make fun of a certain WWE Shop commercial. The premise involved a line of people waiting to get into a hip nightclub. The bouncer would reject all except those wearing official WWE T-shirts available on WWE.com.

I hadn't spent a ton of time in New York City nightclubs, but I had waited on enough lines to know that if you were wearing, say, a Rikishi "Back Dat Ass Up" T-shirt you most definitely were not getting in. But at Gas Panic you'd be whisked to the front of the line. As we stood inside the bar with techno music blaring, I looked up at the TV monitors and my jaw dropped. It was a replay of a *Raw* featuring a match between Christian and Eugene. It was being played non-ironically. It was like an *SNL* Stefan bit. "This place has *everything*—foam, to-go bags from the Hard Rock Café ... a poem by Heidenreich!"

These fans were so grateful just to be associated with anyone WWE that the experience changed their lives forever. How do I know this? Because they told us as much in a handwritten letter sent to our offices in Stamford a few weeks later, which included pictures I had no recollection of posing for. Again, a stark contrast to the "you are no one" clap-clap-clap-clap-clap chants we'd get from our U.S. fans as we'd walk out of the arena.

Once back, we communicated with Vince as he gave us notes on the phone from his hospital bed, and though we didn't actually go through with re-creating the classic scene of a babyface attacking Vince in the hospital with a bedpan à la Steve Austin, we at least took comfort in knowing it would've gotten over *huge* on the Japanese club scene.

* * *

As I got more comfortable at WWE, I began to do things I wouldn't have considered when I started…like pulling a "rib." "Ribbing"—the wrestling word for "practical joke"—was something usually done by the wrestlers. And while I could never be as hardcore as Classie Freddie Blassie, who allegedly stuffed toilet paper in a young Roddy Piper's bagpipes, ruining his Madison Square Garden debut, one time I did muster the courage to commit a rib of my own.

Candice Michelle was a new WWE Diva making her debut in 2004. When I found out this former model and actress was childhood friends with Jessie Ward, my friend and WWE stage manager, I decided to have some fun.

She would debut on TV, and I let Candice know we had a great idea for her that Vince loved. She would be the first Diva in WWE history… without a tongue. I forgot the specific reason *why*—possibly due to accidentally drinking lava.

Either way, we'd shoot these extravagant vignettes touting her arrival, shot with sexy music and lighting, and then when it was finally time for her to speak, she'd grab the mic, slowly raise it to her lips, and…give a guttural hiss like a tortured vampire.

I could see the look of confusion/panic on Candice's face, but she just nodded politely. And it got better. I also told her that over time people would start to understand her—like Chewbacca! I gave her the following example of an exchange she should expect:

MICKIE JAMES: Hey Candice! Ready for our tag match?
CANDICE: Hhhhhggggghaaaaaaa!
MICKIE JAMES: I agree…the situation in Bosnia *is* tenuous, but we need to head to the ring.

CANDICE: Chaaaaagggfffffaaaa.

MICKIE JAMES: Okay, fine, you can start the match and then tag me in when we get the advantage.

I somehow said this all with a straight face, to the point where Candice actually believed it (or at least believed we'd be dumb enough to try it). Later in the day, I told her the truth and felt the high of pulling off a genuine wrestling rib. Eventually Candice debuted, tongue intact. Years later she got some measure of revenge when she completely hustled me in pool, resulting in me having to piggyback her from the dive bar back to the TV hotel in full view of some massively perplexed WWE wrestlers and staff. Yeah, it's not in the same rib category as Mr. Fuji supposedly serving a wrestler a cooked stray dog, but at least it's my own. By the way, I believe "accidentally drinking lava" was a deleted scene in *Joe Versus the Volcano*.*

* * *

In addition to being the greatest ring announcer of all time, Howard Finkel was by far one of the nicest human beings of all time. A fellow diehard Mets fan, all Howard wanted to do was ring announce in front of the camera and do his job in Talent Relations behind it.

He was one of those performers who truly brought out the fan in you. Growing up, nothing was as goose-bump-inducing as hearing Howard announce a "newwwwwwwww" WWE Champion. I loved watching him announce the upcoming card on the Madison Square Garden Network:

"The Mighty Hercules [long pause for crowd to boo] will do battle with . . . the Junkyard Dog [massive cheer]."

But it was the little things he did that always caught my attention. To me, nothing was funnier than when Lanny Poffo, aka "the Genius," dressed in a graduation cap and gown, would enter the ring and whisper in Howard's ear before his match, resulting in Howard rolling his eyes and saying:

---

*And there it is! Number three! As if there was any doubt. Okay, I'll stop now.

"Ladies and gentlemen, I've just been informed... [shakes head] 'The Genius' has a poem for us all."

That personality quirk was taken to the next level a few months before I started at WWE when Howard became the new sidekick, or "stooge," for Chris Jericho. It was genuinely hilarious to see him in heel mode. I don't know if everyone thought it amusing, but I found it hysterical and fun to write. The more I got into it, the more ridiculous Howard's character became. Eventually Howard would find himself feuding with some of the WWE Divas, resulting in me writing him bon mots such as this:

"Trish, it's a dog-eat-dog world... You with your puppies and I with... my *wiener*."

Or after Stacy Keibler sarcastically telling Howard what he was saying was "really moving," having Howard respond with:

"You're moving something right now... in my trousers."

On the surface these very inappropriate lines are completely cringeworthy, and yet coming out of Howard's booming ring announcer voice, they were never not funny. In fact, at one point I literally fell out of my seat in Gorilla Position laughing—the only time that ever happened.

Howard himself was the ultimate company man playing his role, gamely culminating in an on-screen issue with fellow ring announcer Lilian Garcia.

The two ring announcers were supposed to be having their own rivalry over who would preside over *Monday Night Raw*. The angle was supposed to end with Eric Bischoff, as the heel GM, siccing 3-Minute Warning, aka Jamal and Rosey, aka two Samoan wrestlers from the famed Anoa'i family, on them. Rosey (Matt) was the older brother of Roman Reigns, and Jamal (Eddie) a brother of Rikishi. Their gimmick was working as Bischoff's hired muscle, physically decimating anyone who crossed him. Bischoff would invariably work the phrase "three minutes" into a promo, and that was the signal for Jamal and Rosey to embark on a serious ass kicking.

The story line originally had 3-Minute Warning laying waste to both Howard and Lilian. Howard had participated in some comedy "tuxedo matches" and in fact had a "tuxedo vs. evening gown match" with Lilian, but neither of them were bump takers. Vince doesn't make any talent do something they're not comfortable with, and Howard definitely wasn't comfortable with this.

"The heart is saying yes, the body is saying no," Howard lamented backstage on the night of the show. It was understandable. Howard was fifty-three at the time and had some knee issues. Even though Matt and Eddie were complete pros, they *did* weigh over 750 combined pounds, and taking bumps from them was something anyone, especially a non-wrestler, would feel nervous about.

Lilian, however, was all systems go. She herself had sometimes been the victim of scorn backstage. I always found her to be cool and friendly, but some saw her as a little full of herself. Knowing how quickly perception could turn into reality, I could relate to her plight.

The night of the show, after Howard bowed out, we pivoted. Instead of 3-Minute Warning attacking both Howard and Lilian, we had Howard do what I probably would've done in real life—shove Lilian into the Samoans and run for his life.

Lilian then took her bumps (a sick-looking Samoan drop and a devastating splash from the top rope) like a champ, and was congratulated backstage afterward, treated like a conquering hero by everyone. Well, almost everyone.

I could see Howard was a little upset. It wasn't necessarily the heaps of praise being bestowed upon Lilian (and deservedly so), but more about his entire state of being. It was something existential. In my obsession in writing for "heel" Howard, I had failed to see that unlike many heels, Howard genuinely did not like to be booed. On the contrary, he very much wanted to be loved and would go to great lengths to rationalize his dastardly actions.

As I watched Lilian receive a big hug from Vince, Howard approached me.

"You know, Brian, it was Eric Bischoff's intent to have 3-Minute Warning attack the both of us. By upending those plans I essentially was acting the role of a babyface."

"Um, Howard? You shoved a defenseless woman into two monsters, then ran as she was beaten and stretchered out of the ring. There is no scenario on the planet where that's the action of a babyface."

"But Eric as a heel wanted to get both of us and I stopped that from happening."

It was at this point I realized that as fun as it was to write heel Howard Finkel, this character needed to come to an abrupt end. My idea of fun was clearly warping this poor man's psyche, so the idea of a heel announcer would go into storage and I vowed never to try something like that again...until we made straitlaced announcer Michael Cole an even more despicable heel a few years later.

The "evil heel announcer" was apparently an idea too good to be considered "once in a lifetime." Fortunately, there was another slightly more prominent story line that fit that description.

Chapter 19

Once in a Lifetime

With all due respect to the "It's still real to me" guy, I believe as they get older, wrestling fans become more cynical. It's like a self-defense mechanism to combat the never-ending taunts of "You know it's not real, right?" which is something that's unique to wrestling. No one pulls aside a fan of, say, *The Boys* on Amazon Prime and dismissively says, "You know that guy in the cape can't *really* melt another person's face off, right?"

But wrestling has been and always will be different. Whenever someone says it's "fake," it's like they're letting you in on some huge secret despite everyone pretty much knowing what the deal is by the time they hit puberty.

When *WrestleMania 29*'s Rock vs. John Cena Championship rematch at MetLife Stadium was announced, some fans quickly unleashed their inner snark to scoff at the previous years' *WrestleMania* tagline "Once in a Lifetime."

"How could it be *once* in a lifetime if it's happening twice?" they'd say on Twitter with an aura of self-satisfaction, as if they were sitting around the wrestling version of the Algonquin Round Table.

Well I'm here to tell you those people are wrong. The Rock vs. John Cena in Miami at *WrestleMania 28* and in New Jersey for *WrestleMania 29* (all set up by the Rock hosting *WrestleMania 27*) truly were once-in-a-lifetime events. In my sixteen years at WWE, I had never experienced anything like them, and I'm willing to bet those currently on the WWE creative team never will.

There have been plenty of story lines that were quasi "shoots," where elements of real life seeped their way in. There have been plenty of angles where the opponents didn't like each other personally but were willing to put their animosity aside in order to do business. There have been programs where one person didn't know what the other was going to do and didn't care.

But there had never been something with all those things converging into a three-year *WrestleMania* main event program. One of the biggest global stars in the world taking on the biggest star in the company. A program where practically everything *but* the match itself was 100 percent real. The promos were real, the passion was real, and the writer caught in the middle slowly but surely losing his mind was most definitely real.

Unlike most modern WWE wrestling story lines that began as an idea on paper, usually in Stamford, this all started with a real-life John Cena interview with the UK *Sun* in 2008. Cena was asked what he thought of the Rock, and he gave his honest answer: to paraphrase, John said while the Rock is a genuinely nice guy and a fantastic human being, there was no reason why the Rock couldn't come back to WWE for an occasional appearance. Okay, maybe it was actually phrased a little more forcefully:

"Associating with sports entertainment doesn't do much for his acting career…so I get why he doesn't come back. Just don't fuck me around and tell me that you love this when you are just doing this to do something else…He just doesn't give anything back, man. I wish he'd just show up, just say 'Hi' and leave, it's all he's gotta do. Do the eyebrow once and get out of town. That's one thing that sweats me."

Rock had been a fan of John's, and to hear these comments really didn't sit well. It would be one thing if John expressed these things face-to-face, but for Rock to hear them in a radio interview was jarring. The message *I'd love to see the Rock come back to WWE* in and of itself is fine. But it was compounded and overshadowed by the messaging of *When Rock says he loves WWE, he's really full of shit—just come back, do your schtick, and then you can go back to your beloved Hollywood.*

For Rock, that last part crossed the line. When it happened, I talked to Rock about it and he told me point-blank he was surprised and actually shocked that the guy who took his place as the face of the company was so flippant—and so disrespectful—with his words. Rock knew one day he'd see John and hold him accountable. Make no mistake, there would be a day of reckoning.

Before getting too deep, I should point out that John is one of the most stand-up guys I know. I'll go one step further: I freaking love John Cena. So does virtually every person backstage who has ever worked with him. There's not a shred of phoniness about him. He has admitted his initial comments were something he truly regrets saying, stating in another interview: "It was stupid of me. It genuinely was. That was my perspective at the time. For me to not be able to see Dwayne's vision on what he wanted to do personally, and how his personal success could affect a growing global brand, that was just ignorant on my part."

While John's comments might've been a mistake, they nonetheless set the stage for what was about to come. WWE is in Rock's blood,* and after years away he was itching to make a return, but the timing both from a business and a scheduling standpoint needed to be just right. If Rock was coming back, it had to be big. Actually, *big* would be underselling it. It needed to be historically epic. That opportunity presented itself in 2010.

Rock reached out to Vince. He didn't just want to come back. He wanted to give back to the business and asked Vince what he could do. Vince asked Rock about a match, which Rock wasn't feeling. Rock had something bigger in mind. He couldn't fuel his passion with a single match. Rock told Vince he couldn't give back to the business and impact the WWE's bottom line economically with a single match. Vince heard this and proposed something pretty much unprecedented—a three-*year* story line that would occupy the main event slots of three consecutive *WrestleMania*s.

Rock heard the idea and realized, *That's it*. A three-year *Wrestle-Mania* main event story line would satisfy all the things Rock wanted to

---

*As seen on the hit NBC show *Young Rock*. Seasons 1 and 2 are now streaming on Peacock.

accomplish. The question of "Who would be the opponent?" was never a question at all. There was only one choice.

Having faced Hulk Hogan in the *WrestleMania 18* Icon vs. Icon classic, Rock knew the only opponent who would be worthy of this type of commitment was the biggest star in WWE—John Cena. Yes, it just so happened John had made those public comments a year earlier, but even if he hadn't, Rock vs. Cena was easily the most exciting, never-before-seen, money-drawing match on the table.

A match with Triple H? Classic rivalry, but we've seen it.

Trying to break the Undertaker's streak? Intriguing, but Taker was already involved in a major multiyear story line with Triple H and Shawn Michaels.

Facing Fandango in a dance-off? The world would not be able to handle it.

No, *the* match was the Rock vs. John Cena. It was something Rock could truly sink his teeth into. He told me what he wanted for the story, and it was stronger and realer than anything you could make up. For Rock the story was simple: *I love this business, I was born in this business, John Cena ran his mouth about me, he disrespected me, and now I'm back—talk your shit now.*

* * *

The plan was for Rock to come back to serve as "host" of *WrestleMania 27* and interact with John in the main event. Whatever would happen there would set the stage for Rock and John working together in Rock's hometown of Miami for *WrestleMania 28*, and then again in a rematch at *WrestleMania 29*. At some point in between *WrestleMania*s 28 and 29, Rock would win the WWE title so the rematch would be a Championship match (upping the stakes). At this point, specifics were TBD, finishes TBD, but the blueprint was there and dollars were set to be made.

The Rock was coming back to host *WrestleMania*, and Vince wanted this to be a big deal. Very few people knew it was going to be the Rock, whose music would hit on a live *Raw* in Anaheim to mark his return after a seven-year absence. In fact, the strong online buzz was that it was going to be Justin Bieber! Rock's name wasn't written into that night's script.

His name wasn't mentioned in the production meeting. We couldn't risk this leaking if we wanted it to be a true surprise. Seeing thousands of fans chant "Rocky" before his music hit would've made the moment anticlimactic.

Rock and I had worked on the promo during the week and rehearsed it at Rock's hotel in Anaheim the day of the show. Rock basically got to the arena that night, went straight to the dressing room that was set up for him for a brief period of time, and then headed to the ring.

Vince knew about it. Stephanie knew. Executive producer Kevin Dunn and a select few in the production truck knew. Some of the writers and I knew, but there was one person who had no idea of what was about to happen—John Cena.

John did stop by Rock's dressing room earlier to say hello. Rock even buzzed him that he was going to say some shit about John in his promo (Rock didn't want to sugarcoat anything). John responded "Great!" John gets it: He knew it wouldn't be a Rock promo if he didn't talk shit about people, especially about John, based on what John had said.

We didn't *have* to go that way. Sure, you can ignore the real-life comments and do an angle about the Rock wanting to face the very best WWE had to offer, the proverbial "spirit of competition," but I'm falling asleep just typing that. Having Rock come out with a legit *reason* to have an issue with John made the story way more intriguing. The promo itself wasn't anything *personal*, but in classic Rock fashion he took aim at Cena's "You can't see me" catchphrase as well as his multicolored shirts ("You look like a big fat bowl of Fruity Pebbles!"). Earlier in the promo he went after John's opponent that year, the Miz, so the stage was set pretty nicely. Cena challenging Miz for the WWE Championship with the Rock, having issue with both of them, being that evening's host.

The audience absolutely loved the promo. Did John? I'm not so sure.

Promo-wise, there probably wasn't anything he'd take offense to. From a bigger-picture business standpoint, I don't believe John had been clued in on the three-year plan and what was about to happen.

For Cena, a guy who was the ultimate company man, who did literally everything asked of him and who happened to be WWE's top star for over a decade, to watch the Rock return and take aim at him on live television without being given a heads-up on what would be the biggest program of his career probably felt...well, a little messed up.

This was one of those things where no one was technically wrong. John's feelings came from a real place, Rock's response to John's feelings also came from a real place, and Vince truly wanted to keep this historic moment of Rock returning with the intent to headline three straight *WrestleMania*s to be as big a surprise as possible. And it was. Despite things being leaked out on the internet all the time, no one knew this was coming.

Now that the stage was set, and the egos were a little bruised, it became time for the task at hand—time to do record-breaking business.

I really did think that if Rock and Cena got to know each other and see how much they had in common—incredible work ethics, off-the-chart promo skills, underappreciated wrestling skills (aka "workrate"), and an overall love and respect for the business—they would actually become friends. I told each of them separately how the other really was a great guy, but what I didn't fully comprehend at the time was that the Rock and John Cena, despite everything they have in common, were just two *very* different people, with completely different DNA and wiring. You can see it even today. John dressed up as his Peacemaker character at the premiere of *The Suicide Squad*, and it *worked* because the people knew John and knew that was exactly something he would do. I don't have any inside information, but I'm pretty sure Rock's not dressing up as Black Adam for that movie's premiere. Not because that's beneath him but simply because that's not who Dwayne Johnson is. If he did, the audience would be massively confused and think the Rock's lost his mind. Their differences work in their favor. You can't possibly lump "former WWE stars now movie stars" into a single group for many reasons, but the top one would be because Dwayne Johnson is a completely different human being than John Cena and vice versa. (For what it's worth, Dave Bautista is a completely unique specimen as well.)

In 2010, my trying to will a friendship between the two just wasn't going to happen. You can't force something like that. Just because Dracula and Frankenstein are legendary monsters doesn't mean they'd enjoy hanging out on weekends.* Rock and Cena were more than happy to do business (as it turned out, massive business) so getting off to a good start was going to be key.

Unfortunately, things went off the rails pretty much from the beginning, thanks to the staunch moral code of a rapping fifth grader.

* * *

To kick off the story line for *WrestleMania 27*, we had arranged to do an off-site vignette with a kid dressed as John Cena. This was pretty important, as it was going to set the tone for the three-year promotion. The kid (ostensibly Cena) was going to approach Rock and do a decidedly un-PG rap that insulted Rock, Miz (Cena's opponent for that *WrestleMania*) and for the most part Cena himself. Inspired by the Funny or Die video "The Landlord," in which Will Ferrell gets verbally abused by a toddler, the kid was supposed to curse up a storm, which we'd bleep in postproduction, and say inappropriate things, straddling the line but not crossing it. I read the rap to Vince while waiting for my rental car in LA, and his laugh boomed through the phone so loud I was giddy (for this vignette Vince was willing to bend the newly installed "TV-PG" rules).**

Then we got to the shoot. The kid hired to play Cena, an actual kid rapper, was very sweet, but his father took a look at the script and, as the cameras and lighting were being set up, looked at me and said flatly:

"My son's not going to say any of this."

Nothing like the launch of a multi-year, multi-million-dollar story line suddenly being in the hands of a rapping ten-year-old's dad. I tried to explain how it's a parody of John Cena's character. Rock tried to give

---

*I wrote for *Big Wolf on Campus*. I know these things.

**This involved a shift to a more family-friendly show, with the rating going from TV-14 to TV-PG, though many argue in the beginning it was more "G" than "PG."

a big-picture perspective, assuring the father how it wouldn't reflect on the child himself, and as a performer it would show the kid's versatility.

But nothing we could say would make the kid's father change his mind, and it was too late to hire another child actor-rapper. We were shooting this the day of the show and had taken one of the *Raw* camera crews, so the clock was ticking. We needed to shoot this thing *now*.

Rock and I regrouped and quickly put something together that while entertaining was, in hindsight, less fun and more mean-spirited than what we initially intended, with Rock telling child Cena point-blank, "He's just not that talented." I can't imagine John was pleased when he watched this air. John had done a rap the week before on *Raw* and taken some pointed shots at Rock, so story line wise, the vignette made sense. It just wasn't what was originally planned, which was much better and way more entertaining. Vince must've felt the same way because when he saw it, the decision was made to enhance it with goofy comedic sound effects.

The angle didn't get off to the start we had envisioned, but we did make a child cry on camera, so at least there was that.

* * *

We got through the first phase of the three-part *WrestleMania* plan; Rock cost John Cena the match and Miz won the main event.* The following night on *Raw*, we made the unprecedented move of announcing the *WrestleMania 28* main event a full year in advance. Rock and Cena were respectful toward each other during the build, but they had by no means become friends. I had a sinking feeling this would get worse before it got better as we went into the promotion for the one-on-one "Once in a Lifetime" match between Rock and Cena the following year. Sure enough, it did get worse, pretty much immediately.

Again, I want to point out as far as this real-life story goes, there are no "babyfaces" and "heels." No good guys and bad guys. What we had

---

*A fact I believe is printed on Miz's business cards.

was two people, each with a legit claim to being the biggest star in the industry, with a deep personal issue that happened to be playing out each week on live television.

Things very quickly went to another level. It started when John cut a promo at a WWE live event in Australia, with the gist being John was physically there at the show and Rock wasn't; John even went so far as to say Rock lied when he said he was back and was never going to leave. This prompted an intense Facebook retort by Rock (with zero goofy comedic sound effects) where he unloaded on this line of thinking. This was pure passion, some of it clearly in character, some not. Rock talked about how he had done everything Cena had done (only better), and coming back to WWE wasn't meant to be taken literally every show, every week.

Whether it was by design or simply a by-product of the real-life heat, people were talking. And not just the wrestling audience—the story was being picked up by media outlets worldwide. This wasn't Ted DiBiase paying a referee to get plastic surgery to screw over Hulk Hogan (though admittedly that angle was awesome). This was serious, boiling tension playing out in real time in front of a worldwide audience to the point that after the Facebook video, Vince had to tell both Rock and Cena to go radio silent until it was time to do business in the ring and on television again.

Like the rest of the world, I watched this all go down while asking the very poignant question: What the hell is happening?!

Again, to set the stage, Cena (thanks to a Rock Bottom in the *Wrestle-Mania 27* main event) had been screwed out of the WWE title and was scheduled to face Rock himself at *WrestleMania 28*, with the finish still to be determined. Even though the writing team had an idea of what the finish would be (Rock "going over") it wasn't officially decided until the day of the show. In real life, I'd imagine John felt he was working day in and day out and feeling unappreciated both by WWE and large segments of the WWE fans. In general, kids and women loved him and adult men didn't. Hence a lot of dueling chants of "Let's go Cena"—"Cena Sucks."

Normally John's attitude was *That's cool. As long as they're reacting it's a good thing.* And while that still was the case, this time the "Cena sucks" chants were the embodiment of the Rock and his fans, and John simply wasn't going to smile and take it.

John was going to make damn sure if he was headed into battle he was going to go in on his terms, as an equal if not better. There were no rules, only results. I believe that was John's attitude, and I can't say I blame him.

As year two of the *WrestleMania* program began, Hiram Garcia and I worked with Rock on his "return to *Raw*" promo, and it was a long one. Simultaneously, I had written an outline for John, but he was going to basically make it his own, not only because that was what he always did (from the very start of his WWE career and with great success) but also because on principle there was also no way in hell he was going to let "the Rock's writer" do his promo for him.

That was the stressful situation I found myself in. Technically I was a guy with no dog in the fight, but if perception was reality, then by all appearances I was squarely on Team Rock. Okay, reality being reality, I *was* on Team Rock, but it wasn't as if I was anti-Cena—even if that was the perception, which of course is reality. My head is spinning just thinking about it.

In Portland, on *Raw*, in that first night back since teaming with Cena at *Survivor Series* three months earlier, John once again stopped by Rock's locker room to say hello. Everything was very friendly and cordial. Rock offered to show John the promo he was going to say, but John said he was good. He had the basic outline and said he didn't need to see what Rock was going to say—he'd rather be surprised. To that point, Rock had a basic idea but didn't know what John was going to say to him, either.

Again, there is no other form of scripted televised entertainment where anything like this happens. Josh Brolin's Thanos doesn't tell Robert Downey Jr.'s Iron Man, *I pretty much know what we're supposed to do, so let's call it out on the green screen.* Something like this can work *if* the two people performing have the utmost trust and respect for each other. We hadn't quite gotten there just yet. Not even close.

What happened next was that infamous moment where Cena came out and called out the fact that Rock had written bullet points on his wrist, live in the middle of the ring, a move that was pretty much unprecedented. Not the act of writing words on your wrist, but betraying your dance partner's trust by pointing it out on live television. Writing notes on body parts was actually an old-school thing. I don't know for certain if Roddy Piper did it back in the day, but he certainly did it all the time when he was back in the company starting in 2003. Again, when you've essentially got a day to memorize a twenty-minute monologue, live on television with no cue cards or teleprompters, and you haven't done it in a while, it's a helpful tool to keep track of where you are.

I was in Gorilla on headset communicating to the truck when Cena caught the notes on Rock's arm on one of the screens. Rock was cutting his promo solo before John's music hit, and thanks to the wonder of high-definition television you could see something was written there if you were looking for it. John either caught it himself or someone buzzed him, because right then and there he made a decision—if it's on TV, it's fair game.

How do I know this? Because after the segment was over, he burst through the curtain, pointed at me, and shouted, "If it's on TV, it's fair game."

Again, that's not to paint John as the bad guy. I can only assume from his perspective, he wasn't just facing the Rock at *WrestleMania*. He was facing the Rock, the head writer of *Raw*, the WWE fans, and Vince McMahon. *The Art of War*, written in China in the fifth century, says "Never back your enemy in a corner" for a reason.

For "smart" fans, this was of course a huge deal. Internally, it was also a pretty big deal because whatever remnants of trust existed between two of the biggest stars in WWE history was obliterated on the *first* night of year two of their program.

For the general audience? I don't think this was considered a seismic event, mainly because most fans didn't know if what John said was true or not. But there was a bigger issue at play. I don't think most fans bought into John's central argument about the Rock not being there all the time. The majority of the audience got the fact that Rock had his great run during the Attitude Era, went on to pursue the next chapter of his life, and was never going to be in WWE every week. They were just happy to have him back now.

Personally, as big a fan as I was (and still am) of John's, I thought he didn't need to go there. Despite what the PG child rapping Cena said a year earlier, Cena really *is* that talented, and I don't think the "oooooh" moment was worth it. Of course, it's easy to look back on it and have that perspective *now*. I wasn't the one who was being serenaded with "Frui-ty Peb-ble" in every city in America.

Afterward, I could tell Rock was *not* happy, but there are no do-overs on live television. What's done is done. John drew his line in the sand. Now the question was: How was the Rock going to respond?

* * *

The gloves were now off. Unlike the first week, now Rock and Cena didn't bother to meet to discuss their promo segment beforehand. Rock did his thing and Cena did his. Sure, I was in the middle, giving both men the gist of that night's segment and trying to fill everyone in on what was happening while trying to keep a rosy, positive attitude, but for the most part it was each man for himself, which was how they both preferred it. Both Rock and Cena had a huge amount of self-confidence. Rock didn't complain about the wrist thing to Vince or raise a stink. Instead his attitude (and John's as well) was *I don't care what the other guy does, because my stuff is going to be better.* To take it a step further, Rock's attitude was *I will sharpen a knife, stick it in him, and slowly push it in and twist.* This was intense but honestly, from my point of view, coming from an era not too far removed from *Call Florence Henderson's reps and see what she wants to do on* Raw *as the guest host this week*, this added an element of danger and realism to *Raw* that was sorely needed.

Strong, believable on-screen tension is a very cool dynamic in wrestling, but when two guys aren't on the same page in real life it can cause headaches. When Rock went around Boston visiting historic landmarks while knocking Cena, the idea was for Rock to have his fun off-site. But once he and John got into the ring it would be time for the serious money-making part of the promo.

This is where meeting beforehand and getting on the same page would've been helpful. When they finally confronted each other in the ring, they were out of sync with each other. The more serious Rock got, the more Cena would smirk and undercut the tension. Rock was in the ring glaring and trying to create a serious moment while John was going the opposite way, countering the laughs Rock got earlier in the night with laughs of his own, eventually making a *Tooth Fairy* joke.

Tonally this segment was just off. It was like having Johnny Knoxville and the cast of *Jackass* show up in the middle of the movie *1917*. John did cut a serious, impassioned promo, but only after Rock had left the ring.

Things started to get worse. In a week Rock wasn't there, he did a pretaped promo at Vince's request (again, something he personally hated doing). John cut his promo, then unleashed a doctored Rock T-shirt reading, "I Bring It...via Satellite."

When Cena got back through the curtain he whipped the shirt at me while I was seated in Gorilla Position on headset (I still have it). That should've given me the impression that Cena was not happy with me personally. But I really got the message weeks later, when John might or might not have tried to murder me on a go-kart track.

Let me back up for a second.

Even though I was a Rock guy, I had always gotten along with Cena. I had never written a Cena rap, but I did get props from John when I wrote Kurt Angle's intentionally ridiculous rap, ending with Kurt embracing John as part of "Basic Huganomics." Years later, John and I actually sat in a room, just the two of us, and watched a final cut of his first starring movie role in *The Marine* weeks before it came out. We sat in silence after it was over, both of us realizing it didn't really capitalize on John's strengths and probably wasn't going to make any year-end best picture lists. Finally John broke the tension by saying, "We need to go drink." We then proceeded to do so at Bobby V's in Stamford, well into the night.

We even once got stuck on his bus in NYC in the middle of a major snowstorm, and along with the driver we attempted to push the bus out of a snow bank. Truth be told, I'm pretty sure I did most of the work.*

But this was a different time. The night before *Raw*, John had rented out a go-kart track on a weekend after hours for a large group of us (wrestlers, writers, WWE crew). Naively thinking his main beef was with Rock and not myself, I happily fastened my seat belt and started driving. I had never done go-kart racing before,** and I quickly spun out. With my car sideways, I tried to figure how to straighten myself out when I looked up to see John barreling toward my go-kart at full speed. He T-boned me as hard as physics would allow, sending me and my car spinning out of control before other drivers, unable to get out of the way, crashed into me as well. One car actually landed on top of my bumper, inches away from my face.

That was it for me. I was done with the go-kart, not just for that night but forever. "Where you going?" John shouted repeatedly as I walked off the track.

What about our Marine *moment?* I thought to myself, suppressing the urge to start crying. Then I remembered I had written a joke for Rock years ago that Rock gave while inducting his father and grandfather into the WWE Hall of Fame. Something about WWE going to Iraq and being accused of torture—by making prisoners watch copies of *The Marine*.

Holy shit, maybe it was *me* who betrayed our *Marine* moment first! I don't know if that line warranted attempted homicide with a go-kart, but again, wrestlers never forget. It then occurred to me John might have reason to think of me as the enemy. In my defense, the joke was hilarious and years later resulted in a Cena meme that's become a go-to for expressing mock surprise.

---

*Somehow *The Marine* still spawned *five* sequels. Four of them starred the Miz, which kept him off TV for long stretches of time, so I guess it wasn't all bad.

**Since I lived in NYC I rarely drove, period.

In John's defense, years later I found out I was far from the first guy he T-boned on a go-kart track.

Either way, the peace I had tried to maintain was now disintegrating. Something needed to change, and it needed to change quickly. Rock and John were set to have one of the most important matches in WWE history, and getting them on the same page was a top priority of mine with only two weeks before *Mania*.

In Cleveland, Rock, Hiram, and I stayed up into the wee hours of the morning writing the lyrics to "The Rock Concert." Cena was to perform a rap early on *Raw*, then Rock would have his segment with a song making fun of John. Again, neither Rock nor Cena had any idea what the other was going to say. Cena hadn't done a rap since the one he'd done a year earlier, but they were always a highlight. John would never use a WWE writer; he would sometimes collaborate with his cousin via phone, and when he performed, his timing and delivery were always impeccable. It was what famously "got him over" in the first place, and it had resulted in him eventually making a successful rap album. Check out "Bad, Bad Man"—it still, as the kids say, "slaps."

Rock, Hiram, and I watched from Rock's locker room. John had some solid shots once again, culminating with John threatening Rock with a "Cleveland Steamer" and putting his nuts in Rock's face. It was remarkable considering, again, this was the start of the ultraconservative "PG Era" in WWE, with Vince looking to tone things down in the hopes of attracting more mainstream advertisers. This was like tuning into *The Muppet Show* only to see Kermit making fun of Fozzy's balls for a solid fifteen minutes.

Rock watched the rap and responded with . . . a smile. He knew what he had later that night would be far more memorable.

In a song set to the "Jailhouse Rock" theme, Rock made fun of Cena's rapping, his fans ("I know you love Chewbacca and Frodo, too, but you're a walking virgin and you're forty-two"), the day of his birth ("April twenty-third, 1977, the doctor shouted—send that baby back to heaven"), before finally settling on the fact that Rock had sex with Cena's mother.

We honestly didn't know how it would be received. Would a "Rock Concert," which hadn't been done in years, be considered dated and even "old-fashioned" compared to John's rap? You truly never know.

We quickly got our answer. Within the first few chords of Rock playing guitar the crowd went absolutely nuts. They wanted to see this and were into every line from beginning to end. It was satisfying to see the crowd respond so vocally, as putting it together was one of the most fun nights Rock, Hiram, and myself ever had, most of the stuff pitched being way too unsuitable for television.

Before the segment, I sat in my usual spot on headset in Gorilla Position communicating to the production truck when John Cena walked through the curtain. I really didn't know how John would react to all this, but to my surprise Cena watched with a huge grin.

"That's the Rock I've been waiting for!" he shouted. Personally, I didn't think the spirit of the song was all that different from what we had been doing all along, but he was right—this segment connected with the audience* in a visceral way. John seemed to genuinely enjoy it, and for the first time in this promotion he waited in Gorilla to congratulate Rock once he stepped through the curtain.

Everything got easier from that point. The following week there were no promos, just in-ring physicality. Then, for the final "go home" week, the time for trash-talking was over, and John and Rock, now on the same page, cut serious promos on each other with one goal in mind—sell as many tickets and pay-per-views as possible. We even gathered in the same room and went over it as a group for the first time ever.

Compared to the buildup, the event itself, *WrestleMania 28* was a cakewalk. (Well, for me at least, since I didn't have to actually wrestle a half-hour-long match in front of seventy-eight thousand people.) After the match Rock and Cena were buzzing—thrilled with the match and the reaction from the fans. They met backstage afterward, and it was there I saw a true mutual respect grow between them.

---

*Except for child-rapping Cena's dad, who I can only assume was appalled.

Which was a good thing, because we were doing it all over again as planned for *next* year's *WrestleMania*, this time with Rock as Champion.

Suffice to say the third time was the charm as far as backstage cohesion. Rock and Cena being on the same page behind the scenes might've been felt by the audience. That real-life tension in their promos just wasn't the same (though they still got plenty of shots in). On the bright side, all our lives were now running a lot smoother. Rock passed the torch at *WrestleMania 29*, the pay-per-view did great business and John never got the urge to invite me to a funplex with murderous intent.

Overall, the night was a huge success . . . except for the fact that Rock tore his adductor and his quadriceps fifteen minutes into the thirty-minute match. In fact, they were torn straight from his pelvis. I'm not a doctor but I can tell you tearing both those things and continuing to wrestle does not make things better. As Rock would tell me, everything else in your body overcompensates. When John hit his final "Attitude Adjustment" for the pin, Rock experienced three tears in his abdomen and needed to get emergency surgery, which must've been incredibly painful. It delayed the start of filming for his next movie, *Hercules*, a film shooting in Budapest with a hundred-million-dollar budget.

But other than that . . . !

The three-year odyssey ended with physical and emotional scars for both Rock and John (with me experiencing mini nervous breakdowns along the way).

Was it all worth it? At the end of the day, no matter what you want to say about how they got there, Rock and John Cena broke an *all-time* pay-per-view buyrate record, one that will never be broken.*

Not only that, they took fans on a ride that will never be forgotten. Plus, John legitimately landed on a box of Fruity Pebbles when all was said and done, so I'd say hell yeah, it was worth it.

Will we ever see anything like this again? Two once-in-a-generation

---

*With WWE's pay-per-view model completely changing via the WWE network and Peacock, this record will stand the test of time.

megastars with serious real-life issues, locked in a multi-year angle head-lining three straight *WrestleMania*s? Nothing's impossible, but I highly doubt it. Something like this truly only happens "once in a Lifetime."

* * *

John Cena became the new WWE Champion that night in New Jersey. Then a funny thing happened—more movie roles started coming in for him as well as commercials, hosting *Saturday Night Live*, and starring in his own *Peacemaker* TV series on HBO Max (which might contain the single greatest opening credit sequence in television history). Slowly but surely, John Cena became the very thing he had first called Rock out on—a guy who'll always be loyal to WWE but won't be in the ring week after week, year after year.

That didn't go unnoticed with John who, again, took full ownership for those initial comments and regularly goes out of his way to publicly praise Rock for paving the way for so many WWE stars who've gone into film—something I know Rock appreciates.

My relationship with John improved after that as well. I'm happy to report that when I see him now there's no mistrust or paranoia. It's more like the U.S. and England decades after the War of 1812—can you believe we set fire to your capital!? What were we *thinking*?!

It all worked out in the end, and it only took about ten years off my life. Trying to navigate the real-life tension between two of the biggest stars in the business while still being responsible for writing the flagship show was pretty stressful, but on the bright side, you become much stron-ger. Mini-crises on the set of *Young Rock*, for instance, like a character's wardrobe not looking right, are downright quaint by comparison.

That final Rock vs. John Cena *WrestleMania* match started the count-down for John to eventually leave WWE, which finally happened in 2017. He had achieved all he could in WWE, and while he and Rock would always come back for special appearances, it was time for John to embark on the next chapter of his career.

It was during this time in 2010 that I started to feel the same way about my life and my career. But unlike John's and Rock's relatively seamless departures from WWE, mine wasn't going to be as simple or as pleasant.

CHAPTER 20

Schmucky the Clown

Some say working one year for Vince McMahon is like working four years for any other boss as far as the stress level goes. That may be accurate, but I don't think the stress Vince induces comes out of malevolence. He wants your passion to equal his, or at least come close. I've found a lot of the Vince stories percolating over the years from ex-employees to be accurate—you're always on call, there's not a ton of sleep, there is no "sick," you should avoid wearing "dungarees" in his presence (and you should avoid reminding him that no one has called them "dungarees" since 1977).

And just when you think you're in his good graces, one ill-timed reaction, facial expression, or offhand remark can throw your entire relationship into a tailspin.

And yet, for the most part, over the course of a decade and a half, Vince and I got along just fine.

Probably better than fine. In fact, at one point, Stephanie McMahon said to me, "I wish he'd listen to me the way he listens to you."

That's not because my ideas were brilliant or anything. It's just that Vince was *always* toughest on Stephanie and Shane. It was almost as if he were telling the world, *You think I just give high-profile jobs to my kids out of nepotism? I'll damn well make sure they earn it.*

I found the three keys to pleasing Vince were:

1. actually come up with good creative ideas,

2. pitch in a clear, concise manner, and

3. don't be "Schmucky the Clown."

I first heard that term in a stand-up bit from Lewis Black, but its reach goes even further. Urban Dictionary defines "Schmucky the Clown" as:

A derogatory name for a person or persons who, though at times may be amusing, are really just a useless flap of skin that nobody really wants to deal with and is generally good for nothing.

There was *always* someone in our writers meetings who unknowingly took on that role in Vince's eyes. Sometimes it was a new writer, sometimes, fairly or not, it was a veteran like Paul Heyman. That's not to say the person unlucky to have that title was pitching bad ideas. It was more that person, for whatever reason, just fell on Vince's bad side. When you became Schmucky the Clown, Vince would react as if everything coming out of your mouth was literally the *last* thing we should do.

Don't get me wrong—I got into my fair share of arguments with Vince. One time, at the end of a heated conference call Vince suggested I "go have a good cry." I got so angry I threw my phone into my apartment wall and made a small hole.

But generally speaking, I was rarely in Schmucky land. If anything, I was the guy Vince would give a look to when that day's Schmucky the Clown made the fatal mistake of opening his or her mouth.

Dealing with Vince could be a tricky labyrinth, but over the years I grew to admire him as a role model. In many ways he was everything I wasn't—brash, fearless, extroverted, impeccably dressed, and possessing inhuman willpower when it came to complex carbohydrates. Plus, unlike me, he *loved* confrontation. I remember him telling me how he actually looked forward to getting pulled over by a cop when he was speeding down the highway. By contrast, after going to the movie theater to see the first trailer for *Star Wars: The Phantom Menace*, I drove back home in my '95 Saturn, driving as if it were the Millennium Falcon, promptly got pulled over, couldn't find my registration, and had such a sad look on my face, the cop correctly surmised I had bigger problems in life and let me off with a warning.

I sometimes wished I could live my life for one day with Vince McMahon's mindset. The life lessons one accrues by just watching him in action are invaluable. I always enjoyed working with him when he was a performer.* And while I would occasionally get chewed out for a promo that went south, I had gained something few people do—his trust.

In fact, I'd go so far as to say the greatest compliment Vince would ever give me (or anyone) as a writer wasn't the proverbial "This is good shit" or a thumbs-up after a good segment. No, the biggest compliment a writer can get from Vince occurs before the show even starts. When he's poring over every line, every graphic, every camera angle, of that night's script and, after waiting your turn, you finally present him with whatever promo you've been working on and his reaction is:

"I don't need to see it. I trust you."

That is the highest level of honor Vince McMahon can bestow on a writer and when it came my way, I felt unstoppable. That, for the most part, was my relationship with Vince for a good ten-year period. It was like Tony and his "nephew" Christopher in *The Sopranos*. Technically not related, but mentor and apprentice in the trenches together.

Then it started turning into the Tony-Christopher relationship in the *last* season of *The Sopranos*, and I knew something needed to change before I got proverbially strangled to death in my own minivan.

But I'm getting ahead of myself.

* * *

The turning point in my relationship with Vince was around 2010, but the wheels probably started turning in 2005. Then I was six years into my tenure, thirty-two years old, and head writer of the flagship show, yet I felt like something was missing.

---

*The Mr. America "lie detector test" and the vignettes in the Church with Shane when he was preparing to face Shawn Michaels and "G-d" were probably my favorites. "Dr. Heinie," shot in a terrible-smelling veterinary office, was . . . not.

In Hollywood, as a writer you go through a trajectory. Start out as a staff writer and work your way up the chain with the hope of someday creating your own show. Obviously not everyone gets to make that climb, but it's all there in front of you and there's any number of places you can go.

In WWE, once you reach the pinnacle of head writer, there's really nowhere else to go. In 2005 I was getting the itch to do something, anything, else. Perhaps sensing this and aware of just how common burnout is among the writers, Vince and Stephanie were extremely generous in letting me have three months paid time off in order to go off and write the Eugene movie.

Eugene, aka Nick Dinsmore, was unique. Unlike any other wrestler who came before him, he was a "special needs" character who became a WWE savant by watching nothing but wrestling as a kid. The character was controversial when he first debuted, but Nick played him with such innocence, sweetness, and passion that he endeared himself to the fans pretty much immediately. The character who some prognosticated would go down as one of WWE's all-time flops was all over the show every week and eventually had a *SummerSlam* pay-per-view match against Triple H. (Probably not Triple H's first choice for opponent, but even he couldn't deny Eugene's popularity.)

The idea of writing a *Pee-Wee's Big Adventure*–type Eugene origin story came from Vince himself. He told me to meet with WWE Films, which at the time was mainly reading scripts about ex-bikers trying to go straight but being lured back into a life of crime after rival bikers kidnap and sexually torture their girlfriends. The feel-good movies of the summer!

Like most of Hollywood at the time, the executives at WWE Films didn't really want to make any movie associated with wrestling let alone a Eugene movie. Why they didn't want to tap into their already established fan base, who were willing to spend their hard-earned money on everything from WWE cologne to WWE garden gnomes to oversized foam urns, was beyond me. The only advice I got from WWE Films was "watch *Dumb and Dumber*."

The break from day-to-day WWE actually did wonders for me physically and mentally. It's a little like *The Shawshank Redemption* in that you get so used to working at WWE you become institutionalized. And while the Eugene movie was not quite on par with *Shawshank*,* I was proud of what I wrote. I was actually putting the finishing touches on the first draft when I tuned into *SummerSlam 2005* (one year after the Eugene–Triple H match) to see Eugene face off against my old friend Kurt Angle.

I had just finished a tough three-months-to-write screenplay, the first screenplay I had ever attempted, only to see the crowd booing the ever-loving shit out of Eugene.

It appears the clock had struck midnight on the character, and the fans who once adored Eugene were now thoroughly sick of him. My theory? WWE used him too much too soon. I once went to a live event where they had Eugene out in front of the people four times in one night. All that exposure eventually caused the fans to grow tired of him.

WWE fans made it very clear: *We don't care if you're an inspirational character with special needs—if you get on our nerves, we will end you.*

In the end, Vince pulled me aside and said he couldn't commit to making a movie based on that character. He then asked if it was possible to rewrite it and just make it a different character but with Tourette's syndrome.

It wasn't.

The weird thing I noticed was that while Vince couldn't have been more supportive when I was off writing the movie, answering all questions and providing encouragement, I could tell something changed when I came back. It was almost like he resented me for taking so much time off while others were in the proverbial foxhole with him. When I came back, for the first time I found myself in the extended role of Schmucky the Clown. It was not fun.

---

*Despite a brilliant opening scene of Jim Ross and Jerry Lawler up in a tree wearing colonial outfits and calling a heel turn from Abe Lincoln to George Washington, in one of Eugene's dream sequences.

"Hey Vince should we breathe oxygen today?"

"That's literally the *last* thing we should be doing." (Dismissive, angered grunt.)

I weathered the storm and things slowly went back to normal, but I was still feeling unfulfilled professionally. Again, it was never my dream to become a "WWE writer," and as I saw all my friends branch out in Hollywood with their writing careers, and I was spending the weekend writing another script for another *Raw*, I started to wonder, *Is this all there is?*

Stephanie got it. She tried to be accommodating. Years later, the two of us came up with an idea that I would almost immediately regret—leave the writing team and move up into WWE senior management. The idea would be that as Stephanie was moving up in the company herself, I would essentially take her role of overseeing the creative team, attend WWE Senior Executive meetings, weigh in on marketing decisions, etc. On paper it's a fine corporate trajectory, but it wasn't for me. I attended management classes in New York City, went to WWE exec meetings, reviewed performance appraisals for both *Raw* and *Smackdown* teams, attended meetings with Creative Services (the team that decides things from T-shirt designs to who goes on the sides of the production trucks). For a while I did it all. The one thing I didn't do was find my replacement as the lead writer, in part because I didn't feel there were any ideal candidates and, probably in larger part, because I didn't want to abdicate my last connection to the creative process.

What came to be was a situation where I was one person doing two extremely full-time jobs. One day, push came to shove and I had to choose—attend a fourth-floor executive meeting or write that week's show. I ended up writing the show. In my mind, I felt it was more vital to get the show done than sit silently as a bunch of suits reviewed sales and marketing numbers. But that really wasn't the point. The whole reason for this promotion/plan was for me to learn and absorb every facet of the company, even the stuff I personally wasn't interested in, and instead I just skipped the meeting to work on that week's show.

Vince heard about it and was understandably enraged. From his point of view, WWE was giving me this tremendous opportunity and I was squandering it. It was insulting not to attend that type of meeting. It was the equivalent of me saying, *Yeah thanks, Vince and Steph, I'm sure your company is fascinating, but the truth is, I really don't give a shit.* My point of view was very shortsighted and stupid. In my head, I knew corporate WWE was a path I wasn't passionate about, and I told myself Vince was going to get mad at me either for not being in the meeting or for not having the show being written, so I might as well do the one thing I was actually good at.

In hindsight, Vince was right. I should've found a way to do both or cut bait on the experiment way sooner. But that wasn't my mindset then.

Tensions started to rise—which leads me back to the *Sopranos* analogy. The thing about Tony and Christopher was they'd greet each other, exchange hugs and kisses, talk on the surface as if everything was great, but there was something ugly boiling underneath.

Christopher thought Tony was too set in his ways and getting out of touch. Tony *knew* Christopher felt that way about him but never confronted him on it. That was basically the dynamic happening with me and Vince. The tension was palpable as we reviewed weekly creative, which soon became my only job once again as Stephanie mercifully ended things on the corporate side. She basically told me, *You were supposed to find your replacement for* Raw *lead writer and you didn't, so we're hiring someone else to take on the management role* (which was fine by me).

Instead of being grateful that Vince didn't just let me go altogether, I decided to get mad. I couldn't do a suplex if my life depended on it, but I could do spite better than anyone. Instead of being angry at what I didn't do, I felt he should have been way more appreciative of what I did do. I was in my own head a lot at this time. In fact, I pulled a "reverse Schmucky," so to speak, reacting internally at every creative idea Vince had as if it was the hackiest thing ever uttered. I never actually said as much, but I think Vince could sense it in my body language. He'd tell me something I had written needed to be "more sophisticated." Out loud I would say, "Okay."

However, my facial expression would convey, *You wouldn't know "sophisticated" if someone shoved a cane, a monocle, and a copy of the* New Yorker *up your ass*. Vince, who can read body language better than most, knew exactly what I was feeling. The tension came to a head in November 2010 during the production meeting of *Survivor Series*, in what now is known in the annals of WWE history as "the Dwyane Wade Incident."

CHAPTER 21

The Dwyane Wade Incident

It was a simple line in a promo designed to get cheap heat, like thousands of promos that had come before it.

In 2010, LeBron James had just taken his talents to South Beach, and we happened to be in Miami, where the Heat were surprisingly struggling. It was *Survivor Series*, and we had the Miz in a solo promo segment for which I had written a line where Miz calls LeBron, their new savior who had yet to save, a disappointment. For all his hype he was nothing more than "Dwyane Wade's sidekick" (and yes, I was still very bitter LeBron didn't join the Knicks).

It was a line in the normal wheelhouse of the Miz, who had been known to rile up the local fans with cheap heat in the past and happened to be a real-life Cavs fan stung by LeBron's exodus. Seemed simple enough, except for one thing…

Vince had no idea who Dwyane Wade was.

"Dammit, Brian, just because *you're* a sports fan doesn't mean the audience is. You think our audience likes *sports*?" Vince asked, looking particularly disgusted.

Based on our ratings going down when *Monday Night Football* was on, going up when it was over, and going down during the NBA playoffs, as well as pages upon pages of marketing research and our constant attempts to create a *"SportsCenter* Moment," plus what I saw with my own two eyes whenever I'd watch the show from the crowd, I believed the answer to be a solid yes. Not all fans, but certainly more than enough to get the reference.

I didn't say that. But I also didn't do the simple thing, which would've been to say *Copy that* and take the stupid line out. Instead, I did the one thing you should never do—I protested. In and of itself that wouldn't be a big deal, but this was at the head table during a pay-per-view production meeting in a room full of about fifty people. As the room was sitting there in uncomfortable silence, I turned to Vince and referenced them:

"Why is this a two-person debate? You have a room full of people sitting here—why not ask any of them?"

Vince slammed his hand on the table. "I'm not talking to them, I'm talking to *you!*"

I don't remember the rest of the argument, but I do remember the subtext:

ME: You're completely out of touch and have no idea what's going on in the world outside of your precious WWE bubble.

VINCE: You're openly defying your boss and trying to show me up in front of a room full of my trusted employees. Who in the holy fuck do you think you are?

This wasn't really about the Miami Heat backcourt. This was tension boiling over at the worst possible time. Vince was itching for a fight, and I was more than happy to give him one. I reached a point where I just didn't care. The argument went on for several excruciating minutes and the meeting ended extremely tense, with the tension carrying over into the next day when usually cooler heads usually prevailed and apologies were made. Not this time.

As we came in to present *Raw* to the room Vince sat next to me and commented how yesterday was *not* good. This is where ninety-nine out of a hundred times I'd agree and apologize for losing my head. Instead I commented, "I thought it was great—healthy debate is a good thing." Vince shook his head in disappointment. Now I was the one itching for a fight. It's one thing to lose your cool in the heat of the moment but this was a full day later, and my lack of contrition probably pissed Vince off more than the actual argument itself. And sure, I always remembered what Vince had said to me early on: "If you fight me you're going to lose, every time." But in that moment my feeling was: *Sounds like a challenge!*

Was I actually looking to get on Vince's bad side? Secretly hoping to get fired and have no choice but go back to Hollywood and resume the sitcom career I had left over ten years before? I didn't think that was the case, but I was certainly angry. Angry at Vince for not appreciating me more, angry at myself for messing up the whole management thing, angry at Dwyane Wade on principle. Mentally I was stuck in a rut. The thing about WWE is you need to be passionate about it. Vince has kept that passion going strong for over forty years. For me that passion was burning out. I was now looking at WWE as a job. I was still putting maximum effort into every WWE script and promo, but the spark that I felt when I had started out was gone. I knew I had crossed a line. Vince will allow you to make mistakes. He'll put up with personality quirks and instances of poor judgment, but the one thing he won't stand for is being disrespected. I was making every day feel like the Vince–Bob Costas 2001 XFL interview.

Tensions rode high as we headed into *WrestleMania* season. The good news was ratings had gone up, thanks to the season end of *Monday Night Football* and a great deal of sports fans who make up our audience returning (sorry, I couldn't help myself). We had a productive week in the office where we had laid out the Michael Cole–Jerry Lawler *WrestleMania* story line which Vince had taken an extremely strong interest in.

We had arranged for Stone Cold Steve Austin to be named the special guest referee in week three of the five-week buildup. But during a production meeting (in week one) Vince forgot what we had laid out, suggesting we name Stone Cold the referee that night. I made the mistake of correcting him in the production meeting. I started laying out what we had talked about week by week when Vince cut me off, saying:

"Jeeeeesus Christ, we *get* it."

This was a case of Vince feeling once again I was trying to show him up, but unlike the Dwyane Wade Incident, this time I truly wasn't. Vince felt otherwise.

Again, a big theme both in front of and behind the cameras in WWE is "Perception is reality." If something is taken a certain way, that's the way it is, regardless of intention.

Perception was certainly reality here. I read the rest of the show in a trance because, while the words of what would transpire on *Raw* came out of my mouth, my thoughts were on only one thing:

If I took this cup of ice water, threw it in Vince's face, and ran, which aisle of the meeting room would be easiest for me to escape? Triple H would almost surely tackle me. John Laurinaitis would want to make a good showing and do the same. Arn Anderson might not know what the hell is going on. I'll make a break for the Arn row!

Of course, I didn't do that, but what I did do was stay behind after the meeting was over. Unlike the Dwyane Wade Incident, I didn't want the bad feelings to linger. If I was going to get the brunt of Vince's wrath, it should be because I deserved it, and I truly felt this wasn't the case.

It was just the two of us when Vince, as I suspected, accused me of trying to show him up, which I emphatically denied. I then told him he was always asking me to have the newer writers speak up in these production meetings and not be tentative.

"Vince, if they see you snapping at me, someone who's been here over ten years, then none of them are going to say anything."

Vince paused as if truly comprehending what I was saying. I was hoping for this to be the moment where he would apologize, I would apologize, we'd hug, and then things would go on as normal. A moment where all the sniping, second-guessing, and pettiness would melt away in a moment of clarity and understanding. Instead he said this:

"Well if that's how they feel…then fuck them and fuuuuuuuuck youuuuuuuuuuuuuu."

On the one hand I was speechless. On the other hand, I just got the full guttural "Mr. McMahon" treatment, which, believe it or not, rarely happens off camera. Deep down, I felt like Ron Burgundy as I thought, *I'm not even mad, that's amazing!*

If the words "fuck them and fuck you" are ever going to be uttered to you by your own boss, it might as well be done by an angry, practically frothing at the mouth Vince McMahon.

Still, the writing was on the wall. If I were to keep this job, a job I wasn't 100 percent sure I still wanted but a job with a great salary, health insurance, and stock options, I needed to think of something to reverse this course and fast.

* * *

By the end of 2011, I finally got something I had been advocating for approved—the idea of a home writing team and an away writing team. The concept was simple—the creative team was now large enough that you could have one half going on the road and producing the live show, and the other looking ahead, writing out story lines and developing characters. Imagine coming back from a long road trip and, instead of meeting on Wednesday and having to start from scratch (as we typically did), there would be a new script already written!

I was pushing this idea with a bit of an ulterior motive. The thrill of being on the road and the rush of producing a live show had left me years ago. It was fun when I was twenty-six. Now I was thirty-eight and just tired. My relationship with Vince was such that the more time I spent away from him the better. Plus, I truly believed this system would actually translate to double the amount of work getting done. What could go wrong? Well, specifically two things:

1. Vince has a habit of changing a ton of things the day of the show, and if you're not on the road and not there to fight for your ideas, what you write during the week usually isn't worth anything. Nowadays they have the home team hooked up via video conferencing so that they're actually in the production meeting and can contribute, but that was not the case back then.

2. As I've mentioned, Vince is a big "foxhole" guy. If you're in the foxhole with him, you're a soldier worthy of at least a modest level of respect. Vince's take on the home team was not: *Hot dog! I can't*

wait to see the story lines they come up with. It was more like: *Home team? What the hell are they doing all day while those on the road are busting their asses? What kind of sick, lazy son of a bitch wouldn't want to be on the road? They're probably goofing off and eating funnel cake on* my *dime!*

This is all to say my relationship with Vince was getting worse, not better. I might as well have worn a "Schmucky the Clown" name tag. At this point I was simply the lead writer of the home team, which meant I wrote the initial scripts for both *Raw* and *Smackdown*. Eric Pankowski was hired to oversee the teams as a whole in the executive position I had mercifully been told to abdicate. I started leaning on Eric to meet with Vince one-on-one to go over creative so I could be spared the minefield of actually being in a meeting with him.

Finally, the tension was building for too long, and I decided to schedule a meeting with Vince in his office in Stamford and have it out over a number of things. We spent over an hour venting our frustrations to each other, a far cry from our first meeting in that very same office where we laughed over my college friend losing the *Royal Rumble* pool. At one point, Vince accused me of essentially not being a team player and only caring about "my shit."

"Vince, there is no 'my shit.' If I didn't work here, do you really think I'd be poring over every detail of a script on a Saturday night, timing it and reviewing it three times before sending it off? My shit is *your* shit, and you should wish all your employees took as much pride in their work as much as I do!"

We got it all out. I told him what I had been feeling, and he told me his feelings as well. At one point he said there were plenty of times he was ready to show me the door but didn't do it. I, in turn, told him there were plenty of times I felt like walking out that same door but didn't do it, either. Neither of us were lying. It was a weird feeling: Both of us were trying nominally to right the ship, but neither of us wanted to sacrifice an inch of pride.

We ended the meeting with a handshake and a better understanding of each other, but we were by no means cool.

It was at that point two things happened simultaneously: Unbeknownst to me, Vince had Eric (practically as soon as he was hired) start looking for my replacement; and unbeknownst to Vince, I had put the wheels in motion to exit the company.

At *WrestleMania 28* in Miami, the Rock was to wrestle John Cena for the WWE title before he ostensibly went back to Hollywood.

I wanted to go back with him. I had reached out to and met with Rock's manager, business partner, and ex-wife, Dany Garcia, whom I had known for years along with his agent, Brad Slater. There was nothing covert about this as for the past ten years I was working under an at-will contract, meaning I was free to quit WWE anytime I wanted, just as WWE was free to let me go.

Dany talked about how she and Dwayne were starting their own production company, Seven Bucks Productions.*

I was interested in joining them, the sooner the better.

It was a productive meeting. We laid the groundwork for me potentially being part of the team. The only issue being, this was the nascent stages of Seven Bucks, and they weren't ready to hire me full-time just yet. Still, there was light at the end of the tunnel. A full-time position would eventually come; I just needed to figure out a way to reach it.

Turned out, I didn't have to find a way. A way found me in the form of a 2.5 rating for *Raw* in October 2012 (ironically, for a show I didn't write, as I was on vacation that week).

Eric called me into his office after he had been summoned to a meeting with Vince. I always found Eric to be a straight shooter.

He told me Vince wanted to make a change and shake things up. I was being offered two choices—either I could step away from WWE entirely

---

*Named after the seven bucks Dwayne had in his pocket when his dad picked him up in Miami after he'd been cut from the Canadian Football League—and not the amount of venison on his ranch, as I had once inexplicably thought.

and receive a generous severance package, or I could stay on as a creative consultant at a lower salary than what I was currently making but with no end date attached. I could do this potentially for years and, most important, I was allowed to work on outside non-WWE projects, something that wasn't viable when I was working full-time.

Eric told me this somberly, but this was actually perfect—now I could work part-time for Seven Bucks as I got indoctrinated in the television development world while still keeping a job at WWE but without all the responsibilities. I'd work from my actual home, I'd get the WWE scripts to review and propose changes to every weekend, give feedback on the shows that aired, and send suggestions in. All the pressure of looking at a blank page, coming up with what had grown from a weekly two-hour to three-hour show and then pitching them to Vince was magically gone.

I told Dwayne and Dany the news, and they agreed this was the ideal scenario. I called Eric back and let him know I'd be sticking around. The truth was this was an incredibly generous offer by WWE; in a way, it embodied the validation I had been seeking. They could've easily cut the cord and just ended things. By offering the consultant role while allowing me to work on whatever I wanted, they showed their appreciation for me both professionally and personally.

Of course, wrestling being wrestling, word quickly spread with a different story. Soon people were calling me telling me how sorry they were to hear the news. It had been reported on "insider" wrestling sites that not only was I "fired" but Vince sent me home from the road yelling to the poor souls left in my wake, "I want results or I want resignations."* They said the consultant position was just a token role (it wasn't), I wouldn't have any say on the shows (I had plenty), and that I'd be done as soon as my contract expired that year (again, my contract didn't have an end date). Otherwise, it was the precise, high-quality level of reporting that one would expect.

---

*Granted that's an awesome line, but it wasn't uttered by Vince nor by anyone else.

250 • THERE'S JUST ONE PROBLEM...

I kept telling people this was one of the best things that ever happened to me. I don't think they believed me based on the gossip, but it truly was. Vince was right. It *was* time to shake things up. Vince has always felt from on-screen talent to people behind the scenes, "If you're not happy, you shouldn't be here." I had reached that point even if I didn't want to admit it to anyone. Plus, now I was eight months out from turning forty, and I had truly reached a point where it was now or never as far as moving onto something else.

I never had any formal talk, meeting, or conversation with Vince on this whole matter. Eric presented me with two options, I chose one, and the next phase of my WWE life was underway without any words exchanged with the man I had spent the previous twelve years working directly under.

And that was fine by me. Anything we would say would just be awkward, and one wrong turn of phrase or perceived reaction could put the whole thing in jeopardy. Our relationship had hit its nadir, and that was just how it was going to be. Out of sight, out of mind, and then ultimately forgotten about.

But then a funny thing happened.

The less time I spent in Vince's presence, the more our relationship started *improving*. Again, part of my job was to send in feedback of *Raw* after every show Monday night, hours after it aired, so Vince and everyone I sent it to could read it that night. I know how hard people worked on that show, and I know it's very easy to sit at home and pick it apart, but I wasn't about to hold back my opinions and just write things I thought Vince wanted to hear. What would be the point in that? I wrote what I felt worked, what didn't, and what could be done differently next time. There was no hidden subtext or agendas—just honest feedback, which I think Vince appreciated.

Why do I think that? Well, after I had been working entirely from home, Stephanie called and asked me to come to the office again once a week to meet with the writers. One day while at Titan Tower I ran into Triple H, who told me:

"So I'm on the phone with Vince and he starts telling me what he thinks we should do next week to improve *Raw*. As he's talking I'm thinking this all sounds very familiar and then it hit me—he's literally just reading your fucking feedback!"

Paul (I call him Paul now) said this with a laugh and a smile. Over the years we gained a healthy respect for each other, and I think he was glad to see the tide turning in Vince's relationship with me. I know I was.

I was able to do both jobs without too much difficulty. When there was a time I needed to be in Panama to be on hand for *The Hero*, Seven Bucks' first reality show with TNT, WWE let me go do it. When I was needed in Florida for our show *Wake Up Call*, I was allowed to focus on that as well, even if it meant missing a few episodes of *Raw*. I was learning more and more about the television business and what it took to create, pitch, and sell a show as I consulted at WWE. The dual job setup was nice while it lasted, but in 2015 Dwayne called me with the news I had been waiting to hear. He and Dany were ready to come have me join Seven Bucks full-time.

After sixteen years (thirteen full-time and nearly three years part-time) it was time to leave WWE.

I gave my notice, and Stephanie was genuinely happy for me. We had essentially grown up in the business together. Stephanie's a mother of three, and I still buy cereal based on the prize inside, but we've still both grown, dammit.

My final show was June 29, 2015, in Washington, DC, the same arena used for my very first show on November 1, 1999. A lot had changed since Vince walked in late to that first production and read a makeshift show off a piece of scrap paper, and I wanted to make sure I saw him one more time before he headed from the production meeting to Gorilla Position to his limo and then on to the next town for *Smackdown*.

I knew before he went to Gorilla he'd make a quick stop in his office, so I knocked on the door and was told to come in. Inside I found Vince, Triple H, and Stephanie. It started to hit me how much of the last decade and a half I had spent with these three people. I was on hand to celebrate one of the happiest days in Triple H's and Stephanie's lives when I attended their wedding and they were on hand to celebrate one of the happiest days in my life, when Vince postponed the postshow meeting to let me watch Syracuse win the 2003 NCAA National Championship.

Inside Vince's office we reminisced warmly (Vince even made a Dwyane Wade joke!), and then I told them that even though it was my last day, it really wasn't, since WWE would always be a part of me.

If this were an '80s sitcom, there would be a big "awwww" from the studio audience, followed by a freeze frame and applause. If it were live-streamed there would be an avalanche of tweets saying how corny that line was followed by a healthy dose of eye-rolling emojis.

Vince smiled and started to make his way out, but before he did he stopped in front of me and, instead of extending his hand, gave me a big hug and simply said:

"I love you, Brian."

I honestly wasn't expecting that. In fact, I was so unprepared for such an emotional moment, I—the guy responsible for coming up with the perfect comeback—couldn't think of one, even one as obvious as this. Instead I fumbled back with:

"And I . . . also. . . . feel that way . . . as well . . . um . . . I love you too, Vince."

Steph and Paul had a good laugh as Vince headed off to produce the show and I went off to start the next phase of my life.

Full Circle

In the seven years (holy shit) since I left WWE, I've noticed one thing about people—they are hilarious.

Now that I'm back to working in Hollywood (while thankfully still living in New York City) I always find it amusing when an actor/agent/executive/writer/director tries to act all tough. They actually think they're intimidating. It's so cute. Like when people dress their pets in top hats and tuxedos. That's the one thing about working at WWE that's a universal positive once you leave—it's nearly impossible to be intimidated.

My reaction when I find myself in conflict with someone in the television world?

"Buddy, I went toe-to-toe with Vince McMahon for a decade and a half, oftentimes when he hadn't eaten—there is literally nothing you can do or say that's going to leave me shaking."

Thankfully I haven't really worked with many raging assholes in television, but when I do, my WWE armor comes out and I'm grateful that I have it.

In general, I'm grateful for the entire WWE experience. I love going to a WWE show and going backstage when I can. Whenever I do, the first thing everyone tells me is how relaxed I look. Shooting a live backstage vignette, making sure it doesn't exceed its allotted time, praying there's nothing Vince finds objectionable, and hoping the audience responds versus eating popcorn and catching up with old friends? Hell yeah, I'd say I'm relaxed.

It's always fun seeing people I worked with for over a decade who are still there: my friends on the writing team, producers, backstage crew, seamstresses, caterers, still photographers, and, of course, the wrestlers themselves—some of them I've been in the trenches with, some I've never met before. Sometimes I'll run into ex-WWE stars who are themselves visiting. I love the fact I can run into say a Sean Waltman and catch up with him, whatever heat we had in the past genuinely water under the bridge.

When I'm backstage, I always manage to take a step back and just take everything in. Everyone running around, shooting promos, vignettes, going over matches, spots, etc. I'll watch, hum Madonna's "This Used to Be My Playground" to myself until I get interrupted by Kasama, my friend and longtime WWE stage manager, shouting in her unique Thai / Staten Island accent, "Hey! We're about to go live! Stop singing Madonna to yourself!"

Of course, I shouldn't get *too* comfortable. The dynamic can change in an instant the moment the Rock decides to come back to do something for WWE. The last official time we all worked on something was in Staples Center, Los Angeles, for the premiere of *Smackdown* on Fox in 2019 with Becky Lynch and Baron Corbin. We met with Becky the night before at Rock's hotel, and again with her and Corbin the day of, to put the promo on its feet, get everyone's input, and work it all out. The benefit of unofficially working on a WWE promo is you get all the fun, none of the heat. WWE assigns a writer to take the promo we've put together and do all the things I used to do—get it approved by Vince, sit in Gorilla Position to communicate with the truck to give cues and make sure it hits its time. If it goes heavy, all the heat is on the writer, who's really an innocent victim. Meanwhile, I get to watch it from the crowd without a care in the world. Sometimes while drinking an adult beverage—something I could never do when I worked there but oftentimes wanted to.

I get to catch up with the McMahons, which is always nice. Stephanie also seems a lot less stressed. While I can't say for certain and I'm sure it's not an easy job, my guess is "chief brand officer" is less panic inducing than that time she was head of the creative team, a major on-air heel character, and an XFL sideline reporter, all at the same time.

I always try to say hi to Vince as well. On the night of the *Smackdown* premiere it was going to be a challenge. Staples Center (now the Crypto .com Arena) is the worst because everyone in Hollywood with a connection or even a slight interest in WWE is milling around backstage, ready to talk Vince's ear off. That night, once the show was over, Vince was making his way to his limo with full security detail as I raced over. I could see security getting ready to tackle me when I held my *Smackdown* script up and screamed like Lloyd Christmas, "It's okay! I'm a former WWE writer!"

Security had no idea how to react to that, but thankfully Vince smiled, gave me the go-ahead, and we hugged and caught up before he got in his limo and sped off. Finally, the WWE Films advice of "watch *Dumb and Dumber*" paid off.

Nowadays I often get asked how one can get a job as a writer at WWE. The truth is I don't really know. WWE is constantly changing and evolving. The process in place when I was there I'm sure has changed. What I would say is ask yourself the following questions: Are you passionate about WWE? Are you in this for the long haul? If the answer to either of those questions is no, then you're dead in the water before you even get started.

Otherwise, I'd say stick to the basics—write up a sample (be it a story line, an angle, a promo) that you consider to be your best work. If you have an agent, have them make the call on your behalf to WWE and get them to submit it. If you don't, then check the WWE corporate website or LinkedIn because job postings are always popping up. Once you submit your sample, be persistent as far as following up, but don't be too persistent to the point of annoying the hell out of everyone. If you don't have the requisite experience WWE looks for in a writer, try to get a job as a writer's assistant. It's not the most glamorous job in the world, but if you do well, there's no better path to becoming a full-time WWE writer. But probably the most important advice I can give isn't so much what to do if you get the job, but what to do if you *don't* get the job. And that advice is—don't sweat it.

Ever since I saw my uncle's name in the credits of *Taxi* when I was seven years old, I wanted to be a sitcom writer. I got to be one, and then I took what I thought would be a short detour working as a writer at WWE, which turned out to be a decade-and-a-half odyssey.

And what happened once I left?

I've gone full circle.

Twenty-two years after I turned in my last script on *Big Wolf on Campus* I wrote an episode (along with Dwayne and Hiram) of our Seven Bucks–produced NBC sitcom *Young Rock*. Not only that, it's the episode detailing Dwayne's first match in WWE, which means I'm literally writing characters based on real people I've worked with for years—Pat Patterson, Downtown Bruno, Steve Lombardi, Michael Hayes, Bruce Prichard, Steve Austin, Triple H, Mick Foley, and, of course, Vince McMahon.

When I started in WWE I was "the Hollywood guy." In Australia, on the set of *Young Rock*, I'm pretty much known as "the wrestling guy."*

My point in not sweating it is this: Forget about what didn't happen—make the most of what *does* happen because you never know where the hell life is going to take you. I may not have a closet full of Emmys, but I can say I wrote / helped come up with Money in the Bank, Jonathan Coachman dancing the Charleston, and taking Ron Simmons's "Damn" catchphrase and putting it at the end of several hundred random promo segments.

In 1999, I was at my lowest point, feeling miserable after not landing a sitcom writing job and about to start hiding in the bushes for Jack in the Box, when a single call changed everything. Change, like Michael Cole deciding to urinate on a plane with no bathroom, can happen suddenly and without warning.

---

*And the guy who orders Uber Eats for lunch every day instead of eating on-set catering. It's not my fault. In Australia asking for a turkey sandwich is like asking for owl meat. Don't even get me started on the absence of challah bread.

So how best to wrap this up? How to relay one more tale that best sums up my time with WWE? When in doubt always turn to a Michael "PS" Hayes story. The question is, which one?

Maybe it's from my thirtieth birthday party in LA, which I shared with a friend who happened to invite some celebrities. After Michael insulted actor Jaleel White by repeatedly calling him "Urkel," he cut the long line of the single-person bathroom and jammed his way in. Moments later a friend emerged in a daze and said, "A large scary man with a fanny pack just barged in and pissed in the sink."

Or it could be years later when I had another birthday party in NYC and late in the night, we lost Michael. We had no idea where he went until he called us impatiently telling us to pick him up. We asked where he was, and he replied "How the fuck should I know? Something called the FDR." The sight of NYC drivers gazing upon a wild-eyed Michael Hayes wandering aimlessly down the FDR at 2 a.m. is strong imagery to end a book on, but that's not quite it.

It could be the time we almost didn't hire a writer's assistant because he used to intern at *The Howard Stern Show*, and Michael legitimately asked, "How do we know Howard didn't send him here as a spy to get all our secrets?"

Or the time I questioned why he named his dog "Splotif." "Hello?" Michael replied, as if I were an idiot. "It's short for 'Explotif'!" I don't know how a man goes his entire life without ever hearing the word *explosive*, but Michael managed to do it, and his dog reaped the benefits.

Okay, I'm now realizing I have about twenty-five more of these, so I better wrap it up with just one more.

We were in a *Raw* production meeting trying to come up with a new tagline for the show. Something announcers can repeat and that we could put on advertisements and billboards. Vince had asked everyone to come in with their top suggestions, and Michael had what he was convinced was the one. This was during the Guest Host Era, so Michael thought of this:

"The entertainment show the *entertainers* go to when they want to be entertained."

Michael was bragging about it to everyone beforehand, and Vince got word of it before the meeting (probably from me). A huge smile came across his face. In the meeting he asked the room for their suggestions as Michael's hand shot up. Michael said his line with an absurd amount of confidence. He stood at home plate, flipped his bat, and posed triumphantly as his home run sailed into the bleachers.

Vince looked at Michael and nodded, saying, "Strong, Michael. Damn strong." Vince then kept a straight face for as long as he could (as did we all) as Michael continued to beam. That's when Vince burst out laughing, which caused the entire room to do the same.

Credit to Michael, who stood his ground as the laughter rained down and said, "Fuck y'all, that's a good line."

That story sums up all the feelings I experienced at WWE: high-stakes pressure, misplaced confidence, immense satisfaction, pure exasperation, some mild humiliation, and, ultimately, acceptance. I competed in a sixteen-year Iron Man match and somehow came out of it stronger, wiser, and ready to take on any new challenge life has to offer. Why? Because ultimately pro wrestling is life and life is pro wrestling.

Now ring the damn bell.

ACKNOWLEDGMENTS

Wrestling writers aren't used to "acknowledgments." Their jobs are almost never acknowledged, at least publicly. There is no Slammy Award for "Best Written Promo," and WWE shockingly never took out a "For Your Consideration" page in *Variety* during Emmy Awards season for Eugene's Musical Chairs segment.

I, however, have a lot of people to acknowledge for helping this book become a reality, starting with my family:

My parents, Donna and Ed, for a lifetime of unwavering support; my uncle Howard, for teaching me so much; and my sister Randi who, despite her husband, Scott, being a Yankees fan, has decided to raise their daughter—my niece, Maia—as a Mets fan. That's probably the most important thing…that and making the call that led to me getting hired by MTV and later WWE, without which none of this happens. But mainly the Mets thing.

When you work on the WWE creative team you're pretty much spending every waking second with your fellow writers, so it's nice when you actually like and respect each other. With that in mind, I'd like to thank the WWE creative team members I worked with over the years for not only being great, underappreciated writers but essentially serving as my road family for over a decade: Ed Koskey, Dave Kapoor, Bruce Prichard, Michael Hayes, Tommy Blacha, Jen Bloodsworth, Ryan Ward, Chris DeJoesph, Nick Manfredini, and Julian Kheel, among MANY others. There's no group of people I'd rather hear scream in terror when driving between towns and I'd invariably fall asleep behind the wheel fifteen minutes into the trip.

There are absolutely too many wrestlers I want to thank—essentially everyone mentioned in this book and everyone I've ever worked with. I truly am in awe of your abilities, and I appreciate every second we got to work together. Except, of course, for the Miz…okay fine, dammit, even the Miz.

Of course, none of this happens without Stephanie, Shane, Linda, and Vince McMahon. Seven years after leaving WWE, not a day goes by that I don't apply one of your quotes or life lessons. Even the weird ones. Thanks for bringing me in and forcing me to grow as a writer and occasionally as a human being.

All of this started with an email to Dwayne Johnson and Dany Garcia, asking them what they thought of the idea of me writing a book. I was nervous sending that email because, let's face it, neither of them have a lot going on in life and the potential success of this book could make them feel extremely insecure. Thankfully they thought it was a great idea and told me to pursue it. Their support—not just for this book but for everything throughout the last twenty-plus years, both in WWE and at Seven Bucks—has been invaluable, inspirational, and truly appreciated. Thanks to them, Hiram, and the entire Seven Bucks team.

After that email I reached out to "Cousin Sal" Iacono. Despite me being the creative mastermind behind his first and only WWE victory, he did not list me among the eighty-three people (damn right I counted) acknowledged in his book, *You Can't Lose Them All*. To make up for this tremendous oversight, Sal put me in touch with Sean Desmond at Twelve, who decided to take a chance on a first-time author with a bunch of crazy wrestling stories. Sean also gave me incredible notes and insights, making this process easy, painless, and, dare I say, fun. Thank you to Sean and the entire team at Twelve: Jim Datz, Megan Perritt-Jacobson, Estefania Acquaviva, Bob Castillo, and Zohal Karimy. I'm proud to have worked with you and equally proud to have set an all-time record for most double negatives in a first draft.

I also want to thank the following people for their encouragement and advice, for reading early chapters, and for sending me pictures, since I sure as hell didn't have any:

Kasama Bhasathiti, Sam Ford, Adam Copeland, Jay Reso, Jason Oremland, Jessie Whitney, Matthew Mitchell, Liz Pena, Amanda Rosenberg, Bradley Smith, Eve Atttermann, Jonathan Lyons, Conrad Thompson, and Mickie F'n James.

And a special thank-you to Michael Cole, whom I specifically texted to ask if I could tell the plane toilet story, and he responded:

"Use my name, I don't give a shit, dude. It happened, why hide it lol."

I can't think of a better sentiment on which to end.

INDEX

ABOUT THE AUTHOR

Currently senior vice president of development at Dwayne Johnson and Dany Garcia's Seven Bucks Productions, **Brian Gewirtz** was formerly head writer for Vince McMahon's World Wrestling Entertainment. He's written for several television shows and has served as executive producer on NBC's *The Titan Games*, *Behind the Attraction* on Disney Plus, and on NBC's *Young Rock*, which is based on the life of Dwayne "the Rock" Johnson.